RUSS & DAUGHTERS

RUSS & DAUGHTERS

100 YEARS OF APPETIZING

NIKI RUSS FEDERMAN & JOSH RUSS TUPPER

with Joshua David Stein
Photography by Gentl & Hyers

FLATIRON
BOOKS
NEW YORK

RUSS & DAUGHTERS

Copyright © 2025 by Niki Russ Federman and Josh Russ Tupper with Joshua David Stein. Photographs copyright © 2025 by Gentl & Hyers. Illustrations copyright © Jason Polan, LLC.

All rights reserved. Printed in China.

For information, address
Flatiron Books, 120 Broadway, New York, NY 10271.
www.flatironbooks.com

Image credits: PAGE 16, Mark Russ Federman by Harvey Wang. PAGE 18, Anne Russ Federman by Edmund V. Gillon Jr., Tenement Museum Collection.

Interior and cover design by Portrait

Library of Congress Cataloging-in-Publication Data

Names: Federman, Niki Russ, author. | Tupper, Josh Russ, author. | Stein, Joshua David, author.
Title: Russ & Daughters : 100 years of appetizing / Niki Russ Federman & Josh Russ Tupper with Joshua David Stein.
Other titles: Russ and Daughters
Description: First edition. | New York : Flatiron Books, 2025. | Includes index.
Identifiers: LCCN 2024059654 | ISBN 9781250886675 (paper over board) | ISBN 9781250886682 (ebook)
Subjects: LCSH: Russ & Daughters—History. | Jewish cooking—New York (State)—New York. | Appetizers—New York (State)—New York. | LCGFT: Cookbooks.
Classification: LCC TX945.5.R86 F43 2025 | DDC 641.5/67609747—dc23/eng/20250131
LC record available at https://lccn.loc.gov/2024059654

Our books may be purchased in bulk for promotional, educational, or business use. Please contact your local bookseller or the Macmillan Corporate and Premium Sales Department at 1-800-221-7945, extension 5442, or by email at MacmillanSpecialMarkets@macmillan.com.

First Edition: 2025

10 9 8 7 6 5 4 3 2 1

To the generations of families—ours and yours—
who have sustained Russ & Daughters

STORE

Original Appetizing
for Gatherings

1
Introduction

9
Genesis: A History of the Family Russ

39
SOUPS

Smoked Whitefish Chowder
Gazpacho
Potato Leek Soup
Matzo Ball Soup
Roasted Vegetable Stock
Mushroom Barley Soup
Chilled Borscht
Hot Borscht

54
SMOKED & CURED FISH

A Guide to Herring

Sauces for Herring
Classic New Catch Holland
Herring Sandwich
Schmaltz & a Shot
Beet, Apple & Herring Salad

A Guide to Smoked & Cured Salmon

How to Slice a Salmon

Gravlax, Apples & Honey
Hot Smoke / Cold Smoke

A Guide to Other Specialty Smoked Fish

Sardine Toast with Avocado Mousse & Olive Tapenade
Whitefish & Baked Salmon Salad
Whitefish Croquettes
Smoked Trout Mousse

92
CAVIAR

A Guide to Caviar & Roe

Notes on Storing, Serving & Enjoying Caviar

Caviar & Blini
Caviar Lovers Black & White
Hasselback Potato with Caviar

107
SIDES

Sour (& Half-Sour) Pickles
Chopped Liver
Vegetarian Chopped Liver
Romanian Eggplant Salad
Health Salad
Cabbage Salad
New Potato Salad
Egg Salad

How to Assemble a Platter

124
BAGEL SANDWICHES

A Classic with the Works
Daughters' Delight
Pastrami Russ
Super Heebster
Fancy Delancey

From the Archives

CAFE

Haimish Meals (& Drinks) to Comfort

156
NOSHES & SALADS

Potato Knishes
Everything Spiced Almonds
Potato Latkes
Kasha Varnishkas
Chopped Salad
Red & Golden Beet Salad

173
EGGS

Eggs Benny
Nova & Cream Cheese Omelet
Matzo Brei with Applesauce
& Sour Cream
Soft Scrambled Eggs with Caviar
Lox, Eggs & Onions (LEO)

188
DINNER SPECIALS

Aunt Ida's Stuffed Cabbage
Vegetarian Stuffed Cabbage
Pickled Carrots
with Cumin & Caraway
Chicken Paprikash
Kippered Salmon Mac & Cheese
Shissel Chicken Cutlets
with Tartar Sauce
Roasted Cauliflower with
Garlic Labneh

204
PASSOVER SEDER

Tsimmes
Charoset
Salmon & Whitefish Gefilte Fish
Potato Kugel
Brisket
Chocolate Toffee Matzo
Flourless Chocolate Cake
Coconut Macaroons

221
SWEETS

Blintzes
Noodle Kugel
Lemon Sorbet with
Poppy Seeds
Ice Creams
Blueberry Kasha Crumble
Babka French Toast

235
DRINKS

Egg Creams
Shrubs
Sodas
Cocktails

BAKERY

Bagels, Bialys & Other Baked Goods

266
BAGELS & BIALYS

Plain
Cinnamon Raisin
Egg
Pumpernickel
Whole Wheat
Bagel Chips
Bialys

285
BREADS

Challah
Shissel Rye
Pumpernickel
Marble Rye

296
BAKED GOODS

Rugelach
Black & White Cookies
Chocolate (or Cinnamon) Babka
Challah Bread Pudding
Hamantaschen
Sour Cream Coffee Cake
Honey Cake
Plum (or Apple) Cake
Fruit Strudel

326
Acknowledgments

332
Index

Introduction

In New York City, time functions differently. Fortunes are made and lost in seconds; fame comes and goes in fifteen-minute intervals; skyscrapers appear overnight, and neighborhoods change like the tides at Coney Island. New Yorkers guard their history fiercely because it is so often buried under the ceaselessly shifting sands of progress. A store, a restaurant, a theater, a home, a bakery, a bar, a flophouse shutters, is perhaps torn down. Within days it has a new face and a new name. So what last, what *actually* last, are slender synapses connecting us to all the New Yorkers of the past. The longer they stretch, the more precious they become.

Our great-grandfather Joel Russ, a tireless man, founded what would become Russ & Daughters over 110 years ago. That's old for trees, ancient for humans, and in New York years, an epoch. And yet we're still here, the fourth generation, continuing the tradition of appetizing that once nourished the denizens of the Lower East Side's tenements, back when, instead of condos and coffeeshops, the quarter was thought of as the New York shtetl.

At one time there were forty appetizing stores on the Lower East Side—some kosher, some kosher-style—crammed into the crowded blocks that housed families of Eastern European immigrants in dank, dark apartments. But today we are the last remaining one. Passed from father to daughters, then sons-in-law to son and daughter-in-law, then to a daughter again—and a nephew!—we have survived and even flourished. Our continued existence is based on wafer-thin slices of lox, pre-dawn visits to our smokehouses to assure quality, endlessly returning to and refining recipes, and the accumulation of daily interactions and slowly forged relationships with life-long customers and long-term employees. Though exacting and at times exasperating, four generations of refusing to let *anything* slide, slip, or atrophy, four generations of devotion to the art of appetizing, four generations of holding tightly to tradition but never giving up the Russ family hustle, has ensured our survival today and tomorrow.

Russ & Daughters draws a continuous line, an unbroken chain of custody, from the Lower East Side pushcart laden with schmaltz herring that our great-grandfather pushed down Orchard Street. But of course, Russ & Daughters isn't just *our* story. For thousands of families—some of whom still call New York

From left to right: Herb Federman (behind the counter), an unidentified man, Murray Gold, an unidentified man, and Joel Russ during the 1949 renovation

home, many who don't—Russ & Daughters serves as a kind of bridge to their own family histories. How rare and precious a thing it is to be able to open the very same glass doors your parents, grandparents, and great-grandparents did, to call out the same orders—whitefish, make it a fat one! a quarter pound of Gaspe! herring! halvah!—to smell the same smells they did, and to taste what they tasted—what *you* tasted when you were young too.

Because New York moves frenetically, ours seems an even more stately pace. Let the cars zoom across Houston and the blur of bodies rush by. Condos come and condos go, yet we remain still. It's not that we don't change, but we do so deliberately. It took us, for instance, a hundred years to open a restaurant. It took us more than one hundred and ten to write our first cookbook.

This volume is a comprehensive guide not just to Russ & Daughters, the legendary store itself, our restaurant, our bakery, and the characters you'll find on both sides of the counter, but also to the nearly lost world of appetizing itself. It is a book full of history, guides, family recipes, insider anecdotes, and first-person accounts of how we're bringing a beloved institution into the future while respecting the past. In these pages, you'll find a century's worth of expertise in everything from how to slice a side of lox to how to prepare the perfect sandwich. There are recipes for dishes from the familiar, like latkes and borscht, to imaginative evolutions of modern appetizing, like shissel-crusted chicken and halvah ice cream. Herring will be explained. Babka will be baked. A road map for rugelach will be provided.

We begin at the Store, the ancestral heart, our first home, and, by a century, the oldest. Here you'll find the most traditional of our appetizing offerings: herring, whitefish, and pickled lox, as well as recipes for soups, salads, pickles, egg salad, and more. Everything you need to entertain—not coincidentally, the raison d'être for appetizing—will be provided. Besides the classics we've been serving for years, you'll find guides to some of our most recognizable products like smoked and cured salmon, herring, and caviar. Though a relatively new addition, you'll also find here our bagel sandwiches, since in the modern era we do a brisk business in them over the counter.

The second section is devoted to the Cafe. In 2014, we made our first major expansion, taking over a storefront stretching from Orchard to Allen Streets just above Delancey and turning it into Russ & Daughters Cafe, a full-service sit-down restaurant with a cocktail program and caviar service. The menu showcases the best of our appetizing interpreted as plated restaurant fare. Here you'll find recipes for noshes like our fluffy knishes and crispy latkes, our famous eggs (soft scrambled with caviar, with lox and onions, etc.), our takes on classic cocktails, and a few dinner specials. You'll also find recipes for our famous Second Seder, a recent tradition in which we invite Russ & Daughters friends and family for a special Passover meal, accompanied by music and storytelling. The music you'll have to make yourself, but now you'll have the stories and recipes.

At right: Joel Russ at the register with Murray Gold behind him, circa 1940

JULY 22, 1968   40 CENTS

Introducing the Dog of the Year

Dick Goodwin: Incredible Leaping Politician

New York

A Gentile's Guide To Jewish Food
By the Underground Gourmet

A 1968 cover of *New York* magazine by Milton Glaser

The final section, Bakery, is drawn from recipes developed at our largest project to date: In 2018, we took over 18,000 square feet in the Brooklyn Navy Yard, transforming the once industrial space into the hub of all of our cooking and baking. Here we make the famous bagels, bialys, challahs, rugelach, babkas, rye breads, and pumpernickels that supply not just the store and the Cafe but that are shipped nationally. You'll find those recipes adapted for the home baker so you too can awake to the intoxicatingly yeasty smell of fresh bagels.

Over 110 years, Russ & Daughters has touched hundreds of thousands of people. Our food has been present at births and deaths, at brunches and breakfasts, at all manner of gatherings that bring human beings together. First, we fed the poor Jewish immigrants, compatriots of Joel Russ. As the Lower East Side has changed, we've fed all of our neighbors. For many families, a visit to our store on East Houston has become a tradition, the passing of a bagel and lox to a new generation. For others, it's a weekly or daily ritual. Yet not everyone can walk through our doors, and even those who do often yearn for a keepsake that lasts longer than a bagel. Nothing can ever replace the experience of taking a number, waiting patiently (or not so patiently) on line, kibbitzing with a slicer, and ordering your whitefish or belly lox. Yet we hope this book captures some of the Russ & Daughters experience and, most important, brings families and friends together around the table.

"WHAT IS APPETIZING?" YOU ASK.

"WHAT IS APPETIZING?" THEY ASK!? The appetizing tradition grows from the ancient Hebrew dietary laws known as kashrut. Among the many prohibitions of kosher laws is this one, found in Exodus 34:26: "Thou shalt not boil a kid in its mother's milk." This one law neatly bifurcates Jewish cuisine into meat on one side and dairy on the other. (A third category, *pareve*, consists of "neutral" foods that can be eaten with either meat or dairy.) This is true in the home, where families who keep kosher have two sets of dishes, and outside of the home, in the form of appetizing stores and delicatessens. A delicatessen, which is what we are *not*, serves meat, but not dairy and rarely fish. An appetizing store, meanwhile, begins with smoked and cured fish—with the exception, of course, of forbidden seafood like shellfish—which occupy the pareve or neutral territory. Because fish can be served with dairy, a concomitant flourishing of dairy products also became part of the appetizing tradition. Cream cheese and lox? Kosher. Muenster and corned beef? *Trayf* (forbidden). Corned beef and lox? Technically okay, but why would you do that? We have never been, or claimed to be, strictly kosher (except for our now-closed outpost at the Jewish Museum). We are, instead, kosher-style, meaning we follow the spirit if not the letter of the laws of kashrut. In the debate between delicatessen and appetizing, delicatessen has thus far triumphed in the American lexicon. (This has, we think, as much to do with linguistic expediency as it does with meat consumption. *Delicatessen* can be shortened to *deli*; *appetizing* must remain *appetizing*.) But we are proud to carry on the appetizing tradition and to play a part in revitalizing it. The word itself is becoming more common. Though we still correct customers daily—at one point we considered T-shirts that read, "Don't call us a deli"—appetizing is making a comeback. And not a moment too soon.

The Russ Daughters

Q. *I often pass an old-fashioned smoked fish emporium on East Houston Street called Russ & Daughters. Why did Mr. Russ take the unusual step of sharing top billing with his daughters?*

A. It was business. Joel Russ, a Galician Jew from a village in what is now eastern Poland, began his career on the Lower East Side in 1911, peddling Polish mushrooms from a horse-drawn wagon. He established his "Cut-Rate Appetizing Store" on Orchard Street in 1914, but the gruff, hard-working Mr. Russ had little patience with his finicky customers, and business suffered until he put his three pretty, smiling young daughters, Ida, Anne and Hattie, behind the counters. (He had no sons.)

Renamed Russ & Daughters, the store moved to its present location at 179 East Houston Street, between Orchard and Allen Streets, in the 1940's, according to Maria Federman, wife of Mark Russ Federman, present owner of the store and son of Joel Russ's daughter Anne. It still sells fresh Mallossol caviar and 50 varieties of smoked and salted fish prepared on premises from recipes unchanged in this century: like lox, smoked salmon (including sweet-smoked Gaspé), smoked whitefish and lake sturgeon, matjes herring and the rather sweet chopped herring salad.

Ms. Federman said each of the three daughters met her husband while working at Russ & Daughters. Today a portrait of the Russ daughters, all now retired and living in Florida, still adorns a wall of the store, and hanging in the window are

URBAN Jewish EATING

AS AMERICAN AS CHICKEN SOUP

Fast-food ethnic is the American style: We gulp down old-world cuisines at a single bite. Which is why there are Jewish delis everywhere.

The Jewish kitchen was the original carryout counter. As a nomadic people, Jews cooked food to eat on the run. Literally. The most famous example is the unleavened crackerlike matzoh: Seems Moses led the Jews from Egyptian bondage so fast there wasn't time to let the bread rise. So, traditionally, Jewish food was prepared to travel — pickled, smoked and long cooked.

As the food crossed borders with the people, the cuisine became flavored with each local style, and by now it's international. Every family has prized recipes handed down to daughters (and sons) by mothers and grandmothers — all of whom came from someplace else. But the equation is always the same: Food equals love.

"TRY IT, YOU'LL LIKE IT"

Russ & Daughters, Inc., on New York's Lower East Side for 65 years, is among the few remaining old-style delis. Ann Federman (right) and her husband Herb carry on her father's business, bantering with loyal patrons who come from far and wide for the experience as well as the food. But, like the old-country dishes, the real delis are fast

---

THE NEW YORK TIMES, WEDNESDAY, AUGUST 12, 1953.

News of Food
Smoked Fish Makes Ideal Summer Dish — Red Salmon Supply Seen Off This Year

By JANE NICKERSON

Those with a taste for smoked fish and the energy to seek it out might make their way to Russ and Daughters, a famous little shop at 179 East Houston Street.

Daughters, it turns out, are to be taken literally; the word is not the name of Mr. Russ' partner. Joel Russ, who came here from Austria almost forty years ago, had two little girls who showed such an interest in fish that he decided to let people know that his daughters were part of his enterprise. Now they are grown and married, and the husband of one, Morris H. Gold, manages the store.

It is a good store to know about at any time, particularly those

supply point in his opinion for that variety.

There are at least a dozen kinds of smoked fish in the scrubbed glass cases, some from as far off as Alaska, Scotland and Newfoundland. Russ and Daughters has such curiosities as pickled anchovies in barrels from Norway.

The canned sardines with bone from France are aged in somewhat the way the French gourmets do it — by turning the tins regularly and letting them stand some time, so that the bones (which are thought to contribute to flavor) soften and the entire fish mellows.

Red Salmon Haul Disappointing

So far this fishing season, the

The mom-and-pop store:
Can it outlast its founding parents?

by LINDA ABRAMS

"AS LONG AS THERE'S A Canterino, there will be a Halfnote," said Rosemarie Canterino as she swirled on a bar stool in her family's jazz club on W. 54th St.

It looks like the Canterinos will be around for a long time. Rosemarie's parents, Frank and Jean, although retired, make the Italian sauce for lunch on Fridays. Their son Mike is the bartender and books the musicians. Rosemarie is bookkeeper and hostess. Their grandsons work there too: Dominick runs the back bar every night and Frankie, who works full time at Con Edison, is the cashier on weekends. Sonny, Rosemarie's big brother, is the boss. And Sonny and his wife Tita work in the kitchen making veal parmigiana, ravioli and tuna salad on Fridays.

In an era when the family business is dissolving, the family-owned business struggles to survive. There is no census taken on the number of

tions with the older generation in a family business who reluctantly want to sell their business but had hoped their children would take over," Rivera said. "My father had a grocery store and I wasn't attracted to that business at all.

"If young people take over the family business they want to make it a corporation right away. And that is how a store loses its flavor as a ma-and-pa business. But it is a real necessity. If ma gets sick, sometimes they have to close the shop. Lack of depth in management is the biggest problem for the family."

Perhaps that's the clue to how the Canterinos have beaten the trend. While turning their ma-and-pa jazz club into big time, they have kept the family flavor by finding a depth of management within the bloodline. When Sonny, the boss, walked through the door, a broad-shouldered man with a well-fed belly, he gave everyone a kiss.

younger brother Mike walked in late, and the Canterinos teased him about being more interested in his family than in the business.

The elder Canterinos owned an Italian bar and restaurant called Frank and Jean's on Spring St., a favorite hangout for longshoremen. They started that business 28 years ago. "Before I knew it," said Frank, "Mike and Sonny took the bar down and put up a bandstand made out of Coca Cola boxes and bought a piano."

Frank and Jean's was renamed the Halfnote and the restaurant with its oilcloth-covered tables became a hangout for musicians, a meeting place for jazz fans and home to the Canterinos. Rosemarie said she almost gave birth to Michael on the steps of the Halfnote. After he was born she kept him in a carriage next to the cash register where she worked. Rosemarie is so much a Canterino that, when she was divorced shortly after

The loose atmosphere of Spring St. turned more formal uptown, but, as before, each member of the family has a duty to perform. "The beautiful part of this family business is that wherever one of us is standing, behind the cash register, or at the door, we can take care of it," said Rosemarie. "If the waiter doesn't show up, you become the waiter. I can't mix drinks but I had to tend bar one night."

Although some members of the family have tried careers outside the club, it never made them happy. When Rosemarie was married she worked as a legal secretary for three and a half years and didn't like it. Her son Michael says that when he gets out of the Air Force he wants to apply his skills as a tree surgeon, carpenter and mason. "I want to buy a piece of land and build a house in the mountains," he said.

His grandfather Frank doesn't believe Michael will really take to

---

The selling uniforms of the eight college girls who met yesterday for a round-table

"We argued for 20 minutes. He won."
Pat Brennan, University of Pennsylvania

What would they like to have of the merchandise they're selling? One of the fur

"beautiful"—which is the only way to pronounce it in collegese.

Everything From Caviar to Lox Can Be Found in Lower East Side Shops

By NAN ICKERINGILL

SUNDAY is far from being a day of rest on the Lower

is more salty and everyone is diet-conscious," one of the best sellers at the store is the herring that is pickled on the

full of water by comparison") and Hawaiian pineapple cores ("They taste so pineapply") and then walked out chewing on a

Business was scarcely less bustling at Ben's Dairy products next door. A realm rich in butter and cheese, it is ruled

he continued, pushing forward another nibble. "That's made from cream cheese, Roquefort and a little Gorgonzola. Just

ever dreamed of being, is sold at Ben's in many forms—plain, with vegetables, with caraway, with scallions or with chives

An Appetizing Story

Mark Russ Federman, Maria Federman and
Anne Russ Federman of RUSS & DAUGHTERS

Interview by **Joan Wilen & Lydia Wilen** / Photograph by **Janette Beckman**

ARK, proprietor, third generation: The business was ...nded by my grandfather, Joel Russ. He came to ...nerica around the turn of the century from Eastern ...rope, to escape from the Russian draft. He started in ... Jewish ghetto on the Lower East Side, with a ...rse and wagon, peddling Polish mushrooms. It was a ...ple then and they were cheap. We have them ...nging in the window now; they're $150 a pound. Russ' Cut-rate Appetizing Store was officially ...ablished in 1914. My grandfather was a good ...sinessman, but he had no patience for the public. ...en he started bringing his three daughters to work, ...ople came to see these young, pretty and charming ...men picking herrings out of a barrel and the business ...rted to grow. In the 1920s, it became Russ & ...ughters.

...NE, one of the three original Russ Daughters, and

were talking about selling Russ and Daughters. Thi... was in 1977 when my parents were running the business. I said I'd help out and practice law on my own on the side. The day I came here was probably ... last day I practiced law.

At first, my wife kind of resented it. Maria is from ... South American high society and she thought she married a lawyer, not a herring man. She's not Jewish and she never saw a herring before.

MARIA, Partner, and Mark's wife: When I was dating Mark we used to come here every Saturday night an... they would give us food for Sunday brunch and I loved it. We ate it more then than we eat it now.

MARK: Maria got sandbagged, but I couldn't have done it without her. She's in charge of all the paperwork and the bills. She also handles the candy ...

Smoked salmon at the venerable Forman & Son in London, above, and, inset, a specialty of the house at Russ & Daughte... on Houston Street.

So Pink, So New York

Salmon is the heart of a classic Sunday brunch.
Its long and winding route to the bagel is a quintessential city tale.

By ERIKA KINETZ

THE seriousness of fall, with its early twilights, overbooked restaurants and new television shows, has descended, and the simple, enduring rituals of city life that seemed impertinent in the heat are reviving. In other words, brunch is back.

The quintessential New York brunch involves a deceptively simple triumvirate: bagel, cream cheese and lox. It is salmon that lies at the heart of this classic dish, and salmon that lies at the heart of its mystery. Those innocent pink ribbons of flesh could tell a tale of battered national pride, ecological battles, ethnic inauthenticity, economic flux and jousting connoisseurs, a tale that spans the globe and the centuries.

The history of a fish is bound to be blurry. But the story of where smoked salmon comes from and how it became a symbol of New York is especially elusive.

A sign behind the cool glass counter at Russ & Daughters, a Houston Street delicatessen that began life in 1905 as a pickled herring pushcart, reads, "Lox et veritas." Both are in short supply these days.

Mark Russ Federman, the 57-year-old owner, grandson of the original Russ, pointed to a meaty, deep pink chunk of fish: lox, which in his store means the rich, brine-cured belly of a wild Pacific salmon. "That's where it all started," he said.

But today, lox accounts for only a small fraction of his salmon sales.

"People use lox as a general term — bagel and lox — but what is traditional and genuine lox is not smoked salmon at all," said Mr. Federman's daughter Niki, who also works at the shop. "It is a salmon cured in salt brine. No refrigeration needed. When people come into the store, they ask for lox, and we say, 'Are you sure?' "

Terry Huggins, charcuterie manager at Dean & DeLuca, has not sold a piece of lox since 1980. Even at Barney Greengrass, that emporium of nostalgia, lox doesn't sell well, and Saul Zabar himself prefers the more modern, Nova-style smoked fish. Today, most of the Sunday-morning salmon sold in New York — 2,500 pounds each week at Zabar's alone — is not lox, but lightly salted and smoked salmon.

For some traditionalists, the dainty stuff now in vogue will not do.

"When I'm in the mood, this is the only one that's satisfying," Mr. Federman said. "My grandfather started with this. Somehow that on a bagel makes it for me." His lox oozes with ocean, begging for cream cheese to counter the saltiness. "It is roots and nostalgia, that salt

Continued on Page 12

Show-off Season for Smoked Fish

Lenten Favorites Shipped From Houston Street to Hollywood

By Clementine Paddleford

Tons of smoked fish are in the market for Lent. Yes, here the year around, but Lent is their show-off season. A pity it is that few cooks born and raised in America know about the adaptability, the flavor, the variety of these deliciously cured fish.

Since the coming of the cocktail hour smoked salmon, smoked sturgeon, and smoked shrimp are in popularity, a "shoe horn" for cocktails. But there are so many others in the clan which may well take important place in winter menus.

To many, smoked fish means simply finnan haddie. To others it is kippers eaten for breakfast in English novels. Here in New York smoked fish to millions means lox to accompany the bagel. Sturgeon, white fish, smoked mackerel, butter fish, bloaters, carp are also much around.

Smoked fish was known and appreciated by the Indian before the coming of the white man and there has been romance in its history since the white man arrived. Channel Island fishermen from Guernsey and Jersey settled in and near Marblehead in the early 1600s Dissenters from England came to Gloucester, and fishermen from both towns sailed to the Grand Banks and brought back their glistening loads. Smoke from the smoke houses between the two ports has perfumed the salty air these three hundred years and more.

Gloucester bloaters are known the year around. Bloaters are just herring (as are kippers) caught in Newfoundland and smoked in ...

A Gentile's Guide to Jewish Food
Part I:
The Appetizing Store

By Milton Glaser and Jerome Snyder

"Along with an array of fish, the store offers fruits and candy. Halvah is beautiful, and tastes like a sweet straw placemat."

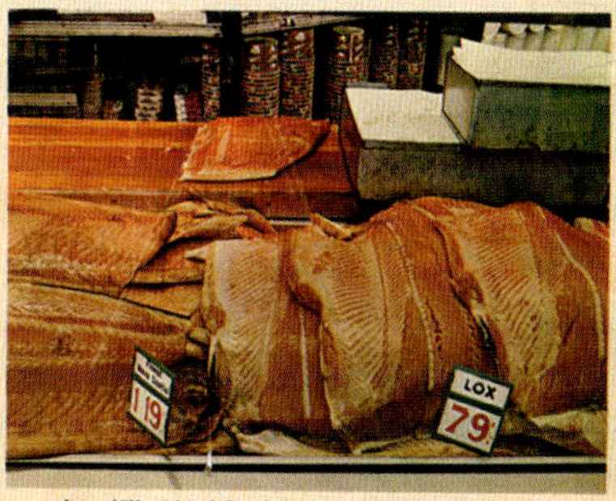

Lox and "Novy" lying belly to belly at Russ and Daughters appetizing store.

"Go to the appetizing and get halfa quarter belly." For those of Jewish background, this Saturday night injunction has a familiar ring. Translated for others it means "go to the appetizing store and purchase an eighth of a pound (2 ounces) of smoked salmon." Belly is the term that refers specifically to the under part of the common smoked salmon. The cut from that section of the salmon's anatomy is fattier, saltier, cheaper and deeper in color than the more expensive smoked salmon called Nova Scotia, which is essentially the same species of fish but debrined and slightly sweetened. In New York both varieties are called "lox", the latter more precisely "novy". Along with bagels and possibly cream cheese, lox is the most familiar Jewish fish delicacy known to Gentiles. The appetizing store, a repository for myriad other lesser known and equally delicious items, is a unique and wonderful institution. To be precise, the items in an appetizing store were and are not necessarily Jewish inventions. The Jews exercise an international gastronomic curatorship by bringing together and developing foods of Scandinavian, Middle European and Near Eastern origins.

The basic stock in the appetizing stores (sometimes called appetizers) consists of an impressive array of ready-to-eat pickled, smoked and salted fish, fish and vegetable salads, sour pickles, tomatoes, peppers, sauerkraut, a variety of breads and rolls, dried fruits, nuts and candies. All these wares are generally displayed and dispensed before a multi-colored background wall of canned specialty foods. To return to lox, most of the salted variety is shipped down from Alaskan waters, while the Aristocratic Nova Scotia comes from around the Gaspé Peninsula in Quebec. If lox is king in the appetizing hierarchy, then sturgeon must be emperor. The firm, white flesh which comes from this prehistoric fish species has a deliciously distinctive, nutty flavor. At one time in the not long past, sturgeon fishing was a viable industry in the Hudson River before its tragic pollution. Present supplies of the fish come from the Great Lakes. Sturgeon, not always in great supply, is treated reverently, cut in paper-thin slices and sold anywhere from $8.00 to $12.00 per pound. Because of its high price, a cheaper substitute has been developed, which might somewhat liberally be called "poor man's sturgeon": sable, which is a smoked California black cod, at $1.60 to $2.00 per pound.

Smoked winter carp which comes in thick golden brown chop-like slabs is another surrogate sturgeon which has many advocates because of its insistent fishy and oily flavor. Carp, like sable, is sold both as chunks and sliced from a large de-boned

Photographs by Sol Mednick

Holiday Season Is No Holiday in Caviar Wars

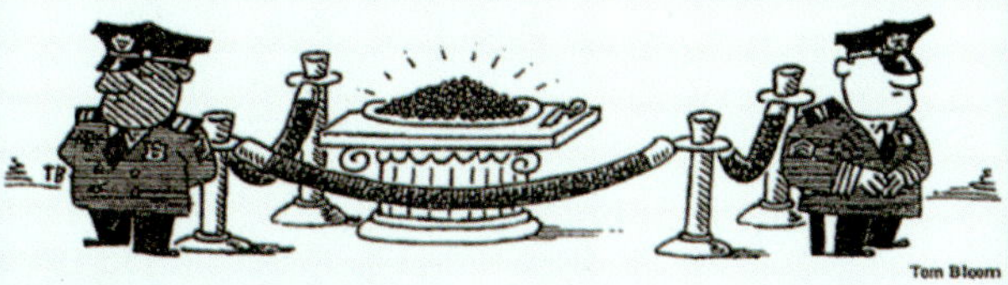

Tom Bloom

FRESH caviar supplies are tight this year, and prices in many places have increased by up to 25 percent. Nonetheless, Macy's, Zabar's tradition-al foe, is armed to the teeth with low prices. And this year, Citarella is challenging Zabar's for the first time.

But Zabar's is not changing its prices. "I'm out of the caviar wars this year," said Saul Zabar, an owner. "We're doing the best we can with quality caviar."

On a price-to-quality basis, the caviar to buy is osetra, the nutty tasting medium-size roe that is 10 to 20 percent more expensive than the darker, smaller sevruga. It is half the price of large, delicate beluga. The smaller the tin, the more the caviar costs per ounce.

These are the prices for a 14-ounce tin (except where otherwise noted):

Caviarteria, 502 Park Avenue (59th Street): sevruga $279, osetra $349, beluga $695.

Citarella, 2135 Broadway (75th Street): sevruga $125, osetra $165, beluga $265.

Macy's Herald Square: sevruga $105, osetra $121, beluga $235.

Petrossian (17.5 ounces), 182 West 58th Street: sevruga $375, osetra $495, beluga $1,100.

Russ & Daughters, 179 East Houston Street (Allen Street): sevruga $199, osetra $249, beluga $498.

Urbani Truffle, at Terra Mare, 22 East 65th Street: sevruga $160, osetra $165, beluga $289.

Vinegar Factory, 431 East 91st Street: sevruga $127, osetra $159, beluga $269.

Zabar's, 2245 Broadway (80th Street): sevruga $127, osetra $165, beluga $269.

Daughters who fill dad's shoes

SUNDAY, MARCH 20, 1977

By CONSTANCE ROSENBLUM

WHEN A WOMEN'S group once tried to find a business whose sign read "So-and-so and Daughter" for an ad campaign, it had to fake it by doctoring a "Father and Son" sign. The New York daughter who goes into daddy's business is a rare breed.

But the city has a *few* such teams—ranging from lawyers to undertakers—and as the women's movement propels *more* women into the work force, there'll be more.

One finger in the wind might be "The Feather and Father Gang," a new TV series about a father-daughter partnership on NBC. While it's not necessarily an arrangement to emulate—Feather's a lawyer, her father's a sweet but scheming con artist—it may at least suggest the drift of things to come.

•

youngest, remains, with her husband, Herb Federman, who married into the business 37 years ago.

Anne, a short, no-nonsense person like her late father, says joining the family firm was a natural step for a girl growing up during the Depression. And, as her father often told her, "They don't teach sechel (common sense) in college."

Joel Russ died in 1961. But his portrait dominates the store, staring down on customers like Zero Mostel and Bella Abzug, who come in for Beluga caviar, sturgeon, dried figs and other delicacies.

•

What kind of lawyer calls her partner daddy?

Elsie Reilly, for one. She calls him daddy, rather than sir or a more formal father, because the pair are partners in a father-daughter law firm.

When Elsie, a striking, articulate woman, graduated from St. John's law school in 1953, there was never any doubt where she would work.

"I'd have felt almost guilty going someplace else," she says of the decision to join her father's Manhattan

Local residents were shocked: was this a job for a lady? Even Rose's husband, Pasquale, who ran a movie theater, wasn't keen on the idea. But her father, Vincent, was solidly behind her.

As Vincent grew older, and after his death, Mrs. Scotto took a more commanding role in the business. Her husband eventually sold his theater and joined the business, too, but he died recently. Today Mrs. Scotto, 73, and her son, Buddy, are partners in the Court St. firm.

Mrs. Scotto thinks a woman's touch adds something special. "People like it, especially if it's a woman who has died."

Often, Mrs. Scotto says, people ask for her or her daughter, who takes an active part in the business. "We feel we're wanted, which is nice. Once we thought we weren't."

•

James McGovern always dreamed that his sons would take over his Park Slope flower store and, with six boys, he thought he had a pretty good chance.

Genesis: A History of the Family Russ

Haimish. If there's one word that defines Russ & Daughters it's this Yiddish term for home-like and humble. Haimish is a feeling as much as it is a philosophy. To us it means never straying far from our roots. So what are our roots, the long history that connects us to the pushcarts and herring barrels of the past?

The story of Russ & Daughters is at heart one of the interplay between ambition and passion, duty and desire, continuity and change. Each generation of Russ & Daughters had its own relationship with the business. For our great-grandfather Joel Russ, what became Russ & Daughters was a way to escape the impoverished shtetlach of Eastern Europe and to make it to (the impoverished shtetlach of) New York City. For his children—the titular daughters—the business was both an imposition from an early age and a means of survival. For the third generation, embodied by Mark, who is Anne's son and was a lawyer before entering the business, Russ & Daughters was a choice, although at the time not thought of as a very glamorous one. And for us, the fourth generation, Russ & Daughters has become something that not only we chose to enter into, but something precious we know is our duty to protect. For four generations, Russ & Daughters has been our family's life's work. Sometimes that has meant hanging on; today that means flourishing. Always it has meant honoring the soulful plain-spoken haimish spirit of the business, established so many years ago by Joel Russ, even as we bring Russ & Daughters into the twenty-first century.

Joel was one of the over 200,000 Jews from Galicia (modern-day southeastern Poland and western Ukraine) who emigrated to New York between 1881 and 1910. In the winter of 1907, Joel arrived from a small shtetl called Strzyzov, at the age of 21. He had been summoned by his eldest sister, Channah, who had already emigrated to the United States. Though Joel had apprenticed to be a shoemaker in Strzyzov, Channah's husband, Moishe, ran a herring stand on the Lower East Side. When he quit the business to study the Talmud, leaving Channah to manage both herring and caring for their eight children, Channah sponsored her younger brother to help with herring. He was given a barrel of herring and told to make a living. (Had Moishe been, instead, a shoemaker, we might have been the fourth-generation of Russ & Daughters Cobbler.)

East Houston Street, 1929

Joel was a hardworking, studious, and serious salesman. From a single barrel of schmaltz herring, Joel graduated to a pushcart, then a horse-and-wagon, and finally to a sliver of a shop of his own. Adept as he was at catering to the herring desires of his fellow immigrants, squeezing words out of Joel Russ was a difficult task. Friendly banter an impossible one. Thankfully the herring spoke for itself. By 1909 he had made enough money to not only pay Channah back the sponsorship fee but to engage a matchmaker. Soon he was married to a fellow Galician, Bella Spier. Joel struck out on his own. After a brief interlude as a candy store owner on Myrtle Avenue in Brooklyn, Joel returned to the Lower East Side in 1914 to open Russ's Cut Rate Appetizing—originally J. Russ National Appetizing, revealing his ambitions—in a dark and narrow storefront at 187 Orchard Street.

If you had walked down Orchard Street back then, threading your way around the vendors that crowded the street, you might not have thought twice about the store. Crowded with barrels of pickled herring, strings of dried Polish mushrooms called *borowic,* and sun-dried uneviserated smoked whitefish called *kapchunka*, their fat dripping slowly onto the sawdust floors, Russ's Cut Rate Appetizing was just one of many bakeries, appetizing stores, dairies, butcher shops, tailors, shoemakers, and rag traders that both catered to and were owned by poor immigrants. Nor would Joel himself—bespectacled, mustachioed, standing at the threshold of his business—strike you as exceptional. His story was just one of thousands of similar narratives. Like many immigrant shopkeepers, he and his rapidly growing family lived in a small apartment behind the store that furnished them a meager living. It was there where the first three of their four children were born: Morris, a son, in 1908; Hattie, in 1913; and Ida in 1915. It was there where Morris died just shy of his second birthday during the typhoid epidemic of 1910. Thankfully, by the time Anne, the last of the Russ daughters, was born in 1921, Joel had scrounged enough to move to a fourth-floor tenement across the street. It was cramped, dark, cold in the winter, and unbearable in the summer. Nevertheless, it was a step up.

Two years later, when Joel took over a former storage facility at 179 East Houston Street, Russ's Cut Rate Appetizing found its forever home. Though only sixteen feet wide by forty feet deep, the store was a major improvement from the original location, sitting as it did on the southern side of a busy street. Joel lined the walls with cans of tinned fish from floor to ceiling on one side and staples like dried mushrooms on the other. He installed a long counter topped with a scale. Every morning he'd visit the smokehouses in Brooklyn to source the best whitefish, chubs, and sides of salmon belly lox. The roughneck smokers grew to grudgingly respect his keen evaluative eye; his customers found that, while not always polite, Joel delivered them the best product.

By 1926, such was the success of Russ's Cut Rate Appetizing that Joel again moved his family. This time out of the Lower East Side to the somewhat more idyllic Flatbush/Midwood section of Brooklyn. Sadly, few triumphs are quick and fewer long lasting. Only nine years later, during the nadir of the Great Depression, Joel, unable to make mortgage payments, was given the option by the bank to sell either house or his business. Joel is said to have replied, "Vi nempt men parnosa?" From where do we take our living? This has, since then, become a family motto, a way of orienting ourselves and the business, to keep ourselves firmly grounded.

Hattie, Anne, and Ida, 1927

Much to the consternation of Bella and the children, Joel sold the house and moved the family back to a tenement apartment on the Lower East Side. Though the store was saved, Bella, as the family lore goes, never recovered from the move, and spent the rest of her life in a diminished state. Like Sisyphus, again Joel began to climb, spending every moment of his life devoted to the store, from those pre-dawn smokehouse visits to the late-night cleaning. In a few years, he saved up enough to move the family to a slightly larger apartment in the Lower East Side's Ageloff Towers.

Anne behind the counter, 1937

While Joel toiled, his daughters balanced the demands of their schooling and an incipient sense of freedom with their father's expectation that they work in the store. Weekdays after school, every weekend, every holiday the daughters spent at the store. (The only exception was Passover, when the shop was closed.) As soon as each graduated high school, they were conscripted to work. The sisters approached the task with varying degrees of enthusiasm. Always responsible, the eldest, Hattie, dutifully took her place among the barrels. Rebellious Ida bucked at her father's authority. Anne, the youngest and most eager to please, accepted her fate stoically. Joel, meanwhile, noticed that his daughters could schmooze, a task he either couldn't or didn't want to do.

Joel Russ might not have been a progressive man but he was a canny one. In 1935, he formally changed the name of the business to Russ & Daughters and made Hattie, Anne, and Ida partners. Alone among the appetizing stores on the Lower East Side, only his was publicly entrusted to his daughters. To many of his neighbors, the choice was *meshuge*. To others, who assumed there must have been a Mr. Daughters, it was simply confusing. To some, including future Supreme Court Justice Ruth Bader Ginsburg, it was inspiring. "Before I knew the word *feminism*," she told us in the 2014 Russ & Daughters documentary *The Sturgeon Queens*, "seeing a sign for *Russ & Daughters* taught me that women could matter just like men in an enterprise." Joel's instincts, whether noble or not, were right. The presence of the three lovely young ladies, arms deep in the herring barrel, proved popular with his customers.

Hattie, Joel, Ida, and Anne, circa 1955

Soon enough the daughters were married. Ida to Max, Hattie to Murray, and Anne to Herbie, whose own mother—shockingly—had dubbed him the Prince of Brooklyn. The Sturgeon Queen and the Prince of Brooklyn. It was, according to family lore, *bashert*. The two younger daughters and their husbands worked at the store under Joel's ever-watchful eye. Shortly after World War II, Joel bought a two-family house in Far Rockaway. Anne's family lived on the first floor, Hattie's on the second. Joel and Bella in a red cottage in the back. By this time Ida had left the business with her husband Max but, along with their daughter Lolly, joined the Rockaway exodus shortly after, living nearby in their own house.

In 1949, just three years before he (barely) retired, Joel took over the space occupied by Baskin's Bakery next door, renovating the store for the first time in thirty years. The narrow store almost doubled in width. A candy aisle was added, with bins of hard candies meant to soothe restless children. The window was taken up with a toothsome display of all sorts of dried fruit from around the world. Over this new and expanded spread, Murray and Herbie were largely responsible. For though the Russ daughters were titularly in charge, Joel still thought of his sons-in-law as the true operators. In 1952, the sixty-six-year-old Joel had tired of the daily grind of Russ & Daughters and started coming in only four or five days a week, to sit in his red armchair and bark orders to all those who would listen.

Of this second-generation Russ & Daughters we know little. The store was not yet an icon. Fishmongering had not the poetic patina it has today. So why keep track? Russ & Daughters was just the family business. We do know it was a time of transition. After World War II, the demographics of the Lower East Side began to change, as the largely Eastern European immigrants from the turn of the century gave way to Puerto Rican and Dominican arrivals. Within the four walls of Russ & Daughters, much remained the same. The slicers were a mix of old-timers, like the gruff World War II veteran Sidney, a holdover from Joel's later era; and his sidekick, a rotund man named Steiny. But newcomers, guys like the Dominican cousins Herman Vargas and Jose Reyes, came from the neighborhood. Herbie, though not as cute as the Russ daughters, proved himself adept at their art of schmoozing. Even as our traditional clientele moved to the suburbs—or otherwise fled the tenements of their youth—many returned every week to Russ & Daughters. But it would not be correct to say the business was booming. It survived and that was, perhaps, enough. Dayenu.

From a first-generation immigrant's perspective, Russ & Daughters had served its purpose. It had been the engine that had propelled Joel Russ from penniless immigrant to a somewhat prosperous home-owning patriarch. By the time he died, in 1961, he and his kin were firmly ensconced in the middle class. Herbie and Anne's children—Tara (1943), Mark (1945), and Hope (1949)—worked their time at the store; it was after all a family business. But each had a path as far from the Lower East Side as could be. After graduating college—college!—Tara and Hope moved upstate, to live in an ashram and pursue a spiritual life. Mark,

Herb and Anne, 1972

From left to right: Maria, pregnant with her son, Noah; Mark; Anne; Uma, holding the balloon; and Tara, holding Josh, 1975

to the great joy of all the Russes before him, from Strzyzov to the Rockaways, became an attorney. The American dream had been achieved.

After Hattie and Murray retired in 1976, Anne and Herbie were left to run the increasingly sleepy store alone. Herbie was saddled with heart problems. Anne, who hadn't so much chosen Russ & Daughters as acquiesced to it, was tired of a life spent with lox. Most businesses don't last even one generation. Russ & Daughters had lasted two. Perhaps it was time to call it a day.

For their son Mark, however, the thought of the store he had grown up in ceasing to exist was untenable and he was ready to change his life to ensure that didn't happen. Like Joel Russ, Mark wore a suit to work every day. Unlike Joel, he didn't smell of herring. As a trial attorney for a fancy boutique Manhattan law firm, Mark's days were taken up preparing for court appearances, poring over legal briefs, and fielding calls from clients. On one hand, this was the stuff his forebearers had dreamt of for him. On the other, for Mark himself, it felt isolating and overwhelming. He remembers sitting at the dinner table, exhausted and preoccupied, while his wife, Maria Carvajal, a Colombian research chemist, tried to engage him in conversation, and two young children, Noah and Niki, vied for his attention. He could focus on neither the conversation nor the food. If he did step into his father's shoes at Russ & Daughters, he thought, he'd be solving two problems at once. First, the store would survive. Second, he'd have his life back. For how all-consuming could fish possibly be?

Mark in the store, 1993

In 1978, Mark agreed to come back to Russ & Daughters part-time while still practicing law. That arrangement, never tenable, unsurprisingly failed to materialize. Like his mother and father before him, Mark took his place behind the counter. The transition of the Lower East Side of the 1950s had given way to a general decline by the '60s, '70s, and '80s. The neighborhood, like much of New York, was beset by high crime and low property values. The Lower East Side—which sticklers will note referred to the area stretching from Chinatown to 14th Street—was particularly hard hit. Buildings sat empty and abandoned, many smoldering; city services had all but fully retreated. Many, if not all, of the bakeries, appetizing stores, and delicatessens that once crowded the streets had disappeared.

For us, it was an era of simple survival. Not that it was easy. Mark walked into a business bearing his name but he did so as an outsider (and, until 1986, an hourly employee). Customers dismissed him as a *schlemiel*, incredulous that he would abandon law for lox. Slicers from his father's era resented him as a newcomer. Smokehouse men, remembering him as a boy at his father's side, had to be convinced that he could tell a good fish from a bad one.

Yet day in and day out, he was the Russ behind the counter, the Russ you could count on. And so eventually, as it had in every previous generation, the business became his. By the mid-1990s, the Lower East Side had turned a corner. Demographic shifts and crime had driven out its residents. But those same high vacancy rates made the tenement buildings palatable for a young generation of artists and musicians. And everyone came to Russ & Daughters: the vanguard of the new LES as well as the longtime residents whose rent-controlled apartments insulated them from the increasing gentrification. By this time, august personages like the *New Yorker* writer Calvin Trillin, *New York* magazine's Milton Glaser, and Martha Stewart, who grew up coming to the shop, among many others, had featured us in the pages of their publications and that attention kept a steady stream of the curious pushing open our doors. They left as acolytes of appetizing. Families drove in, parking on Houston Street, no longer quite as afraid that their hubcaps would be stolen. When Mark had time to look up from the counter, he saw tourists, filling the store with accents foreign to the four walls. More and more, Russ & Daughters came to be seen as an institution, an embassy of a bygone world, one of the last haimish stores on the Lower East Side.

The store was flourishing but needed attention. In 1995—during the annual Russ family vacation—Mark and Maria undertook the store's second renovation in eighty years. He installed a new forty-foot counter, replaced the worn-through linoleum with tile, softened the lighting, and made, as he says, Russ & Daughters truly his. This refreshed Russ & Daughters regained its vigor and as the fortunes of the Lower East Side rose, so too did ours. But as the twentieth century gave on to the twenty-first, Mark was getting older and thinking of the next generation. This is where our story—the story of Josh and Niki—begins.

Jose Reyes, 1981

Anne Russ Federman, circa 1970s

Herb Federman, 1965

Maria Federman, 1985

Nina Gold, 1954

Herman Vargas, 2016

Josh, Mark, and Niki, 2010

Ron Riccio, 2014

Autumn Starr, 2024

Niki (five) pushed by Walter Reynosa, 1982

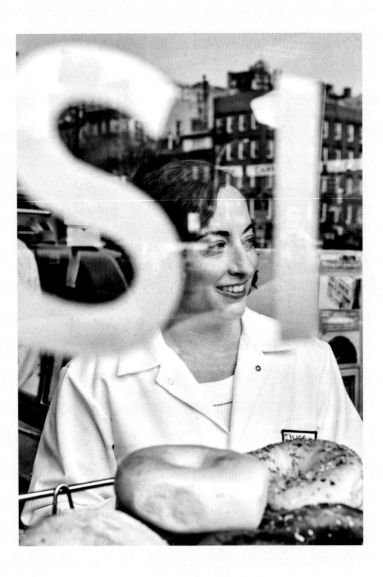

NIKI RUSS FEDERMAN

I AM THE FOURTH-GENERATION owner of Russ & Daughters, the great-granddaughter of Joel Russ, the granddaughter of his youngest daughter, Anne, and the daughter of her only son, Mark. Lox, as my father likes to say, is in my blood. For most of the world Russ & Daughters is, as *The New York Times* called it, "the most hallowed shrine to the miracle of caviar, smoked salmon, ethereal herring and silken chopped liver." It is that. But for me, it's also my home and legacy.

Like Anne and her sisters, Hattie and Ida, the original daughters, I grew up in the store, riding pallets of potatoes and onions as a toddler, running errands for my mom and dad to the neighboring dairies and bakeries. I was witness to millions of exchanges: of fish, of gossip, of lore, of shoptalk. But I never thought my own life would lead me back to East Houston Street.

For years, I tried as hard as I could to avoid ending up back at Russ & Daughters. To me, Russ & Daughters wasn't a glamorous place. It was an appetizing shop on the Lower East Side. For much of my life, it was a struggling shop on a dismal block, one that ate up my weekends and holidays. To my parents' credit, they never insisted I join the business. In fact, like so many Lower East Siders—and the progeny of Lower East Siders—all the blood, sweat, and tears of my ancestors seemed orchestrated so I wouldn't have to return. And it almost worked. Most of my twenties were spent blazing my own path. I worked in arts administration at a museum in San Francisco and for a nonprofit in New York. True, for some time in the early aughts, I lived above the store and helped out, but when Dad asked if I wanted the business, back in 2002, I saw my entire future collapse into this one store and said no thanks. Instead I enrolled in the Yale School of Management and fled to Connecticut. Even upon learning business school wasn't for me, I stayed in New Haven. I worked in a divorce attorney's office. I taught yoga. I worked a series of odd jobs. Any job, in fact, seemed better than returning to Russ & Daughters.

And yet, this seemingly wayward period proved to be the ground on which I re-engaged with my family's business. It was then, with no eyes upon me, that I began to contemplate the idea of lineage, what it meant. What occurred to me in a thousand little moments was that it needn't be a burden. It wasn't a weight pulling me down, but a support buoying me up. My lineage was, instead, a rare gift, an opportunity. How often does one get the chance to steward and preserve a century's worth of family tradition while also getting the chance, because I was of it and effortlessly a part of it, to put their own stamp on it? So by 2006, with my father now seriously retiring, I asked him whether I could rejoin Russ & Daughters, not as I did as a child—that is, without a choice—but as an adult. By then, my cousin Josh had come in to learn the business and was working alongside our longtime manager, Herman Vargas. Of course, my dad being my dad, was still at the store nearly every day. Some things are hard to let go.

So at the age of twenty-seven, I finally returned to Russ & Daughters, the fourth generation of Russes to find themselves behind the counter. It wasn't exactly the path for my life I had imagined. But, unlike my grandmother or her sisters, it was 100 percent my choice. This is my lineage, my heritage. As I see Grandma Anne and Great-Grandfather Joel gazing out at me now from the pictures lining the walls of the store, twenty years later, I no longer see in their eyes judgment or expectation, but silent support. Not that I have too much time to contemplate. There's lox to slice, customers to serve, and a business to run.

JOSH RUSS TUPPER

I'M A RUSS THROUGH-AND-THROUGH, but of a different stripe than Niki. I'm the eldest son of Anne's eldest daughter, Tara. But the very nature of a family tree is that, from one central trunk, branches spread wide. My mother grew up in the store on East Houston. She too rode pallets of potatoes and onions. She too knew the difference between Gaspe Nova and western Nova before most kids knew their colors. But she scrammed as soon as she could and never looked back. First, as a teen, to a kibbutz in Israel, then to Italy to paint, and finally, to a spiritual community in Upstate New York, where my sisters and I were born. Since we lived in a vegetarian ashram, I didn't know appetizing from Adam.

The only glimpses of the family business I had came on our occasional visits to Grandma Anne, who lived in Gramercy. Though we lived a mere two hours north of Manhattan, we made the trip no more than a few times a year. Russ & Daughters meant getting to see my cousins, standing behind the counter and "stealing" candy. (I eventually realized our stealing was sanctioned.) My mother, somewhat grudgingly, would order platters of lox, herring, and whitefish, then we'd all head to Grandma Anne's, where, ever the shopkeeper, she'd look over the spread. What I remember most from those days is my competition with my cousin Dave to see who could make the most massive sandwich, piling all there was to pile onto bagels then shoving the things into our mouths. We loved the game as much as my grandmother hated it.

Other than those few visits, Russ & Daughters was in the periphery of my life. At age ten, we left the ashram and I discovered ice hockey, eventually getting a scholarship to a prestigious boarding school in Minnesota. I returned to Upstate New York to go to college and, after I studied chemical engineering, moved to Portland, Oregon, where I worked as an engineer designing factories for the likes of Intel. I could see my life stretch before me. I was good at my job but not very happy at it. Did I really want my days to be filled with poorly catered meetings with intermittent rounds of golf on the weekend as my only respite? The answer was no. So, when I got word from my mother that Uncle Mark was thinking of selling the business—my mom must have told him I was adrift—I called him and told him I'd love to take over. He was surprised and very skeptical. "You've hardly been in the store at all," he said. "You know, it's very hard work. Six days a week, ten hours a day. That's the way it is." "I know," I said, "but I'm willing to learn. Let's give it a try." He acquiesced. That summer, I packed up all my things and drove back East. I moved into an apartment above the store and thus started a new life as a lox macher. The point is, whereas Niki grew up at the store, and her path seemed to inexorably lead there, mine didn't.

I knew I didn't know much. But, as I said to Mark, I was willing to work and willing to learn. Thankfully both Mark and Herman Vargas were there to help guide me. I listened to the slicers, some of whom, like Jose Reyes, had been there since I was just two or three years old. I also had every regular, who each had an opinion of how things should be done. Some advice I heeded; some I knew enough not to. Mark, of course, was around. Six days a week, ten hours a day at first. But eventually he trusted me more and more. (Not that he'd ever say that; simply not showing up was a measure of trust.) In 2006, after I had been there for about four years, Niki decided to return and we had a long conversation about Russ & Daughters. Niki and I were friendly but not super close, which was, I later realized, the best way we could enter a business relationship. We had total trust in each other but none of the baggage of a closer relationship or rivalry. What became clear was that our visions of Russ & Daughters were aligned. With Mark sufficiently comfortable with the new guard, Niki and I made Russ & Daughters our own. We've tried to keep all innovation unobtrusive. In the same spirit, Great-Grandpa Joel and Grandma Anne's insistence on quality remains present. And though our clientele is much changed from the neighborhood regulars with their heavy Yiddish accents, we continue to do as the Russes have always done: build community over slices of lox, family over dozens of bagels, and communion over cream cheese.

A BISSEL OF RUSSES

IT'S NOT OFTEN that we Russes get together to reminisce. We kibbitz often. We share meals. Mark is a frequent presence at the Cafe; Niki and her family—Christopher, her husband; Maya and Elan, her daughter and son—are often at Mark and Maria's house for dinner. But nostalgia isn't in our bones. In fact, we can't remember a time when we all gathered specifically to look back on our life's work. It's not that Russ & Daughters doesn't come up. It does. The better question is when doesn't it come up. But our conversations tend to be practical: how the fish are coming in; which old-time customers stopped by and sent their regards; when this year's herring catch will arrive; the state of caviar. As far as we know, Joel never contentedly communed with his daughters in reflection. Nor did Mark with his mother and father. Nostalgia is not a Russ trait. But it's a rare thing for a business to reach a fourth generation—only 1 percent of family businesses do—so on a recent afternoon Niki, Josh, Mark, and Maria gathered in a back booth of the Cafe to take stock.

NIKI: I can't believe we've never really sat down before to reflect on Russ & Daughters.

MARK: Reflection is for retirement. That'll be the tagline of my next book.

NIKI: Each of us had our own path into the business. Josh, you came to Russ & Daughters as an adult. Mom, you married into it. Dad and I might have the most in common, since we grew up in the store.

MARK: You couldn't help but be surrounded by Russ lore. You and your brother got it osmotically. What happened at the store during the day was dinner table discussion that night.

NIKI: That's also when I realized I could never marry someone I would work with.

MARK: It has its plusses and minuses. If you're a mom-and-pop shop, you want a mom to go with a pop.

MARIA: I didn't exactly marry into the business, at least not knowingly. When I married your father, he was a lawyer. I had no idea he would quit his job to sell fish!

JOSH: Or that you would go from being a research chemist to running the back end of an appetizing store. How did that happen?

MARIA: After Niki and her brother were born, I didn't go back to work. I started coming into the store more often. At that point, you had to be Jewish to work in the front. Someone with a Colombian accent like me? Forget about it. At that time, the customers weren't very accepting. So I began working in the back, taking care of the accounting and business operations.

MARK: They were barely accepting of me. When a customer came in, they expected, if not my grandfather, then my mother or aunt, my father or my uncles. When I showed up, they said, "Who is this guy?" When they found out that I had been a lawyer they looked at me like, "Were you disbarred?" Eventually I won them over. After all, I had grown up around schmoozing—my father was a world-class schmoozer—so it came natural to me.

Also, even though Maria wasn't as gregarious, she was a tremendous help. I would say we need a soup or a salad or something and she would figure out how to make it and come back with a recipe. The soups, the gefilte fish, and many of the salads were made that way. You know that Jewish joke? My wife is a chemist. She takes money and makes it into *mishegoss*? In my case, she turned it into gefilte fish.

NIKI: I hadn't realized this until listening to the two of you, but running a business like this requires a lot of different elements. In a way, you two are a bit of yin and yang. By absorbing aspects of your complementary personalities, I think I absorbed those skills too. There's the public facing part, which I get from you, Dad: engaging with the public and being the host, the storyteller, the kibitzer. And there's being analytical, being behind the scenes, doing the thinking, the administrative and quantitative work that also underpins everything. That I got from you, Mom.

JOSH: Niki, in some ways you're right about your path and your dad's being similar. If you're talking about the experience of the business growing up, sure. But if you're talking about leaving an established career, that's me. Your dad left being a lawyer to join the family business; I left a career as an engineer and a life in Portland to come try my hand at Russ & Daughters.

MARIA: Mark, were you ner—?

MARK: You don't even have to finish that sentence. Yes, I was very nervous. Josh had never been in the business. What did he know from smoked fish? What did he know about running a family business? On the other hand, how could I object? I hadn't seriously worked in the business before I took over either. One big difference, though, is the trajectories were reversed. By the time I took over, Russ & Daughters—and the entire Lower East Side—was in decline. When Josh came, in 2002, not only the business but the neighborhood was on the rise again.

NIKI: You thought we had it easy.

MARK: I thought you had it easy, but I'm assuming my parents and aunts and uncles thought that I had it easy somehow too.

JOSH: When we took over, the challenges were totally different. For one, there was a clientele transition. Remember all the conversations we had about our customers getting older, moving away, or dying? I remember thinking, "What's going to happen to the business in ten or twenty years?"

NIKI: Josh and I don't approach things with an explicit strategy of how to capture a younger generation. But I do think that the fact that we're carrying on our family tradition resonates with them, whether or not they are Jewish. We realized there was a new generation but they're not going to be the same type of customers we had in the past. Like you said, Dad, previously Russ & Daughters was a Jewish store with Jewish products run by Jewish people and sold to Jewish people. As both our clientele and our staff became more diverse, that was no longer the case.

Also, after September 11th there was a cultural shift. People began to reevaluate what professional success looked like. There was a deeper appreciation for makers, for people who work with their hands. That extended to the world of food. Bankers suddenly wanted to become bakers. We are a reflection of that, too.

MARK: That was a tough transition for me to accept, to be honest. When I was running Russ & Daughters, I was at the counter every day. What that meant is that I couldn't see beyond the store. I knew the neighborhood was changing but I could only sense it. What you two have done is to step back in a way I never was able to, which has let you think about the business from a more panoramic lens.

NIKI: Growing up I watched you, Dad, ride the highs and lows of the business. And I'm sure you saw your parents do that and they saw Joel do that too. But one thing that it made me conscious of is the importance of finding a way to maintain equilibrium. I don't have a plan B. This is my life. I am very conscious of maintaining a balance, of never getting too riled up or too caught up in the moment. If both Josh and I were behind the counter every day, not only would we drive each other (and everybody else) crazy, but it would be hard to think bigger picture.

MARK: I wish I had learned that earlier. I had tried to do some of what you achieved but failed. For instance, I wanted to take over the lease of the adjoining store on Houston to make a sit-down cafe. But for whatever reason it didn't work out. Other projects, such as the bakery, or the online business, or the Midtown location, I never would have thought of. I'm proud of you. I'm *shopping naches.*

JOSH: And for us, we recognize that what we've been able to achieve is because you were there, every day, head down, behind the counter for so many years. You kept Russ & Daughters alive for us.

RUSS & DA

RUSS & DA

SARDINES
in olive oil

Minutes after the metal grates of 179 East Houston creak open, customers begin to push open the glass doors of the store into a Choose Your Own Adventure of Appetizing.

The first, and requisite stop, is the red Take-A-Number ticket dispenser mounted to the left. For years, Russ & Daughters was a free-for-all in which the most insistent elbower managed to order first. We operated on what we called a *see you* system. If a slicer looked up and made eye contact, you were theirs and they were yours. It was, to say the least, lively. The numbered tickets have quelled the chaos. As the numbers begin their inexorable tick higher, they give comfort for the customer.

There is no soundtrack playing, but the store is not quiet. Rather the music of commerce and kibbitzing create an ongoing score. Customers, their eyes roving over sides of salmon, strategize their order. Across the shoulder-high counter, slicers ask for orders, details, clarification, and offer guidance, advice, suggestions. Between the slicers, a sense of camaraderie knits them together and though they rarely chat on the line, they weave behind each other, as if in a delicate dance.

To your left, a counter and display case run the length of the space. First up, laid out in fetching array, are golden whitefish, chubs, trout, sable, sturgeon, and yellowfin tuna. If the first display case is a golden ode, the second is a symphony in white and beige. Containers of spreads, schmears, and cream cheeses; whitefish and baked salmon salads; trout mousse and hot smoke / cold smoke—they beckon like delectable paint swatches. Next to them, tubs of roes—the bright orange trout, the inky pearls of whitefish eggs, the bright green flying fish, and the pale pink salmon roe—add pops of color. As the counter continues, at the very middle of the store, the heart of Russ & Daughters, is our smoked salmon showcase. Pastrami-cured salmon sits in its dark coat of spice beside gravlax in its green garb of dill. Irish organic, Gaspe Nova, Scottish, wild western, and Norwegian are subtle variations of pale peach, orange, and sunset hues. Each wait to be plucked up, laid on the wooden cutting board, and expertly sliced.

Working your way past the salmon you come to our assorted appetizing, a Technicolor display of the foods so often found on your parents' and grandparents' tables: golden latkes on a plate; the burnt umber of chopped liver; the bright yellow egg salad alongside tuna salad, Romanian eggplant salad, new potato salad, and the magenta beet, apple, and herring salad; the gentle pink smoked salmon tartare; emerald pickles; the forest-colored orbs of mixed olives. The final section holds silvery herring, the original fish from whence, as Joel often said, we make our living. Neat fillets of pickled herring are displayed next to accoutrements of cream sauce and pickled onions. Beside them are smaller trays of curried herring, smoked fresh herring, Swedish matjes herring, roll mops.

Since 1950, when Joel took over the adjacent storefront, a former bakery, the west side of the store has been given over to chocolate and sweets. The bounty begins at the window, where tubs of dried plums, pears, apricots, and pineapple rings lure in passersby. A glass display case holds chocolates ranging from the contemporary—almond bark and sea salt caramels—to classics like chocolate-covered jelly rings. On top of the case are baskets full of fresh babka, a tower of halvah, a jar of mandel bread, licorice. On shelves on the back wall are old-fashioned glass jars full of dried figs, Swedish Fish, crystallized ginger, and more. Now, even though it's devoted mostly to baked goods, we still call this the candy side.

Working back from the candy counter, where once there were open barrels of coffee beans, today a refrigerated case holds many of our prepared foods: containers of bright borscht and golden matzo ball soup beckon. Made in our bakery across the river, tins of noodle kugel, trays of blintzes, and stacks of latkes can be picked up. Here you'll also find our famous orange juice, beet and lemon shrub, iced teas, and lemonades.

Beyond that, no customer shall pass through the narrow door to our backroom. A tiny nook of an office, a walk-in, a prep kitchen—in short the workspaces on which the entire operation rests. Glamorous it is not. Haimish it is, which is much more important.

Like guardians, paintings and photographs of Russes past line the upper perimeter of the store. A portrait of Mark painted in 2012, a painting of Joel, artist unknown. Black-and-white photographs of Anne with Zero Mostel, Joel and his daughters, give way to the sepia taupes of the next generation: Herbie in a suit, the Russ daughters as a gray-haired trio of sexagenarians. Between these mementos are other reminders of the past: large empty tins of caviar called OTs are artfully stacked; scales from years past, heavy things from the days before digital, await to be called back to duty. A small placard reading "De gustibus non est disputandum" (In matters of taste there are no disputes) hangs above the register to which we point when customers ask, "What is the best smoked salmon? What is the best bagel?" and we answer, "We wouldn't have it if it wasn't the best and best is whatever your taste buds prefer."

For most of our history, the store was, like a cheesemonger's or a butcher shop, not a place to purchase a finished product but a place to provision for gatherings at home. Be it a whole smoked whitefish (a fatty one please!), a herring, a pound of silky thinly sliced lox, a quart of matzo ball soup, a handful of dried apricots or chocolates or hard candies, what one picked up at Russ & Daughters was meant to be shared. Russ & Daughters products are staples at brises and birthdays, brunches and break fasts. You'll find Russ & Daughters spreads at wakes and at shivas, at Rosh Hashanah, Christmas, New Year's and everything in between. Anywhere people gather, brought together in happiness or in heartbreak, or simply the desire for community, you'll find Russ & Daughters there.

Today we still do a brisk business in pounds of smoked fish, bissels of cream cheese, and tins of caviar. But many of our customers, especially those who have traveled from afar, order a bagel sandwich or two to enjoy on the spot. They stream from the shop onto the benches outside or to the park on Forsythe Street, pausing only to take a photograph of the sandwich with the Russ & Daughters sign in the background before digging in. As always, the soul of Russ & Daughters, one of the reasons so many people hold us so dear, is that essentially our food is for community. In both a literal and figurative sense, families and friends bond *over* our food.

The following recipes, which originate from the store, cover all you'll need to assemble a spread of your own. They constitute the cornerstone of appetizing cuisine: the pickles, the salads, the fish. Herein you'll find both the histories and guides to our most famed offerings: our smoked salmon, sable, sturgeon, our herring and our caviar. And, although a relatively recent addition, also included are our now legendary bagel sandwiches, to enjoy alone or, preferably, in the company of friends.

I GREW UP IN RIVERDALE IN THE BRONX, but we always drove down to the city in our Chevy Impala for our pilgrimage to the Lower East Side. My mother would buy bras and stockings at discount prices from the stores on Orchard Street and we'd buy our essentials from Russ & Daughters. (We also shopped at Lord & Taylor. We weren't completely shtetl.) My parents were born in Belarus and came to America via Palestine, so there's a tremendous resonance and texture of the old country in those streets. These were our people and even more so for my parents. The store was a very sweet memory for me growing up. When the restaurant opened, I loved hanging out there. It represented the best of what they had to offer. MAIRA KALMAN, AUTHOR AND ARTIST

SOUPS

Smoked Whitefish Chowder

MAKES 2 QUARTS, 6 SERVINGS

2 cups heavy cream

2 cups whole milk

2 large Yukon Gold potatoes (about 1 pound), peeled and diced

2 cups flaked smoked whitefish (about 1 pound)

1 bunch fresh thyme, tied into a bundle

1 bay leaf

1½ tablespoons extra-virgin olive oil

1 large carrot, peeled and diced

2 large stalks celery, diced

½ large Spanish onion, diced

Kosher salt, to taste

½ teaspoon garlic powder

¼ teaspoon red pepper flakes

2 cups white wine

Matzo, for serving

Aleppo pepper, for serving

Goyische chowder relies on cream for its comfort, clams for its salinity, and bacon for its smoky richness. Our appetizing version, on the other hand, has at its heart deeply flavored smoked whitefish (and yes, lots of dairy and potatoes to round and soften it out.) Smoked fish chowder isn't exactly new or exclusively Jewish: The Scots have cullen skink, a chowder made with smoked haddock. Seattle has a Northwest-style chowder, pinkish in hue and made with smoked salmon. And the Lower East Side has Smoked Whitefish Chowder.

In a large pot over medium heat, combine the cream, milk, potatoes, 1 cup of the whitefish, the thyme, and the bay leaf. Bring to a simmer and cook until the potatoes are tender, 10 to 15 minutes. Remove the pot from heat and allow to cool to room temperature.

Meanwhile, heat the olive oil in a large skillet over medium-low heat. Once shimmering, add the carrot, celery, and onion. Season with salt and cook for 25 to 30 minutes, until the vegetables are tender. Add the garlic powder and cook, stirring, for 1 minute. Add the red pepper flakes, then the white wine, and raise the heat to medium-high. Bring to a simmer, then cook until reduced by about half, 5 to 10 minutes.

Strain the cream mixture, reserving the whitefish and potatoes. Discard the herbs. Spoon out 1 cup of the potatoes (it's okay if some fish is in there too) and 1 cup of the cream mixture to a blender and blend until smooth. Add this mixture back into the pot in addition to the vegetable mixture and the remaining 1 cup whitefish. Season with salt to taste. Turn the heat to medium and bring to a simmer. Remove from the heat, top with Aleppo pepper, and serve immediately with a side of matzo.

The chowder keeps 3 days covered in the refrigerator or in the freezer for up to 2 months.

IF I COULD CHOOSE, whitefish chowder from Russ & Daughters would be my last meal. LAURIE ANDERSON, ARTIST

Gazpacho

MAKES 8 SERVINGS

2 cloves garlic, finely chopped

½ teaspoon sweet paprika

½ teaspoon ground cumin

¼ teaspoon cayenne pepper

2 tablespoons extra-virgin olive oil, plus more for serving

2 pounds beefsteak tomatoes, stemmed and quartered

1 stalk celery, coarsely chopped

1 large cucumber, coarsely chopped

1 large red bell pepper, stemmed, seeded, and coarsely chopped

½ medium red onion, coarsely chopped

1 (16-ounce) can tomato juice

2 tablespoons chopped fresh cilantro leaves

¼ cup red wine vinegar

1½ tablespoons kosher salt

1 teaspoon freshly ground black pepper

Gazpacho might not seem like an automatic fit for Russ & Daughters. But it isn't so crazy. The chilled tomato soup from Andalusia is not far from a Bloody Mary or tomato juice. In fact, the acidity of the tomato cuts beautifully through the richness of our appetizing fare: bagel, lox, and a swig of gazpacho is perfect picnic food. (We think of gazpacho more like a drinking soup than a slurping one.) This recipe comes from Maria, Niki's mother, who is responsible for most of the recipes from the store. It was born from an embarrassment of tomatoes one summer many years ago. Not wanting them to go to waste, Maria turned them into this tart, spiced, refreshing soup. These days, during our local growing season, we get our tomatoes from the Brooklyn Grange, a one-and-a-half acre rooftop farm in the Brooklyn Navy Yard, not 150 feet away from our bakery. How's that for local?

Mix together the garlic, paprika, cumin, and cayenne. In a small frying pan, warm the oil over medium heat. Add the spice mix and cook, stirring constantly, until fragrant, about 1 minute. Remove from the heat and set aside.

In a large bowl, toss together the tomatoes, celery, cucumber, bell pepper, and onion. Working in batches if necessary, transfer to a blender and blend until smooth.

Combine the spice mix, pureed vegetables, tomato juice, cilantro, vinegar, salt, and pepper in a bowl and mix well. Place the gazpacho in a fridge until chilled, at least 1 hour. Once chilled, taste and adjust seasoning. Serve cold with a drizzle of olive oil.

The gazpacho will keep covered in the refrigerator up to 1 week.

Potato Leek Soup

MAKES 8 SERVINGS

2 tablespoons unsalted butter

3 medium leeks, cleaned and thinly sliced

2 shallots, thinly sliced

Kosher salt and ground white pepper

1½ pounds Yukon Gold potatoes, peeled, halved, and sliced ⅛ inch thick

6 sprigs fresh thyme, tied into a bundle

¼ cup white wine

4 cups Roasted Vegetable Stock (PAGE 47 or use store-bought)

1 cup heavy cream

1 tablespoon lemon juice

Trout roe, for garnish

Crème fraîche, for garnish

Finely chopped fresh chives, for garnish

A potato has never met a leek it hasn't taken a shine to. Leeks and potatoes are the Abbott and Costello of food. One is tall; one is rotund. One is sweet; one is starchy. Together, the pair make magic. Nowhere is the symbiosis more apparent than in this rich and comforting soup. Conceptually, PLS (potato leek soup) can be as haimish or as fancy as you like: Nothing is more humble than a potato, except perhaps a leek. Yet little is more luxurious than the cushion of cream, the battery of butter, or the tricolor trio of trout roe, crème fraîche, and chives to finish it.

Melt the butter in a medium stockpot over medium heat.

Add the leeks and shallots and sweat for 3 minutes, until softened. Season with ½ teaspoon salt.

Add the sliced potatoes and thyme bundle and sweat together for 10 minutes, stirring occasionally. Season with 1 teaspoon salt and a pinch of white pepper.

Add the white wine and scrape the bottom of the pan to deglaze, then reduce until almost dry, 30 seconds or so. Add the stock and an additional ½ teaspoon salt. Bring to a simmer over medium heat and cook until the potatoes are soft, about 15 minutes. Remove from the heat, pick out the thyme bundle and discard, and stir in the cream. With an immersion blender, blend the soup until smooth. Finish with lemon juice and adjust seasoning to taste with salt and white pepper. Serve immediately with the trout roe, crème fraîche, and chives.

The soup will keep covered in the refrigerator for 5 days or in the freezer for 6 weeks.

Matzo Ball Soup

MAKES 10 SERVINGS

FOR THE CHICKEN SOUP

3 chicken legs, about 1¼ pounds

3 bone-in chicken thighs, about 1¼ pounds

1½ pounds chicken feet or 1½ pounds joint section of chicken wings

1 bay leaf

2 cubes Knorr chicken bouillon, or more to taste

1¾ teaspoons kosher salt

2 stalks celery, cut into ½-to-¼-inch dice

½ Spanish onion, cut into ½-to-¼-inch dice

1 large carrot, peeled and cut into ½-to-¼-inch dice

FOR THE MATZO BALLS

1½ cups matzo meal

6 large eggs

¾ cup seltzer water

2 tablespoons canola oil

½ teaspoon kosher salt

⅛ teaspoon freshly ground pepper

Nonstick cooking spray, for scooping

1 small bunch fresh dill, minced, for serving

⁕

Chicken feet can be found at your local butcher shop and many grocery stores. They are an important element of this recipe . . . but if you can't get them, you can't get them. Soup's still delicious with chicken wings.

Like many matters culinary and Jewish, matzo ball soup is the subject of great debate, as well as a source of great comfort. Are there noodles or are there not? Is there chicken or isn't there? Should the matzo balls float or sink? But there's one point on which everyone can agree: There is nothing more nurturing than a bowl of this Jewish penicillin. Customers buy it for their friends who feel sick, for themselves when they're worn out and down. We make thousands and thousands of gallons every year. Our version features matzo balls made with seltzer, which renders the balls light as air, and a homemade chicken stock, which utilizes cartilage-rich chicken feet to add depth and body. Intensely flavorful and not stingy on the vegetables or the fresh dill, our matzo ball soup is care in a cup, love in a bowl.

MAKE CHICKEN SOUP

Place the chicken legs, thighs, and feet along with the bay leaf in a medium stockpot with 12 cups cold water and bring to a boil. Lower the heat and simmer, uncovered and skimming occasionally, for 2 hours, until the chicken has been cooked through.

Remove from the heat and strain through a sieve to remove the solids. Reserve the broth and the chicken legs and thighs but discard the chicken feet (or wings) and other schmutz. Set the chicken aside to cool while you scrub and rinse the pot.

Return the strained broth to the clean pot and bring to a simmer. Season with the bouillon and salt. Add the celery, onion, and carrot. Return to a simmer and cook until the vegetables are tender, 10 to 15 minutes.

While the vegetables are simmering, pick the meat from the chicken legs and thighs, discarding the skin and bones; you should have about 4 cups meat. When the vegetables are soft, add the picked chicken to the pot and remove from the heat. Taste and adjust seasoning if needed.

Makes 4 ½ quarts. The soup can be refrigerated for up to 5 days or frozen for 3 weeks.

CONTINUED →

MAKE MATZO BALLS

Mix all the ingredients in a large bowl until well incorporated. Cover and refrigerate for 20 minutes to firm up.

Bring a large pot of salted water to a boil. Using a 2.7-ounce cookie scoop or a ⅓-cup measure sprayed with cooking spray, work quickly to scoop 8 to 10 balls of the matzo dough directly into the poaching pot. Cover the pot and lower the heat to a simmer. Carefully poach the matzo balls for approximately 25 minutes. Remove one ball to check its texture: The ball should keep its form but feel soft throughout. If it feels dense in the center, return it to the water for another few minutes. (If you're not sure if it's soft throughout, sacrifice one ball and cut it in half to check.) Remove with a slotted spoon and set aside, loosely covered with plastic wrap.

The matzo balls can be kept refrigerated for 5 days, stored on a baking sheet under plastic wrap, but they cannot be frozen (it turns them into mushy garbage).

TO ASSEMBLE

Use a slotted spoon to evenly distribute the chicken and vegetables from the soup among serving bowls, then add the matzo balls. Ladle the broth over and top with dill.

A KNEYDL IN A KHOLEM IZ NIT KEYN KNEYDL, NOR A KHOLEM. A matzo ball in a dream is not a matzo ball, just a dream. YIDDISH PROVERB

Roasted Vegetable Stock

MAKES ABOUT 14 CUPS

6 large carrots, peeled and roughly chopped
1 large onion, roughly chopped
1 leek, sliced in half lengthwise, cleaned, and cut into thirds
1 large bulb fennel, roughly chopped
2 tablespoons extra-virgin olive oil
1 cup white wine
3 large tomatoes, quartered
1 sprig fresh thyme
1 bay leaf
1 teaspoon whole black peppercorns

Worries, according to a Yiddish proverb, go down better with soup. But the cornerstone of a good soup, especially one that doesn't have the benefit of meat to add flavor and body, is a strong stock. This vegetable stock, which is the base for many of our soups including our borschts (PAGES 52 and 53) and Potato Leek Soup (PAGE 43), relies on the browning of the roasted vegetables to add extra body and intense flavor.

Preheat the oven to 450°F.

Toss the carrots, onion, leek, and fennel with the olive oil in a large flameproof roasting pan. Roast, stirring occasionally, until the vegetables are fragrant and browned, 40 to 45 minutes.

Remove the pan from the oven and place over two burners. Cook over medium heat, stirring constantly, for 1 minute. Add the white wine, stirring to pick up any bits of browned vegetables stuck to the bottom of the pan. Continue to cook until the wine has mostly evaporated, 1 to 2 minutes longer.

Transfer the contents to a large pot and add enough water to completely cover the vegetables—the amount depends on the size of your pot—then add the tomatoes, thyme, bay leaf, and peppercorns. Bring the mixture to a boil, then reduce to a simmer and cook, covered, until the vegetables are soft and the flavors have melded, about 90 minutes.

Cool to room temperature, then strain and discard the vegetables.

The stock will keep in an airtight container in the refrigerator for 7 to 10 days or in the freezer for 3 months.

Mushroom Barley Soup

MAKES 10 SERVINGS

1 cup pearl barley

1 ounce dried porcini mushrooms

2 tablespoons unsalted butter

2 tablespoons vegetable oil

4 stalks celery, diced

2 medium carrots, peeled and diced

1 medium Spanish onion, diced

Kosher salt and freshly ground black pepper

1 clove garlic, chopped

1 pound white mushrooms, cleaned and sliced

3 tablespoons all-purpose flour

9 cups store-bought beef broth or Roasted Vegetable Stock (PAGE 47 or use store-bought)

2 tablespoons chopped fresh parsley

Mushroom barley soup is an Ashkenazi classic, made with ingredients both plentiful and cheap (barley) and those that were historically foraged (mushrooms.) *Kropnik*, as barley soup is known in Poland, often contained meat. It was the Jews who, being both poor and in the lumber business, had easy access to the woods and the mushrooms therein. Observant and unable to afford meat even if they weren't, our mushroom barley soup precursors forewent beef for the fungi. In fact, one of the first things Joel sold were strings of dried Polish mushrooms called *borowic*, which many of our customers used as a more affordable substitute for meat in soups like this one. (Today borowic mushrooms run $200 a pound, though we still sell them, strung up on the same hooks as in Joel's time.) The result, a marriage of thrift and fortune, is nutty and rich.

Bring 2 quarts water to a boil in a medium pot. Stir in the barley and return to a simmer. Cook at a strong simmer until slightly chewy, 30 to 45 minutes. Drain and set aside (you should have about 4 cups).

While the barley is cooking, place the porcini mushrooms in a bowl and cover with 2 cups boiling water; set aside to rehydrate.

Meanwhile, melt the butter with the oil in a stockpot over medium heat. Add the celery and sweat, stirring occasionally, until bright green, about 2 minutes. Add the carrots and sweat for another minute. Add the onion and 1 teaspoon salt and cook until the onion is just starting to soften, 3 to 4 minutes. Add the garlic and sauté briefly, about 30 seconds to 1 minute. Gradually add the sliced mushrooms and a pinch of salt and cook, stirring, until they have reduced in volume and almost all of their water has cooked off, 10 to 15 minutes.

Sprinkle the flour over the vegetables and stir to coat the vegetables and soak up the residual butter and oil, scraping the bottom of the pan with a rubber spatula so as not to scorch, for 1 minute.

Add 2 cups beef broth and stir with the spatula, scraping the bottom to dissolve the flour, until the mixture thickens, about 1 minute. Stir in the porcini mushrooms and their water and the remaining beef broth. Season with salt and pepper and bring to a boil. Reduce to a simmer, add the barley, and simmer until the flavors meld and the barley is tender, 15 to 20 minutes.

Add the parsley and adjust seasoning to taste. Serve immediately.

The soup keeps in the refrigerator for 5 days or the freezer for 3 months.

Chilled Borscht

MAKES 6 SERVINGS

2 tablespoons extra-virgin olive oil, plus more for garnish

1 leek, white parts only, cleaned and sliced

1 Spanish onion, thinly sliced

1 stalk celery, thinly sliced

3 large beets, peeled and diced

1 teaspoon kosher salt, plus more to taste

¼ teaspoon freshly ground pepper, plus more to taste

1 bunch fresh parsley

1 sprig fresh thyme

1 bay leaf

2 quarts Roasted Vegetable Stock (PAGE 47 or use store-bought)

3 tablespoons sherry vinegar

1 tablespoon granulated sugar

½ cup sour cream, for garnish

Note: Chilled borscht in small glasses (as borscht shooters) makes for easy entertaining and adds a nice pop of color to any cocktail party.

The word *borscht* comes from the Slavic word for hogweed or cow parsnip, for the soup was initially made with these wild plants, and cut with plenty of vinegar. It often brings to mind bowls of steaming ruby red beet soup (NEXT PAGE), warming the belly on a cold winter's day. But that's just one kind of borscht (albeit the most well-known). There's also a beet-less white borscht made with cabbage, and a green borscht made with sorrel, called *schav*, which we used to sell in 24-ounce jars. There's also this smooth and delicious chilled borscht, also called *svekolnik*, whose tartness cools and refreshes in the oppressive summer heat. We serve chilled borscht as long as we possibly can, holding on to New York's long bright summer days even as the air crisps. And just like the autumnal equinox, when we switch from making chilled borscht to hot borscht, it marks—for us—the official end of summer.

Heat the olive oil in a large stockpot over medium heat. Once shimmering, add the leek, onion, and celery. Turn the heat down to medium-low and sweat the vegetables for 10 minutes, until softened. Add the beets, season with the salt and pepper, and increase the heat to medium. Continue cooking for another 10 minutes.

Meanwhile, tie together the parsley, thyme, and bay leaf with kitchen twine to create a bouquet garni and place in the pot.

Add the vegetable stock and bring to a boil, then lower the heat and let simmer until the beets are tender, about 45 minutes. Stir in the sherry vinegar and sugar and remove from the heat.

Remove and discard the bouquet garni. Carefully blend the soup in a blender until smooth. Season with salt and pepper to taste. Transfer the soup to a nonreactive container and refrigerate, covered, until completely cool. Garnish with sour cream and olive oil to serve.

The borscht will keep covered in the refrigerator for 5 days or in the freezer for 6 weeks.

TSU BORSHT DARF MEN KEYN TSEYNER NIT. To eat borscht, you don't need teeth. YIDDISH PROVERB

Hot Borscht

MAKES 6 SERVINGS

2 to 3 large red beets (1 pound), trimmed and scrubbed

2 tablespoons extra-virgin olive oil

1 medium onion, diced

Kosher salt and freshly ground black pepper, to taste

1 medium carrot, peeled and diced

1 small white turnip, diced

¼ head green cabbage, thinly sliced

1½ cups sauerkraut, drained (juice reserved)

5 sprigs fresh thyme, tied together with butcher twine

8 cups Roasted Vegetable Stock (PAGE 47 or use store-bought)

Lemon juice to taste

Sour cream and fresh dill, for garnish

A soup so famous they named a belt after it, borscht has sustained (and stained) Jews for centuries. First in the Slavic countries of the Old World, where instead of the bright red sugar beets we know today, peasants used foraged cow parsnip, and the soup was constantly replenished and long-lasting. Then, as now, a good amount of acid is needed to brighten up the borscht. Traditionally, this has come from vinegar or lemon juice. (Über-traditionally, it's come from long fermented beet vinegar called *russel*). The secret here is sauerkraut, which for years we kept in pickle barrels at the store. Bursting with lactic acid and a sour flavor, the sauerkraut balances out the sweetness of the beets and adds even more comforting body.

Preheat the oven to 400°F. Wrap each beet individually in aluminum foil and place on a baking sheet. Roast until fork tender, 70 to 90 minutes, depending on the size of the beets. Let cool until cool to the touch. Remove the skins and dice the beets. Set the diced beets aside, along with the ends and smaller pieces.

In a large stockpot, heat the olive oil over medium-high heat. Add the onion and a pinch of salt and sauté, stirring occasionally, until beginning to brown, 5 to 7 minutes. Add the carrot and turnip and continue to cook until they develop color, 5 to 7 minutes longer (you can reduce the heat to medium if browning too quickly). Add the cabbage and season with salt; cook until soft, 3 to 5 minutes.

Add the sauerkraut, thyme, and 7 cups of the vegetable stock. Bring the mixture to a boil over high heat then reduce to a simmer.

Meanwhile, in a blender, puree the reserved beet scraps with the remaining 1 cup vegetable stock. Add the puree to the stockpot. (Add a splash of water to the blender jar and swirl it around to coax out any remaining puree and add that to the pot as well.)

Bring the soup to a simmer, then simmer uncovered, until the soup has reduced a bit and the flavors have melded, about 2 hours. Add the diced beets and remove from the heat immediately.

Adjust the seasoning with salt, black pepper, and sauerkraut juice, if necessary. If needed, add a squeeze of lemon juice to boost acidity. Remove and discard the thyme. Serve, adding a dollop of sour cream and a sprinkle of dill to each bowl as desired.

The borscht will keep covered in the refrigerator for 5 days or in the freezer for 6 weeks.

SMOKED &

CURED FISH

A GUIDE TO HERRING

Bemokem she-eyn ish iz a hering oykh a fish.
Where there is no worthy man, even a herring is a fish.
YIDDISH PROVERB

Nations have been built on the shimmering backs of herring. Trade alliances formed, empires spread, wars fought, and millions fed by the grace of these fish. New York City itself, once a Dutch colony called New Amsterdam, has the herring—and the economic power it afforded the Dutch empire—to thank for its very existence. To this day, herring festivals abound in Northern Europe and the United Kingdom. There are parades and floats dedicated to the fish. In New York City, herring is a hero—at Russ & Daughters, if nowhere else.

If that is the way it must be, so be it. We are proud champions of herring. Ours is a house built on herring. It was herring that drew Joel Russ to America, since he was sponsored by his sister Channah, who had a herring stand tucked into Hester Street. Like thousands of other poor immigrants, Joel got his start packing schmaltz herring into a barrel and selling it on the street corner. Wrapped in day-old copies of the *Forverts*, the local Yiddish paper, herring was a cheap source of protein. (Its omnipresence and humbleness is the source of the Yiddish proverb above.) Few gave a thought to the herring, other than the fact that it could feed their families, not once, but twice. (Typically, the first meal was a slice of bread with herring rubbed onto it, imparting its oils, flavor, and a hint of protein. The second meal was the delectable herring itself.) But if they had, they might realize how miraculous a fish herring is.

Herring are pelagic fish of the northern seas. They are small and silver, shimmering like clouds as they traverse the waters from Scandinavia to Canada. Herring were first fished by the Anglo-Saxons in the thirteenth century. The Hanseatic League, formed in the fourteenth century, came about in part to protect European herring interests. Today herring is a delicacy from northern Europe to the Caribbean. Among Ashkenazi Jews, the fish is both a staple and a symbol, secular and spiritual sustenance. Herring is a prerequisite on the table for a shiva or a kiddush. It swims through the generations so that you feel like your parents or grandparents when you eat it. But is that such a bad thing?

Herring is also a remarkably nutritious fish, even more so than the much ballyhooed salmon. Wild and plentiful, herring is rich in vitamin D, which strengthens bones, and omega-3 fatty acids such as EPA (eicosapentaenoic acid) and DHA (docosahexaenoic acid), which not only help reduce inflammation but promote brain function and reduce the risk of heart disease. It's the rare meeting point of thrift, flavor, and health.

For years, we sold our herring out of wooden barrels. Fishing out the perfect herring, or rather accepting the perfect herring, was a matter of great importance. The ideal schmaltz herring should be head on, large, and fatty. Until the mid-2010s, when New York State Agriculture and Markets regulation prohibited it, uneviscerated fish was preferred. Some people wanted the milt (sperm sac) or roe still inside. Once ordered, we'd cut the head off, clean the guts out, and place the milt or roe in a separate container. When the wooden barrels were replaced by plastic buckets, we transferred our herring selection to the display case, where they live next to the olives and a tray of pickled onions. Nevertheless, the back-and-forth about the right herring continues to be volleyed over the counter.

As is the case with many fish, the desirability of a herring depends on its fat content. The colder the water, the greater the fat, the deeper the flavor. But much also depends on the process by which the herring is preserved. This is more a matter of preference than quality. A herring can range from aggressively oceanic to mild and sweet, depending on its age, where it's from, how it is cured, and in what it is marinated.

I FIRST CAME ACROSS NEW CATCH HOLLAND HERRING early in my years in New York. I was at Russ & Daughters for a Super Heebster (PAGE 135) in June and it just happened to be the beginning of the New Catch season. I saw the glistening herring there and was immediately intrigued. Even more so when I saw how people were popping them in their mouths. I'm always a sucker for taking something by the tail, tilting my head back, and eating it. Since then I've been swept up in the Herring Hurricane. I've written articles about herring and filmed television shows about it. The fish might get a bad rap because so few people—at least in the United States—do herring right. But New Catch is sashimi-grade fish. When it's fresh, as it is at Russ & Daughters, there's nothing better. PERVAIZ SHALLWANI, JOURNALIST AND CHEF

NEW CATCH HOLLAND HERRING

New Catch Holland herring is the gateway herring for many of those who go on to become clupeophiles. For those leery of entering the herring world, we liken New Catch to an immaculate sashimi: It is neither pickled nor sauced but rather lightly salted. Its flesh is buttery and its flavor delicate. At the beginning of every year, we get a call informing us of when the herring harvest will begin. (Typically this is around mid to late June, but due to climate change the harvest is happening later and later.) These herring, which must be at least three years old but still sexually immature, hail from the North Sea and, by law, need to have a minimum of 14 percent fat.

WHEN I MOVED TO NEW YORK FROM ISRAEL sixteen years ago, I found in the schmaltz herring a memory of my youth, growing up on a kibbutz. The food was, generally, terrible but the bright spot was the herring cart. Though the herring at Russ & Daughters is more mild, a schmaltz herring brings me right back to my childhood. NAAMA SHEFI, FOUNDER, JEWISH FOOD SOCIETY

SCHMALTZ HERRING

Schmaltz herring is the original herring, the type of herring on which Joel Russ built Russ & Daughters. Caught in the extremely cold waters off Iceland, these herring are extra fatty. (*Schmaltz* is Yiddish for fat.) Hard cured in salt, schmaltz herring has a strong umami flavor, akin to anchovies, that pairs well with boiled potato and raw onion, its traditional accoutrements. It is often chased with a shot of vodka (See Schmaltz & a Shot, PAGE 65).

ROLL MOPS

Fishy silver pinwheels, roll mops owe their preparation to the Germans, who prefer their herring in a bracingly acidic vinegar. Ours are made with leaner, heavier Bismarck pickled herring, rolled with the skin on around pickled onions on the inside and fastened by a toothpick (which, naturally, must be removed before devouring).

MATJES HERRING

Matjes—or maiden—herring are pre-spawn herring with tremendously tender flesh. With so subtle and sweet a flavor, we steep these Swedish herring in an aromatic brine redolent of cranberries, cinnamon, and cloves. These are best served alone or with a neutral-flavored cracker to savor the sweet subtlety of the fish.

PICKLED HERRING

Lean North Atlantic herring, pickled with sugar and vinegar, is a mild and amiable fish that is often enjoyed with cream sauce and pickled onions—for many Jews this is the only herring—or with curry or mustard sauce (PAGE 62), or chopped in a herring salad (PAGE 66).

FRENCH SMOKED HERRING

Smoking is another major method of preserving herring. French herring, caught off the Côte d'Opal, are fileted, salted for 24 to 48 hours, then smoked in traditional wood ovens, called *coresses*, over oak chips. Also called *hareng doux*, this quite smoky herring is best served with boiled vegetables, such as carrots and potatoes.

HERRING IS MY FATHER'S MADELEINES. He didn't grow up with it but discovered herring while studying in Holland for medical school. I was fifteen when he discovered Russ & Daughters herring. And every year we'd make the journey to the store for New Catch. When I got married, I realized I needed herring at the wedding, to honor my father. But since the wedding was in a synagogue it had to be kosher. I ended up having to hire a mashgiach to certify the herring (and bagels and lox.) It was a nightmare. By far the most expensive thing about the wedding. But it was all worth it to see the sheer joy on my father's face. ALANA NEWHOUSE, FOUNDER, *TABLET* MAGAZINE

Sauces for Herring

Traditionally, pickled herring was served with one of two sauces. The first is a wine sauce, which we now call *Plain Sauce* to avoid confusion since it doesn't contain wine (traditional versions were made with white wine vinegar). Plain sauce is, essentially, just the pickling liquid of the herring. Its acidity bolsters the brightness of the herring. Cream sauce is more straightforward. Slightly sour but rich, it yins the yang of the pickled herring's brininess. Both are appealing and we've found that customers' preference for one over the other depends mostly on how they grew up eating herring. (Niki prefers cream; Josh plain.) Less classic in the appetizing cannon are the Curry and Mustard Dill sauces, both of which date from the time of Mark's herring renaissance (see Herring Pairing sidebar). Though Scandinavian, each has been part of the Russ & Daughters experience for more than forty years now, which means for many of our customers these are the sauces they grew up on too. If, heaven forbid and despite your most valiant efforts, you can't secure herring from Russ & Daughters, your best bet is to find a jar of pickled herring from your supermarket. (The fresh and salted varieties are still a niche product and unlikely to appear on supermarket shelves.) Since herring must remain moist, store them in the brine in which they come. When ready to sauce them, drain off the liquid and add a sauce of your choice.

PLAIN SAUCE

MAKES 2 CUPS

1½ cups white vinegar (high acidity preferred, greater than 7 percent)
½ cup water
¼ cup granulated sugar
1 teaspoon kosher salt
1 cup thinly sliced white onion

In a medium saucepan, combine all the ingredients. Place the saucepan over medium heat and bring the mixture to a simmer, stirring to dissolve the sugar and salt. Remove the pan from heat and let cool to room temperature.

The sauce will keep in the refrigerator for up to 2 weeks.

CREAM SAUCE

MAKES 2 CUPS

1½ tablespoons distilled white vinegar
1 tablespoon granulated sugar
1 cup sour cream
¼ cup buttermilk
Water as needed

In a large mixing bowl, combine the vinegar and sugar until the sugar is dissolved. Whisk in the sour cream and buttermilk and mix until incorporated. Thin the mixture with water, a tablespoon at a time, until it reaches a pourable consistency.

The sauce will keep in the refrigerator for up to 1 week.

CURRY SAUCE

MAKES 3 CUPS

2 cups Cream Sauce (PREVIOUS PAGE)
1 cup mayonnaise
2 tablespoons Swedish mustard (mild or sweet) or Dijon mustard
1 tablespoon whole grain mustard
2 teaspoons freshly squeezed lemon juice
1 teaspoon turmeric
1 to 2 tablespoons curry powder, to taste

Combine all the ingredients in a small bowl and whisk until incorporated. Add additional curry powder if desired.

The sauce will keep in the refrigerator for up to 1 week.

MUSTARD DILL SAUCE

MAKES 2 CUPS

1 cup vegetable oil
1¼ cup Dijon mustard
¼ cup water
5 tablespoons granulated sugar
2 tablespoons finely chopped fresh dill
1 tablespoon honey
2 teaspoons red wine vinegar
Kosher salt and ground black pepper to taste

Combine all the ingredients in a small bowl and whisk until incorporated.

The sauce will keep in the refrigerator for up to 1 week.

HERRING PAIRING

IN THE MID 1990S, Mark befriended a herring-loving Swedish chef named Ulrika Bengtsson and embarked on a herring renaissance that expanded our stable of sauces. For a brief period, we had ten different herring preparations. By July 2009, when we threw our first Herring Pairing at the Roger Smith Hotel in Midtown (where Ulrika was the chef), we had become the epicenter of the herring enlightenment. At the Pairing, true herring lovers were able to sling back their heads and devour the newly arrived New Catch Holland herring in community with one another. It was intended to be a onetime event, but when neurologist, author, and herring fan Oliver Sacks surprised us with a write-up in *The New Yorker*, we realized perhaps the Herring Pairing had legs. Over the years we've invited chefs like Wylie Dufresne, April Bloomfield, Chikara Sono, Jeremiah Stone, and Fabian von Hauske to put their culinary spin on the herring. (Wylie made a frozen herring soup.) Watching guests vamp with the herring in our photo booth, fish in their hands, joy on their face, filled us with *naches*. Since then we've delighted in welcoming schools of herring adherents to the Herring Pairing, and seeing what our guest chefs develop to elevate this humble haimish delicious fish.

SLOWLY, THE HERRING-LOVERS LEFT THE HOTEL, still discussing favorite dishes with fellow-travellers as they went. They sauntered slowly up Lexington Avenue. One does not rush after such a banquet; indeed, one's whole perspective on the world is changed. Some of us, the New Yorkers, will meet again, at Russ & Daughters. But the rest, after they have slept the deep sleep of the consummated herring-eater, will start counting the days to the herring festival of 2010.
OLIVER SACKS, "CLUPEOPHILIA," *THE NEW YORKER*, JULY 13, 2009

Classic New Catch Holland Herring Sandwich

MAKES 1 SERVING

1 New Catch Holland herring
1 potato hot dog bun
1 tablespoon chopped cornichons
1 tablespoon chopped raw sweet onion

Grasping the tail of a New Catch herring, you could simply tilt back your head and slide the fish in its silver slipperiness into your mouth whole. This is the OG and most pure method of enjoying New Catch Holland herring. It is the pose struck by herring devotees from the Lower East Side all the way to Amsterdam's street markets. But it isn't the only way. Laying the herring on a pillowy homemade challah bun and tucking it under a light comforter of cornichons and raw onion is a slightly more restrained way to enjoy the delicately flavored and textured fatty fish. As an at-home delicacy and as a nod to expediency, we think a potato bun works just fine too.

Place the herring on the bun. Evenly spread cornichon and onion atop it. Eat.

Schmaltz & a Shot

MAKES 2 SERVINGS

1 russet potato
1 schmaltz herring fillet, cut into ½-inch chunks
½ small white onion, sliced into thin strips and separated
2 shots of vodka

In a city with no shortage of exclusive venues and members-only clubs—many of which were closed to Jews—perhaps the most haimish and most difficult into which to gain entry was a table set up in the back of Russ & Daughters. There, Joel, and then son-in-law Herbie, would invite friends and loyal customers for schmaltz and a shot from a bottle of schnapps that was discreetly tucked away, swapping tales of the Old World, the new country, and trade secrets that never left the kitchen. By the time we took over, the table was gone and the bottle left empty. But the spirit of schmaltz herring, chased by an ice cold shot of vodka suffused with kinship, has never left.

Put the whole potato into a pot of salted water and bring to boil. Boil for approximately 25 minutes until you can poke through with a fork. Remove the potato from the water, let it cool, then peel it. Cut the potato into quarters.

Find a friend.

Lay the herring and potatoes out.

Also the onions.

Keep the shots near.

Cut a piece of potato and put a piece of herring on top of it and then some onions.

Eat a little. Drink a little.

Kibbitz.

Beet, Apple & Herring Salad

MAKES 8 TO 10 SERVINGS

4 medium beets

1 small russet potato

2 pickled herring fillets or 14 pieces of fillet, cut into ¼-inch dice

1 full-sour pickle, cut into ¼-inch dice

½ Granny Smith apple, cored and cut into ¼-inch dice

½ red onion, minced

3 tablespoons Mustard Dill Sauce (PAGE 62)

We've been serving chopped herring since the 1930s and some version of an apple herring salad since not too long after. For years our great-grandfather Joel Russ used an old apple corer—it was not old when he started using it—to core the Granny Smith apples for this salad. And today that corer/peeler is on long-term loan to the Museum of the City of New York (PAGE 145). The presence of beets is part of the Scandinavian influence of the early 1990s, fostered under Mark. It's a belated but welcome addition. The earthiness of the beets and the tart crispness of the apple complement the sweetness of the herring for an unlikely but unusually delicious salad.

Bring a large stockpot of water to a boil. Add the whole beets and boil for 40 minutes, or until tender. Remove the beets and cool completely. (Reserve the beet water for Russ & Daughters Pickled Beet Juice, PAGE 242). Peel the beets and cut into ¼-inch dice.

Meanwhile, bring a small pot of water to a boil. Add the potato and boil for 15 to 20 minutes, until fork tender. Cool, peel, and cut into ¼-inch dice.

Combine the beets, potato, herring, pickle, apple, and onion in a mixing bowl. Dress with the prepared Mustard Dill sauce and serve immediately.

A GUIDE TO
SMOKED & CURED SALMON

Vu iz do fleysh un fish, dort iz a freylekher tish.
Wherever there is meat and fish is a happy table.
YIDDISH PROVERB

As it is written on our shopping bags, we are the Queens of the Lake Sturgeon. But we are also the stewards of salmon, cured, pickled, and smoked. Glistening sides of the fish occupy prime real estate in our showcase. They are grasped by slicers—an official job title—and laid on the counter. They are thinly sliced with considerable finesse. They underpin the House of Russ. Though salmon was not our first product, over the years smoked and cured salmon—and an array of other fish—have come to define who we are.

Like herring, and many other staples of early twentieth-century tenement dwellers, belly lox in particular, and smoked and cured fish in general, was a long-lasting, well-preserved, nutritious, and cheap source of protein. Cured fish is a culinary legacy of Scandinavia; smoked fish tends more Germanic in origin. Both came to America with their respective immigrant populations. Yet the sides of lox that Grandpa Russ sold were distinctly American. In fact, *lox* as a term—the Americanized spelling of the Yiddish *laks*, meaning salmon—was coined in the New World sometime around the 1930s. At that time, *lox* referred exclusively to cured wild-caught Pacific salmon that made its way across the country via the transcontinental railroad, packed with salt in large barrels. Today, lox has become a generic term for smoked salmon such that today if a customer does indeed want the traditional belly lox, they'll confirm that yes, they know what belly lox is and yes, they know it is salty. For someone who grew up on belly lox, other smoked salmon is too milquetoast for them.

In Great-Grandpa Russ's time and all the way through to the early 1980s, smoked and cured salmon was made with wild-caught fish. But starting in the '80s, as salmon fisheries became depleted and the smoked fish more popular, virtually all salmon became farm-raised. Consequently, our work as providers of smoked salmon has also shifted to focus more on the methods and results of the smoking and curing process and less on naturally occurring variations among wild fish. (The exception is western Nova, which continues to be made with wild-caught Pacific King salmon.)

Russ & Daughters did not and does not smoke or cure our own fish. Rather we have relied on a network of smokehouses, many of which were founded in the early twentieth century, to furnish our product. Our job, therefore, has always been not in production but in careful curation and selection. Like a négociant in wine, we both maintain a house style and demand a pristine level of quality from our suppliers. Conversation is continual. For the first three generations of Russes, it meant visiting the smokehouses that dot the outer boroughs, a fraught and sometimes hostile tour, in order to assure that we were being offered the best and highest quality fish. Smokehouse men, traditionally, have been rough and tumble, and Mark has stories of having to prove himself as a newcomer. These days, the fish come to us on an almost daily basis but the exchanges continue. If a fish does not meet our rigorous criteria, we'll send it back. After more than a hundred years, most of our smokehouse partners know to send only the highest quality salmon. And we often work with them to assure our standards are maintained and the flavor profiles stay consistent.

Meanwhile, from Great-Grandpa Russ's belly lox, we've enlarged our selection of smoked and cured fish. In terms of salmon, our selections range from belly, which has zero smoke but lots of salt, to Scottish, which has the smokiest flavor. Though the names seem to indicate geography—and at some point they did—these days they refer mostly to the flavor profile imparted during the smoking and curing process.

BELLY LOX

The original lox, belly lox, is not smoked but rather cured in salt. Originally belly lox was made from the bellies of wild Pacific salmon. Today the stock is farmed. Though aggressively salty on its own, belly lox is magnificent as part of the trifecta of bagel, cream cheese, and lox since it was the lox of the original combination. (The fat of the cream cheese and the dough of the bagel soften the saltiness.)

GRAVLAX

Gravad means buried in Swedish and, when it was developed in the fourteenth century, gravlax was salmon that was buried beneath lemon, dill, and alcohol to cure. Today, gravlax's cure also includes salt, but it isn't buried but weighed down to help the cure penetrate the fish. The most overtly Scandinavian of our preparations, this nonsmoked fish is mild, slightly sweet, and herbaceous. SEE PAGE 79 for Gravlax, Apples & Honey.

GASPE NOVA

The archetypal New York–style lox, Gaspe Nova traditionally hailed from wild Atlantic salmon caught off the Gaspé Peninsula of Nova Scotia. Unlike belly lox and gravlax, Gaspe Nova is both lightly cured and gently cold-smoked over hardwoods at temperatures which range from 72°F to 80°F. This yields Gaspe Nova's signature delicate flavor and a silken texture.

PASTRAMI-CURED SMOKED SALMON

A relatively recent addition to the smoked salmon canon, pastrami-cured smoked salmon begins its life as a Scottish salmon but is cold-smoked with a spice-rich pastrami rub that includes pepper, coriander, paprika, and mustard seeds. It finds its greatest expression on a bagel, such as in our Pastrami Russ sandwich (PAGE 132).

IRISH SMOKED SALMON

Our Irish cold-smoked salmon, thus called because it originally hailed from Ireland though now it refers to a style more than a provenance, is slightly less smoky and fattier than Norwegian salmon with a silken texture similar to Gaspe Nova.

SCOTTISH SMOKED SALMON

The smokiest of our cold-smoked salmon, the Scottish salmon hails from a Scottish farm and is cold-smoked over apple and cherry woods. It tends to offer the perfect balance of fattiness and silken texture.

WESTERN NOVA

Nearly alone among our smoked salmon offerings, western Nova is made with wild Alaskan King salmon. It is treated in the smokehouse as one might a Gaspe Nova, that is to say, it is lightly cured and cold-smoked. A side-by-side comparison of the two illustrates how a wild salmon is a leaner, more muscular fish, with a tighter texture and an assertive flavor.

KIPPERED HOT-SMOKED SALMON

Unlike cold-smoked salmon, kippered salmon—also known as baked salmon—is hot-smoked at temperatures that range up to 150°F, rendering the intermuscular fat and resulting in a flaky texture. The result is a fish with a consistency more like poached salmon, with a wonderful smoky flavor. SEE PAGE 80 for Hot Smoke / Cold Smoke and PAGE 87 for Whitefish & Baked Salmon Salad.

NORWEGIAN SMOKED SALMON

Perhaps the perfect introductory salmon, our Norwegian smoked salmon tends to be on the leaner side, with a mild flavor and medium smoke. It is made with farmed Atlantic salmon, lightly cured and cold-smoked.

PICKLED LOX

A hidden hero of appetizing, pickled lox is salt-cured and pickled. It is perhaps the most direct descendant of belly lox. We pickle our own lox in the same solution as we do herring. In fact, we serve the lox cut into chunks, as opposed to slices, accompanied by pickled onions and sauce (cream or plain, customer's choice). SEE PAGE 61 for Cream and Plain sauces.

HOW TO SLICE A SALMON

A slice of our smoked salmon should be sliced so thin through it you can read The New York Times.

The closest thing Russ & Daughters has to an altar is the forty-foot-long custom-made refrigerated showcase that runs along the eastern length of the store. On one side of the counter, customers file in and out, gazing at the appetizing before them and waiting patiently (sometimes) with their numbers in hand. On the other side, a team of slicers, each at their own station, administer to the hungry.

As many a slicer will tell you, the most important skills of their chosen profession are interpersonal. Not, that is, between slicer and lox or slicer and whitefish, but between slicer and customer. Our customers have come to think of Russ & Daughters as their own place. We love the enthusiasm. But, seeing as it is their store, they have not hesitated to tell us how to do our jobs, or to give feedback—not always constructive—when they feel we haven't. For generations, it has been a mark of honor to haggle, negotiating for the best piece of smoked whitefish or the fattest herring or the best salmon in the case. These days, as our clientele has shifted from neighborhood Jews doing their daily rounds to foodies from around the world, the dynamic has changed. To the relief of the men and women who wear the white coats and slice the lox, there is much less arguing. Nevertheless, particularly during the holidays, a disarming smile, an inexhaustible good cheer, an ability to defuse through wisecracks, and a selective deaf ear are essential tools in the slicer's belt.

But the core responsibility of a slicer is that he or she can slice our smoked fish into sheets so thin they are nearly translucent. This task requires a sharp knife, practice, patience, a steady hand, and spatial visualization. It takes about three months of training and practice before our slicers are self-sufficient, but years to truly master the art of slicing.

Due to the low temperatures of the cold-smoke process, the flesh of smoked salmon remains silky. (On a molecular level, the proteins are not denatured.) That means when being sliced—especially thinly—salmon can easily tear. A torn sheet of salmon is a *shonda* and is to be avoided at all costs.

Our slicers use long twelve-to-fourteen-inch bladed nonserrated knives. (Both the person slicing and the knife that slices are called slicers.) Each slicer grinds the blade thinner from edge to spine, making it narrower and decreasing the surface area so as to keep the friction to a minimum. The blades are kept as sharp as possible. Regardless of their dominant hand, at Russ & Daughters everyone cuts with their right hand. (Josh, for instance, is a lefty but like everyone else, slices with his right hand.) Counters are, after all, crowded affairs. Can you imagine the chaos if left- and right-handed slicers were allowed to slice willy-nilly?

The act of slicing cannot be rushed. In fact, much of our culture of kibbitzing comes from the fact that it takes even the most skilled slicer eight minutes or so to slice a pound of smoked salmon. (A pound should yield eighteen to twenty-five slices.) You can get to know someone pretty well during that time.

Many are the opinions and vociferously are they expressed about where the best slices come from. There is, to be sure, a bias for and an actual satisfaction in the luxurious curtain-like slices obtained from the middle of a side. And yet, smoked salmon aficionados know that the collars and *flegals* (wings) and the slices from them are often overlooked delicacies. Ditto slices from the tail, which tend to be leaner, with a closer grain, and therefore take on more salt.

Enough. Let's get to the secrets of slicing. For this is what you came.

① Place a whole side of salmon before you. Gently lay a hand atop the side of salmon. Use a pair of sturdy kitchen tweezers (or deft fingers) to remove the pin bones that run along the length of the salmon. (Pin bones, not bones at all, are calficied nerve endings that help with a salmon's proprioception.) Pin bones removed and holding your knife in the opposite hand, start at the tail end. Lay the knife as flat as possible against the skin so you are shaving off the top.

② The first slice should be at as shallow an angle as possible and serves double duty as it removes the pellicle, the thin film of protein found on smoked fish. It goes without saying these slices should be as thin as you can manage.

As you slice, work the blade back and forth in gentle movements, exerting scant downward pressure. This must be a very controlled movement, similar to bowing a violin. Contact between the back of the blade and the flesh of the salmon must be constant. There can be no lateral wiggling. The knife moves forward. The knife moves backward. That is it.

③ As you work toward the center of the side, gradually create a 45-degree angle with the blade, so as to obtain the optimal size slice. Continue working, adjusting to the angle and contours of the fish, until you reach the collar, the area right under the gills. As the shape of the salmon becomes irregular, work the knife angle back to flat, as at the tail.

④ As each slice is completed, transfer it to a platter using the side of the blade. Fold the slice in half then make a singular cut at the bottom, where the flesh is darkest, resulting in a V-shaped notch in the slice. Naturally you'll want to remove as little of the salmon as possible. (This darker flesh is the bloodline. Removing it is purely an aesthetic choice. It is, indeed, edible.) Sounds easy, right? Give it a try and then we'll check in with you in a few years.

Gravlax, Apples & Honey

MAKES 4 SERVINGS

⅔ cup distilled white vinegar

1 tablespoon granulated sugar

2 teaspoons kosher salt

1 medium red onion, thinly sliced

4 sheets matzo

6 tablespoons clarified butter (PAGE 184)

8 ounces whole-milk Greek yogurt

2 Granny Smith apples, cored and thinly sliced

½ pound gravlax, thinly sliced

Freshly ground black pepper to taste

1 to 2 tablespoons honey, to taste

1 tablespoon chopped fresh dill, for garnish

We know. We know. Apples and honey is a Rosh Hashanah thing, when apples dipped in honey are meant to symbolize a sweet New Year. Matzo is, obviously, a Passover thing. So what are these all doing together? Well, if you think of matzo—oven-fried in butter—as simply a delicious cracker (which it is) and apples and honey as a blessed combination of texture and flavor, these little hors d'oeuvres make a lot of sense. When we ran this as a Rosh Hashanah special at the Cafe, we expanded upon the array of flavor by adding silken gravlax along with the bite and crunch of pickled onions and the tartness of Greek yogurt. It works for Rosh Hashanah; it works for Passover; it works whenever you want a simple nourishing snack. (And if, for some reason, you find yourself out of matzo, the snack works just as well on toasted and buttered shissel rye.)

Make the pickled red onion by whisking together the vinegar, sugar, and 1 teaspoon of the salt in a bowl. Place the sliced onion in a container with a lid (a mason jar works well). Pour the vinegar mixture over the onion until all the slices are submerged. Cover and let stand at room temperature for at least 2 hours.

Preheat the oven to 400°F. Line a baking sheet with parchment.

Break each sheet of matzo into four pieces. Melt the clarified butter in a shallow pan set over low heat (or even atop the oven will work.) Dip the matzo in the butter to coat on both sides, and place on the lined baking sheet. Sprinkle all the matzo with the remaining 1 teaspoon salt. Bake for 8 to 10 minutes, until the matzo is golden. Let the matzo cool.

Schmear each piece of toasted matzo with Greek yogurt. Then top each piece with four to six slices of apple, two slices of gravlax, a few turns of pepper, and a few drained pickled red onions. Drizzle with honey and garnish with dill.

The pickled red onions will keep in the refrigerator for 2 weeks.

Hot Smoke / Cold Smoke

MAKES 3½ CUPS, ABOUT 6 SERVINGS

2 tablespoons unsalted butter
1 shallot, minced (½ cup)
1 pound fatty kippered salmon, flaked into ½-inch chunks
⅓ pound Scottish smoked salmon, cut into ¼-inch dice
¼ cup mayonnaise
¼ cup sour cream
½ teaspoon grated lemon zest (about ¼ of a lemon)
1 tablespoon lemon juice
1 tablespoon chopped fresh chives
1 tablespoon chopped fresh dill
1 tablespoon chopped fresh tarragon
Kosher salt and freshly ground black pepper to taste
15 to 18 Bagel Chips (PAGE 280)

This is our version of rillettes, a sort of French confited meat made traditionally with pork and game. Here we use both smoked salmon and kippered salmon. What we love about it is the combination of flavors and textures: the smoked salmon adds silkiness and smoke (obviously), whereas the kippered salmon has a meatier texture and adds heft. Though it's not a classic of the Russ & Daughters repertoire, this recipe began at the Cafe. Soon thereafter, patrons, having enjoyed it there, came looking for it at the shop. When we explained that it was available at the Cafe only, the answer made as little sense to them as it did to us. Now hot smoke / cold smoke is available everywhere. This is somewhere between a schmear and a salad, perfect to spread on bagel chips, an endive leaf, or a slice of cucumber.

Melt the butter in a sauté pan over medium heat. Once the foaming subsides, add the shallot, lower the heat to medium-low, and sweat until translucent, about 5 minutes.

In a large bowl, combine the shallot, kippered salmon, smoked salmon, mayonnaise, sour cream, lemon zest and juice, chives, dill, and tarragon. Mix well until uniform and season with salt and pepper (being mindful that smoked salmon is naturally salty). Serve alongside the bagel chips.

Hot smoke / cold smoke keeps, covered, in the refrigerator for up to 3 days.

Serve with bagel chips.

HOT SMOKE / COLD SMOKE IS THE SLEEPER HIT. It has all that creaminess but with the added smokiness too. It's a deeper schmear but it also has texture. When you do it with a nice organic Scottish, the caviar cream cheese, and wasabi roe, that's the perfect sandwich. I've been lobbying Niki and Josh to call it the Squadron or the Senator. It's the make-no-choices sandwich. DANIEL SQUADRON, FORMER NEW YORK STATE SENATOR

A GUIDE TO OTHER SPECIALTY SMOKED FISH

CHUB

Rich, smoky, and moist, chub—more specifically lake chub—is a rare treat we get only sporadically. Smaller than a whitefish, though often confused for one, smoked chub is an integral part of the appetizing canon. Hailing from the Great Lakes, chubs have become increasingly difficult to catch as the fish seek colder, deeper waters. We maintain a list of chub-loving customers who we alert whenever a shipment comes in.

WHITEFISH

The silver-skinned lake whitefish is native to the Great Lakes, where it has sustained the local economy and peoples for thousands of years. By the time the whitefish arrive at Russ & Daughters, the cured and then hot-smoked fish has taken on a golden hue. The flesh, moistened by its own fat, has turned delicate and flaky. For over a century, hours of back-and-forth debate between customer and slicer have taken place as savvy clients jockey for the fattest, plumpest fish. After much work deboning, we serve them either fileted or whole (the deboning is the fileting), as well as using it for our Whitefish & Baked Salmon Salad (PAGE 87) and Whitefish Croquettes (PAGE 88).

STURGEON

Joel Russ dubbed his daughters the "Queens of Lake Sturgeon" for sturgeon was once the marquee smoked fish at Russ & Daughters. Clean and earthy, sweet and delicate, it is easy to see why. Lake sturgeon (*Acipenser fulvescens*), once plentiful in the Great Lakes, were particularly prized for their mild flesh. By the 1950s, thanks in part to the popularity of caviar, sturgeon stocks had plummeted. Though generally the sturgeon isn't as buttery as in days of yore, we offer hand-selected Private Stock sturgeon that are as tender and tasty as in their heyday.

MACKEREL

Cured and smoked, then seasoned with peppercorns, our wild mackerel fillets are flaky and delicate although there is no denying—nor should there be—mackerel's intense fishy quality. Like most of our cured and smoked fish, mackerel is high in omega-3 fatty acids. The fillets, which come from the North Atlantic, are delicious with a squeeze of lemon and placed on a cracker or atop a salad.

BROOK TROUT

Smokier than our whitefish or chub, our freshwater brook trout is cured then hot-smoked. We serve them whole, though their meat makes for a wonderful Smoked Trout Mousse (PAGE 91) or as an accompaniment to fresh greens.

SABLE

Sablefish, a recent addition to the appetizing canon, arrived in the 1960s, when it was plentiful and cheap. Once known as the *poor man's sturgeon* or *chicken carp*, it has a rich buttery texture and delicate flavor. Ours is line-caught in the waters of the northern Pacific, somewhere between hot- and cold- smoked according to our specifications, and dusted with a thin coat of paprika and garlic, both to seal in the natural moistness and to round out the fish's flavor.

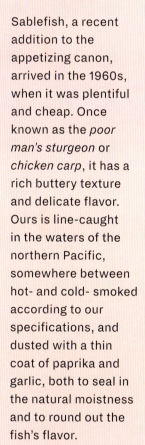

YELLOWFIN TUNA

A new addition to our selection of smoked fish, the rosy-hued yellowfin tuna is cured then medium-smoked for a firm texture, which means it can be enjoyed sans the base of a bread or cracker.

SABLE DOESN'T GET THE SHINE IT DESERVES. You gotta have Eastern European Judaism in you to order. Of all the things that I remember about my grandmother Adele "Ada" Peskowitz, I remember that she loved the smoked sable. She was a brash woman and would talk through the bites. I remember sitting in her kitchen in Brooklyn, with the floral wallpaper and Formica floors, as she waved a bagel around and I was showered with sable. That's a formative memory. JOSH PESKOWITZ, CREATIVE DIRECTOR

Sardine Toast with Avocado Mousse & Olive Tapenade

MAKES A SNACK FOR 4

3 to 4 slices pumpernickel bread, homemade (PAGE 293) or store-bought

1 (4.2-ounce) tin Russ & Daughters (or other) sardines, drained

1 tablespoon minced fresh parsley

FOR THE OLIVE TAPENADE

1½ cups kalamata olives, pitted

2 tablespoons roughly chopped fresh parsley

1½ tablespoons capers

2 cloves garlic, roughly chopped

1 tablespoon pimientos, drained

1 tablespoon lemon juice

3 tablespoons extra-virgin olive oil

FOR THE AVOCADO MOUSSE

1 large ripe avocado, halved, pitted, and peeled

¼ cup whipped cream cheese

1 tablespoon lemon juice

½ teaspoon kosher salt

In the early days of Russ & Daughters, the entirety of the shop was lined from the windows to the walls, the ceiling to the floor, with cans of tinned fish. Moosabecs from Canada, Riga Gold sprats, sardines in lemon, cod liver. It was a tinned fish mosaic. So important were sardines to Joel Russ's business that, during World War II, he ran a sardine speakeasy (to skirt metal rations) around the corner on Ludlow. Customers would whisper into his ear then drive around the corner where their trunks were loaded with the precious tinned cargo. The tinned fish business has waxed and waned over the years, but we have always kept our shelves stocked with sardines, trout, cod liver, and tuna. Today, tinned fish is having a renaissance. A new generation is falling in love with the wonders of the silvery slivers of the sea. Since 2024, we've been importing our own sardines from Spain. This recipe was first developed at the Cafe as a means to showcase the tinned fish offerings at the store.

MAKE OLIVE TAPENADE

Combine the olives, parsley, capers, garlic, pimientos, and lemon juice in the bowl of a food processer. Pulse the mixture two or three times, then scrape down the sides of the bowl with a rubber spatula. Turn the food processor on again and slowly drizzle in the olive oil until the mixture becomes uniform. Remove and reserve until ready to use.

MAKE AVOCADO MOUSSE

Combine all the ingredients in the bowl of a food processor. Process until smooth and set aside.

TO ASSEMBLE

Toast the pumpernickel bread. Spread avocado mousse on the toast, add a layer of sardines, then a few dollops of tapenade. Garnish with the parsley and serve open-faced.

The tapenade lasts a week in the fridge, and leftovers make a great condiment for crudités and charcuterie boards.

Whitefish & Baked Salmon Salad

MAKES 1¼ QUARTS (5 CUPS), 8 TO 10 SERVINGS

1½ pounds smoked whitefish meat, bones removed*

½ pound kippered salmon, skin and bones removed

½ cup mayonnaise

⅓ cup minced white onion

¼ teaspoon onion powder

¼ teaspoon white pepper

---

*
A 2-pound smoked whitefish will yield about 1½ pounds meat.

Whitefish salad has long been an appetizing classic. Noshable, spreadable, creamy, and slightly smoky, it has graced the tables of brises and bar mitzvahs, been laid upon bagels immeasurable, and schmeared all along the journey of our lives. For as long as we can remember we've taken the highly unusual step of adding a small amount of baked (or kippered) salmon to the whitefish. The addition of salmon, in our minds and to our customers' delight, rounds out the flavor of the whitefish and softens what can be its intense flavor. The salad is wildly popular and has become one of our signature recipes.

Place the whitefish and salmon in the bowl of a food processor and pulse until chunky. Depending on the size of your food processor, you may need to do this in two batches. Transfer to a medium bowl and stir in the mayonnaise, onion, onion powder, and pepper. Keep refrigerated until ready to serve.

The salad will keep in the refrigerator for 5 days.

Whitefish Croquettes

MAKES APPROXIMATELY 26 CROQUETTES

1 large or 2 medium Yukon Gold potatoes (about ½ pound)

4 tablespoons (½ stick) unsalted butter

1 large shallot, minced (½ cup)

¼ cup all-purpose flour

2 cups whole milk

Grated zest of ½ lemon (1½ teaspoons)

2¼ teaspoons sherry vinegar

1 whole smoked whitefish (about 2 pounds), picked and bones removed

36 Bagel Chips (PAGE 280)

Kosher salt and freshly ground black pepper

6 large eggs

2 to 3 quarts neutral oil, for frying

½ cup Tartar Sauce (PAGE 201), for serving

*

If frying the croquettes from frozen solid, you will need to place them in a preheated 325° F oven for 10 to 12 minutes before frying. Or thaw them in the refrigerator overnight before frying.

Around the time we were opening the cafe, Josh was eating at Il Buco, a romantic restaurant a little west of us in Noho, a lot. (He is still a regular.) Though the owner, Donna Lennard, is a nice Jewish girl from Chappaqua, the cuisine is inspired by Umbria and Spain and the chef, Roger Martinez, is Barcelonan. One of Josh's favorite dishes was the *bolinas de bacalao*, little fried salt cod fritters that emerged from the kitchen golden and crisp on the outside and creamy within, served with a Meyer lemon aioli. These croquettes are our Iberia-via-Ashkenazi version. We use the milder smoked whitefish rather than the dried—then rehydrated—salt cod. The whitefish imparts a subtle smoky flavor to the croquettes. Though this recipe makes many, we recommend preparing the entire recipe, frying what you want then freezing the remaining (unfried) croquettes for later.*

Add the potatoes to a medium pot of lightly salted cold water. Bring to a boil and cook until fork tender, about 20 minutes total. Drain and allow to cool slightly. When the potatoes are cool enough to handle but still warm, remove the skins. Mash the potatoes with a fork or potato masher until smooth.

Make the béchamel by melting the butter in a medium saucepan over medium heat. Once the foaming subsides, add the shallot, lower the heat to medium-low, and sweat until translucent, about 4 minutes. Stir in the flour, using a rubber spatula to incorporate it into the butter and scraping the bottom of the pan to make sure the roux—that is, the combination of butter and flour—does not burn. Once the roux starts to smell nutty and darkens slightly, 2 to 3 minutes, gradually whisk in the milk. Bring to a gentle simmer (there should be a few bubbles coming up), and cook, whisking, until thickened, 3 to 5 minutes. (The finished sauce should have the consistency of yogurt.) Add the lemon zest and sherry vinegar and stir to incorporate. Remove the pan from the heat and let cool.

Once the béchamel and potatoes are both slightly cooled, combine the fish and béchamel in a large bowl. Add the potatoes and mix until fully combined. Season lightly with salt and pepper. Chill for 1 hour.

Portion the mixture into 1½-ounce balls (each about the size of a golf ball). Cover with plastic wrap and freeze for a minimum of 1 hour, or up to 14 days.

Pulse the bagel chips (a double batch of our recipe) in a food processor until they are fully ground. (Or use a blender or a mortar and pestle.) You should have about 5 cups.

Make the egg wash by whisking together the eggs and ¼ cup water in a shallow bowl.

CONTINUED →

Roll the frozen croquettes in the egg wash, then in the bagel chips. Repeat this process to produce a solid even coating on each ball and lay them out on a tray. Cover with plastic wrap and freeze for a minimum of 1 hour. At this point, the croquettes can be wrapped in plastic and frozen for up to a month.

To fry, fill a Dutch oven halfway up with neutral oil and heat to 325°F. Working in batches of 3 to 4, add the croquettes to the hot oil and fry, turning occasionally, for 3 to 4 minutes, until the croquettes are a deep, rich, golden brown color. Remove with a slotted spoon, drain on paper towels, and season with salt. Serve immediately with tartar sauce.

Smoked Trout Mousse

MAKES 3 CUPS

3 smoked brook trout, about 1 pound total
1½ cups mayonnaise
1 tablespoon onion powder
1 teaspoon granulated sugar
⅛ teaspoon white pepper

For most of human history, food with eyes on it was a symbol of status. Think apple-mouthed pigs staring up from the feasting table, or lambs gazing unseeingly, getting dizzy on the spit. A whole animal, in its natural form, meant the meat—fish, pig, lamb, duck, whatever—had been procured in its entirety. No offcuts or back-alley scraps allowed. For years, partially for this very reason, Russ & Daughters sold our smoked trout mousse as the full fish, head and tail attached. We'd remove the flesh from the trout, while carefully keeping the skin intact, make a mousse out of the meat, and stuff it back into the fish. It was a fish-stuffed fish and it graced countless Shabbat tables, admired before being devoured. Things have changed. As many of our customers climbed their way from the tenements of the Lower East Side to middle- and upper-middle-class Jewry—and later to include the broader gentile world—the need to *prove* provenance receded in importance. The new luxury was to consume our meat with the least possible reminder of its living form. So, we did away with the fish and its eyes and its tail and its skin, but kept the delicious mousse which transforms the trout into a creamy, schmearable spread for crackers, matzo, bagel chips, rye chips, and toast.

Carefully pick all the meat off the trout, making sure to remove all the small pin bones. Place the trout meat and the rest of the ingredients in the bowl of a food processor and pulse until the mousse is smooth.

The mousse keeps in the refrigerator for 3 to 5 days.

/IAR

That as haimish a concern as Russ & Daughters sells as luxurious a product as caviar—which comes from the Persian *khav-yar* meaning "cake of power"—may seem incongruous. Yet, the journey from smoked herring to these small elegant pearls of salted fish eggs mirrors the journey of the American Jewish experience, the narrative of the Lower East Side, and the history of caviar itself.

Sturgeon, a slow-moving shockingly large ponderous order of fish, has been around for millions of years. Caviar, which is made by salting the eggs of the sturgeon, has been around for almost a thousand. The first usage of the word can be traced to Batu Khan, a grandson of Genghis, who wrote of a visit to Uglich, north of Moscow, in which he enjoyed eel paste, pierogi, and an "apple and caviar preparation." For centuries the vast majority of the global caviar trade centered around the Caspian Sea, where four of the twenty-six sturgeon species—beluga (*Huso huso*), osetra (*Acipenser gueldenstaedtii*), sevruga (*Acipenser stellatus*), and ship (*Acipenser nudiventris*)—provided the majority of the world's caviar production. In the modern era, the countries surrounding the sea, notably Russia and Iran, became powerhouses in the caviar trade. In Russia and much of Europe, since at least the time of the czars, granular caviar—as distinguished from salty pressed roe, called *payusnaya*—has been synonymous with luxury.

Not in America. In the early nineteenth century, caviar was an unfancy bar snack in New York. Atlantic sturgeon (*Acipenser oxyrhynchus*) was once plentiful in the waterways from the St. Lawrence River to the Gulf of Mexico. Lake sturgeon (*Acipenser fulvescens*) once filled the Great Lakes. But the American sturgeon industry didn't really take off until around 1873, when a German immigrant named Henry Schacht founded a caviar export business on the Delaware River. Soon business sprang up along many Northeastern waterways. In the late 1800s, sturgeon—called *Albany beef* for its cheap flavorful meat—was a major resource in New York's Hudson River Valley. Though their flesh was little valued—in fact, it was often boiled down for sturgeon oil—the eggs from female sturgeons were harvested, salted, and sent to Europe. For a time in the 1880s, sturgeon spawned a Caviar Rush on the banks of the Delaware River in New Jersey, which was the world's primary provider of caviar.

CUSTOMER AT RUSS & DAUGHTERS

As was the case for the entire caviar industry, the American caviar boom, sadly, soon resulted in vastly depleted American sturgeon fisheries in as little as twenty to thirty years. Depletion of the stocks of Caspian and Black Sea sturgeon took longer thanks in part to strict control by the U.S.S.R. After the fall of the Soviet Union in 1989, however, the caviar market descended into chaos, and often criminality. Much like how unregulated fishing in the United States had decimated the sturgeon fisheries a century before, the Caspian Sea was rapidly rid of its sturgeon stock. These were the Wild West years of caviar, when nefarious caviar dealers sold poached sturgeon, when visitors would return from the former Soviet Union with suitcases full of caviar, and when mislabeling was rampant. Many a disgraced caviar monger ended up in prison during the feeding frenzy to capitalize on the now unregulated delicacy.

As for when caviar became part of the appetizing canon at Russ & Daughters, we're not sure. Certainly by the 1960s, Mark's father, Herbie, was selling

Russian beluga caviar by the pound. (It cost $69 in 1969.) Along with sturgeon caviar came humbler fish roes like the bright orange salmon roe and trout roe, and the small beaded inky whitefish roe. Though technically caviar refers only to the salted roe of sturgeon, many customers referred and still refer to these alternatives as salmon caviar, trout caviar, whitefish caviar, etc. Less a diffusion line of caviar than its more populist cousins, these roes have their devotees, preferring the more assertive flavors over the buttery (and much more expensive) traditional caviars. Roe or caviar, Mark continued the tradition, putting tins of caviar on ice, wrapping that in aluminum foil and thrusting them to his customers like silvery snowballs. Like everyone else, we've also had to negotiate the changing tides of caviar production. In 2005, beluga (*Huso huso*) was the first of the wild Caspian caviars to be made illegal by the US Fish and Wildlife Service. The following year, the Convention on International Trade in Endangered Species of Wild Fauna and Flora (CITES) installed rigorous guidelines and quotas on the caviar trade from the Caspian and Black Seas.

At Russ & Daughters we have always taken pains to source ethically, no matter where our caviar came from. But after the Iranian boycott and the CITES Act, we focused on the nascent American caviar market, including white sturgeon (*Acipenser transmontanus*) and hackleback, a small sturgeon native to American rivers, and emphasized our paddlefish, a less expensive, more plentiful relative of the sturgeon. Today our selections include a large range of farmed caviar from around the world. Though it took a long incubation period, today's farmed sturgeon offer both a sustainable and a high quality caviar.

Just as it has with farmed salmon, aquaculture has narrowed the range of variation amongst caviar production. However, unlike cured or smoked fish, the species of sturgeon is of a paramount importance. Today sturgeon farms can be found in the United States, China, Italy, France, Poland, Bulgaria, and beyond.

No matter the source of the caviar, we look for certain indicators of quality. This starts with an inspection of the original tins, the so-called *OT*, the 1.8-kilogram circular canisters in which our caviar arrives from the farm. We taste and select from every OT before carefully hand-packing them into smaller tins. Caviar pearls should be intact and round. The interior viscosity—mouthfeel—of each egg should be pleasantly textured, not too watery nor too thick as it bursts in your mouth. Though caviar flavors range from mild and sweet to salty and aggressive, no caviar should leave a sour or bitter taste in one's mouth.

Today we are one of the premier and most trusted caviar purveyors in the country. But our approach remains essentially haimish. We use straightforward labeling, are always scrupulously honest, ensure that our staff is knowledgeable, and work with our guests not to sell them the most expensive caviar, but rather to provide the best caviar for their needs and desires at the right price for them. This has expanded to include even more affordable options like salmon roe, trout roe, flying fish roe, and more. (*Caviar* is the eggs of a sturgeon; *roe* is the eggs of other species of fish.)

We even have a Caviar Express Line for devotees of the delicacy, who shuffle, glide, and doven their way to the back of the store. Occasionally the express line, like all express lines, is mildly misused. For instance, one time when the store was exceedingly crowded, a gentleman used the express line to by a large tin of caviar and four bagels. It was the bagels he wanted but he simply couldn't bear to wait in line. More often, caviar accompanies momentous events in the lives of our customers, events of which we become a part: birthdays, graduations, New Year's Eve (one of our busiest for caviar), Valentine's Day (also huge), first dates, anniversaries, and the million small moments that call for celebration and a tin or two of caviar.

A GUIDE TO CAVIAR & ROE

OSETRA CAVIAR

After beluga's demise, osetra caviar, from the long maturing *Acipenser gueldenstaetdii*, stepped in as the top-tier caviar. Osetra caviar has large pearls that can range in color from dark to golden, with a flavor that ranges from mild to slightly earthy and a long-lasting buttery finish. We sell exclusively golden osetra. Alone among the Caspian varieties, *gueldenstaedtii* tolerates farming quite well.

SIBERIAN CAVIAR

Siberian caviar, harvested from the *Acipenser baerii*, a river sturgeon native to Siberia, is mild and sweet, similar in many ways to osetra. Its eggs are grayish to black with a buttery texture and a sweet briny aftertaste.

AMERICAN TRANSMONTANUS CAVIAR

The white sturgeon (*Acipenser transmontanus*) is native to American waterways and yields large beaded caviar with a dark brown hue, honeyed striations, and a nutty flavor that resembles in many ways a traditional osetra—but at a much more accessible price point.

HACKLEBACK CAVIAR

Our American hackleback caviar comes from shovelnose sturgeons (*Scaphirhynchus platorynchus*) caught in the Mississippi River Valley. It is typically mild flavored with small black, often firm, eggs. Along with paddlefish caviar, hackleback is a wonderful gateway caviar.

PADDLEFISH CAVIAR

Paddlefish belong to the same order as sturgeon (*Acipenseriformes*) but a different family (*Polyodontidae*). Much more affordable and similarly wild caught from the Mississippi River Valley, paddlefish caviar ranges in color from dark gray to light gray with small, often firm beads, and a somewhat intense and saline flavor.

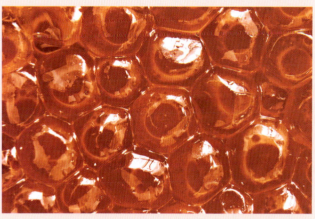

SALMON ROE

The large, shockingly orange eggs of salmon are the most popular and flavorful of caviar alternatives. Ours come from either pink (*Oncorhynchus gorbuscha*) or chum (*Oncorhynchus keta*) salmon, depending on the production each year. Both species have a delicate taste and a bright pop, and are relatively long-lasting.

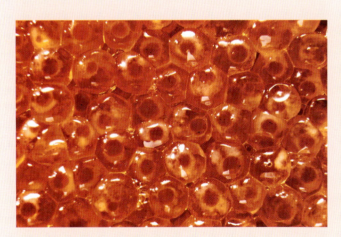

TROUT ROE

Slightly smaller and milder than its migratory cousin salmon roe, trout roe is well loved for its delicate flavor and the pleasing firm consistency of its pearls. Though also made gently smoked, we prefer our trout roe unsmoked and mildly salted.

WASABI-INFUSED FLYING FISH ROE

Don't let the small pearls of flying fish roe fool you. Bright green and bracingly strong, the wasabi-infused eggs have an outsized kick. We find that our newest roe addition works best when served with the softening flavors of, for instance, our whitefish and salmon salad.

NOTES ON STORING, SERVING & ENJOYING CAVIAR

ON CHAMPAGNE AND VODKA: Though champagne is probably the best-known beverage companion for caviar, and in fact aligns nicely with caviar's luxurious profile, traditionally vodka is caviar's closest friend. Vodka cleanses your palette, wiping away the oils so the next bite you take is like the first bite. The best vodka is the cleanest so as not to impart any other flavors to your palate and should be served very cold. If, however, you do enjoy champagne, opt for a dry one. Josh likes a crisp vintage Dom Pérignon; Niki enjoys a Billecart-Salmon.

ON STORAGE: Caviar should be kept refrigerated until five minutes before serving. Keep the tin closed while storing. (Oxidization is your enemy.) Store caviar in the coldest part of your fridge. Stored in this way, unopened caviar will keep in the average refrigerator for about three weeks. Once opened, caviar should be eaten immediately. However, if there are any leftovers, smooth out the surface and then carefully place a piece of plastic wrap on top of the caviar (without pushing down) to create a seal and keep air out. Close with the lid. Refrigerate and finish the rest in the next one to two days.

ON SERVING: Serve caviar cold, from 50°F to 53°F, on top of crushed ice, or in a caviar presentoir, if you have one (this requires removing the caviar from the tin). Avoid using metallic utensils as they can interfere with the natural essence of caviar. For an unadulterated experience,

choose utensils and bowls made from nonreactive materials such as mother-of-pearl, glass, plastic, or wood.

We don't believe in muddying the caviar experience with too many accoutrements. Caviar should be served straight, with nothing to interfere with its flavors. The exceptions are a neutral, or close to neutral, vessel such as a blini or toast points and crème fraîche. Nevertheless our standard caviar service does include chopped hardboiled egg, minced red onion, and chives, since many of our customers do and, as the sign says, "de gustibus non est disputandum."

If, however, for some reason you do want to pair your caviar with a more outré vessel, try a potato chip, preferably one not too salty. The crispiness of the chip and the delicate softness of the caviar is the best of the high-low pairing.

Caviar can either be scooped directly from the tin or it can be made into quenelles. A quenelle, a French term, can be both a food and the shape of that food. The food itself is often a fish mousse (not applicable here) but the shape of it is like a little dumpling. Here we mean the shape. To make a quenelle, use a small spoon—not a teaspoon but a regular one—to scoop up the caviar. Using another spoon of the same size, gently transfer the caviar from one spoon to the other, passing it back and forth with care until it forms a cute little, almost football-like, shape. This is a quenelle.

NOT FOR US

BELUGA CAVIAR: Beluga boast the largest eggs (often graded 000 or 00) and is the mildest of the Caspian caviars, with a luxury price tag to match. But, like all other wild-caught caviar from the Caspian Sea, it is now illegal to sell. Farmed beluga, in which the caviar is milked rather than harvested, is a more sustainable option, but we find that it is an inferior product.

SEVRUGA CAVIAR: Delicate gray eggs from the smallest of the sturgeon *Acipenser stellatus*, sevruga caviar is defined by its assertive flavor and heavier salinity but very clean finish. It is being farmed today in very few locations and the price is very high.

KALUGA CAVIAR: Sourced from *Huso dauricus*, a relative of the beluga sturgeon, Kaluga caviar is lauded for its large golden brown to gray pearls, firm texture, and distinct nutty flavor. But, like farmed beluga and sevruga, we don't find the quality to be worth the price.

BE WARY OF... So-called beluga—Since the beluga sturgeon is critically endangered and caviar derived from it is illegal in the United States, don't trust any caviar labeled *beluga*. Though there is limited beluga (*Huso huso*) farming, beluga hybrids are more prevalent. Labels like Imperial, Tsar, or Royal—In the absence of unified international oversight about the labeling of caviar, some producers and many restaurants add high-falutin adjectives to their caviar descriptions which, though poetic, are meaningless. Look for the species name and origin. Caviar in glass jars—We sell our caviar in tins of varying sizes, from 50 grams all the way to OTs, which can be hold as much as 1.8 kilograms. We only sell fresh, unpasteurized caviar. If you find caviar in glass jars, that usually means it is pasteurized, which extends the shelf life but often makes the eggs overly firm. Caviar not from sturgeon— All caviar is roe but not all roe is caviar. By definition, caviar is the roe of sturgeon family (*Acipenseridae*). Everything else is roe. Though there has been some elasticity in the past over this definition, generally speaking, a product labeled caviar that is not from sturgeon and not clearly indicated as such should be avoided.

Caviar & Blini

MAKES 2 SERVINGS

¼ cup buckwheat flour
1¼ cups all-purpose flour
½ teaspoon kosher salt
½ teaspoon granulated sugar
⅛ teaspoon baking powder
⅛ teaspoon baking soda
1 large egg, separated
1¾ cups whole milk
1 ounce of your favorite caviar
¼ cup crème fraîche

The delicate buckwheat flavor of blini—traditional Russian pancakes—has long been thought of as an ideal, amiable companion to caviar. There are generally two families of blini: the more pancake-y French blini and the Russian blini, which is more similar to a crepe. At the Cafe we make the French style, which we think work better as mini-blinis. As is true with bagels and smoked salmon, the ratio of blini to caviar is key. We keep our blini petite so a respectable but not extravagant 15 g bissel of caviar feels (and is) luxurious. As for the crème fraîche, it's a concession to the modern taste for accoutrements—but it is true that the lushness of the dairy augments, rather than detracts from, the flavors of the caviar.

Sift together the flours, salt, sugar, baking powder, and baking soda in a small bowl.

Whisk the egg white in a small bowl until soft peaks form. In a medium bowl, whisk together the egg yolk and milk until combined. Add the flour mixture to the yolk mixture and whisk until fully mixed, then fold in the beaten egg whites.

Heat a nonstick pan over medium heat. Spoon about 4 quarter-sized dollops of the batter into the pan, being careful not to crowd. Cook for 30 to 45 seconds, until bubbles form across the tops, then flip and cook an additional 30 seconds, until the blini are light golden brown. Transfer to a plate and continue with remaining batter to make the rest of the blini.

Serve the blini with caviar and crème fraîche.

The blini will keep in the refrigerator for 2 days.

Caviar Lover's Black & White

MAKES 5 SERVINGS

5 Potato Latkes (PAGE 163)
50 grams black caviar
Approximately 1 cup crème fraîche

After a century, inspiration and good fortune still occasionally hit us. Such is the case with the Caviar Lover's Black & White. One day during a meeting with an ample spread of appetizing before her—as per usual—Niki put a schmear of crème fraîche atop a latke and covered one half of it with a bissel of caviar. She took a picture and posted it with the caption "Caviar Lover's Black & White." The image, which true enough did resemble the bifurcated coloration of our Black & White Cookie (PAGE 303), was widely shared. It eventually reached Florence Fabricant, the inimitable *New York Times* columnist, who included it in her column, Off the Menu. And suddenly, the Caviar Lover's Black & White went from lark to actual thing. In some ways it's just a neat party preparation, a callback to one of our other iconic offerings. But it also happens to be delicious, with the crispiness of the latke playing contrapuntally to the lush crème fraîche and the delicate caviar.

Preheat the oven to 350°F.

Place the latkes on a baking sheet and bake for 8 to 10 minutes, until the centers are warm.

Spread crème fraîche equally over each latke. Spoon about 10 grams of caviar on one half of each latke.

Hasselback Potatoes with Caviar

MAKES 4 SERVINGS

4 medium russet potatoes
6 tablespoons melted schmaltz, unsalted butter, or neutral oil
1 teaspoon kosher salt
½ bunch fresh chives, minced
One 125-gram tin of your favorite caviar

As mentioned before, we believe caviar, itself a food of excess, is best enjoyed minimally. The exceptions are Soft Scrambled Eggs (PAGE 181), Blini (PAGE 103), Caviar Lover's Black & Whites (PAGE 104), and these spectacular potatoes. When paired with a crispy schmaltz-brushed hasselback potato, caviar comes alive. The potato dish itself—a Swedish preparation originating in Stockholm's Hasselbacken restaurant in 1953—is cut into thin slices that nevertheless remain connected at the base. Brushed in schmaltz (our preference), butter (also acceptable), or oil (fine) then baked, the potato becomes at once crispy and creamy. That texture (somewhere between a chip and a baked potato) and the starchy, rich, creamy flavor make the potato a perfect complement to the salinity and delicacy of caviar.

Add the potatoes to a medium pot and cover with cold water. Bring the water to a boil, then cook for an additional 8 to 10 minutes, until the potatoes are still firm, but can be pierced with a toothpick.

Preheat the oven to 425°F. Once the potatoes are cool, peel and cut each into ⅛-inch-thick slices, but stopping about ⅛ of an inch before you cut through the potato, being careful not to cut all the way through. (Lay two chopsticks on either side of the potato to serve as a stopper for the knife blade.) If you do slice too far, use a toothpick or two to hold the potato together.

Using half the schmaltz, butter, or oil, brush the potatoes inside and out. Season with salt. Place the potatoes in a ceramic baking dish and bake for 15 minutes. Remove and brush the potatoes with the rest of the schmaltz, again being sure to coat both the outsides and the interiors. Return to the potatoes to the oven and bake, removing every 10 to 15 minutes and basting the potatoes with fat from the pan, for a total of 50 to 60 minutes, until the potatoes are light golden brown, crispy on the outside, and tender in the middle.

Allow to cool slightly, then garnish with minced chives and about 30 grams of caviar each. Enjoy immediately.

SIDES

Sour (& Half-Sour) Pickles

MAKES 6 TO 8 PICKLES

6 to 8 Persian or Kirby cucumbers

½ head of garlic, cloves separated and peeled

1 cup fresh dill, stems included

1 teaspoon whole black peppercorns

2 cups distilled water

1½ tablespoons fine sea salt (for half-sours, use ¾ teaspoon)

EQUIPMENT NEEDED

1 (16-ounce) sterilized airtight jar, such as a Ball jar

Once, the streets of the Lower East Side were clogged with pickle pushers, crying out, "Sours for sale!" For as long as we can remember, we've had barrels of pickles at Russ & Daughters. It's one of the threads that connect us to the ecosystem of the neighborhood. Today, there are still some longstanding picklemongers, such as the Pickle Guys on Grand Street. We offer sours and half-sours—the difference being the amount of time the cucumber sits in the brine—to complement our appetizing. These recipes are our home adaptations with simple guidelines. Pickle-making is an endeavor that requires developing a good pickle sense, so feel free to experiment to suit your own taste.

Bring a large pot of water to a boil. Clean the pickle jar with hot soapy water and submerge in the boiling water for 10 minutes. Remove with tongs and let air-dry.

Clean the cucumbers thoroughly with cold water. Place the cucumbers in the jar and add the garlic, dill, and peppercorns.

Combine ½ cup of the distilled water and the salt in a saucepan and bring to a simmer. Remove from the heat and whisk until the salt is completely dissolved. Let the water cool for a few minutes, then whisk it into the remaining 1½ cups distilled water. Allow to cool until close to room temperature.

Pour the brine over the cucumbers until it comes just below the rim. Seal the jar tightly and store in a dark, cool place for 48 hours. (For half-sours, pickle for only 6 to 8 hours.) The longer they sit at room temperature, the more sour your pickles become.

Remove the dill from the jar and transfer the pickles and brine to the refrigerator where they'll keep for up to 1 month.

Notes on Pickling: Fermentation is a tricky and detailed process and many factors can affect the results. But lack of sanitary conditions can endanger the pickling process, the pickle, and you, the pickle eater. Always make sure your work surfaces and utensils are cleaned and sanitized before you begin. And make sure you use fresh, clean ingredients without any blemishes or signs of decay. (Many recipes will tell you to add a head of garlic, cut in half, skin and all. We prefer to peel the cloves to help ensure that there is no mold or decay.) And use only *distilled* water and *sea* salt—no substitutes.

The fermentation process will depend upon the temperature of your home or wherever you choose to ferment. If you're making this recipe during the colder months, pickling may require more time. Likewise, in the summer, be mindful not to leave your ferments unrefrigerated for too long.

Chopped Liver

MAKES 8 TO 10 SERVINGS

3 tablespoons canola oil
2 tablespoons schmaltz, or chicken fat
1 large Spanish onion, chopped
2 teaspoons granulated sugar
Kosher salt and freshly ground black pepper to taste
1 pound chicken livers, cleaned, deveined, and patted dry
2 large eggs, hard-boiled (PAGE 118) and peeled

Chopped liver is nearly as maligned as gefilte fish. Perhaps it is even more so, as it has made its way into common parlance as a literal example of nothing. "What am I, chopped liver?" many a slighted Jewish mother have complained. (The origins of this saying, it should be noted, have more to do with chopped liver being a side dish, and not a main course.) But how unfair it is to knock a thing simply for its worst-made iterations, or because of the horror with which a child contemplates a mushy textured food? Chopped liver—when it is made with high-quality chicken liver that is cooked through in schmaltz and kissed with caramelized onions, as we do—is irresistible. Like gefilte fish, this prized nosh began as an affordable way to extend a cheap piece of meat. Full of protein, chopped liver is as silken and strong as an iron fist in a velvet glove. It has a wide array of year-round acolytes, from keto-followers to the pregnant. But on Passover, everyone orders pints of the stuff. Not only is it tradition, but the richness of the chopped liver compensates for the dryness of matzo.

Heat a large sauté pan over medium heat. Add the canola oil and chicken fat. Once the fat has liquified, add the onion, sugar, and a pinch of salt. Cook, stirring often and reducing the heat if browning too quickly, until the onions are golden, 15 to 20 minutes. Transfer the onions to a bowl.

Raise heat to medium-high and add the chicken livers to the pan. Season generously with salt and pepper and cook, turning occasionally, until there is a deep brown sear on the exterior and the residual liquid has cooked down, 3 to 4 minutes.

Return the onions to the pan and reduce the heat to medium-low. Cook for an additional 5 to 10 minutes, stirring occasionally, until the livers are cooked through without any pink left in the center. Remove from the heat and let cool slightly, about 10 minutes.

Transfer the livers and onions to a food processor. Chop the eggs and add them as well. Pulse until combined: The mixture should be totally combined, uniform in color, but not totally smooth, and have the consistency of cottage cheese. Refrigerate until cold. Enjoy with toast, crackers, or straight up.

The chopped liver will keep, covered and refrigerated, for 3 days.

Vegetarian Chopped Liver

MAKES 6 TO 8 SERVINGS

- ½ pound cremini mushrooms
- ½ pound portobello mushrooms
- 4 tablespoons extra-virgin olive oil
- ¼ pound green beans, trimmed
- ½ cup walnuts
- 1 large Spanish onion, thinly sliced
- 1 (16-ounce) can chickpeas, drained
- 2 tablespoons brown sugar
- Kosher salt and fresh ground black pepper to taste
- 1 large egg, hard-boiled (PAGE 118), peeled, and chopped

At our own locations we have never been—and have never claimed to be—kosher. We're kosher-style, which is different. But when we opened a Russ & Daughters at the Jewish Museum in 2016 (now closed), we had to be certified kosher. So instead of our traditional chopped liver, we returned to our roots with this vegetarian version. Dating back to the 1950s, during the time of our grandmothers, we offered a vegetarian chopped liver that combined mushrooms, nuts, chickpeas, and green beans to create a nonmeat meatiness. Surprisingly, perhaps, over time the vegetarian version proved itself nearly as popular as the original. It earned die-hard devotees who mourn the pandemic-era closure of our outpost at the museum and the resultant fact that this vegetarian chopped liver is no longer regularly on the menu. This recipe, then, is for them, so that they can make it at home whenever they wish.

Preheat the oven to 400°F.

Place the cremini and portobello mushrooms on a baking sheet, toss with two tablespoons olive oil to lightly coat, and season with salt. Roast for 45 minutes, until the mushrooms are beginning to brown and reduced in size by half.

Meanwhile, set a steamer basket in a saucepan with 2 inches of water and heat over high heat until boiling. Reduce the heat to medium, add the green beans to the basket, cover, and steam for 5 to 7 minutes, until softened but not flaccid. Set the green beans aside.

Remove the mushrooms from the oven and reduce the heat to 350°F. Spread the walnuts evenly on a baking sheet and roast for 10 to 12 minutes, stirring occasionally, until lightly roasted. Let cool slightly.

Heat 1 tablespoon of the olive oil in a large sauté pan over medium-high heat until shimmering. Add the onion and cook, stirring frequently, until beginning to caramelize, about 10 minutes. Remove from the heat.

Roughly chop the green beans, mushrooms, and walnuts. Transfer to the bowl of a food processor and add the onions and chickpeas. Roughly blend until slightly chunky and well mixed. Cover and refrigerate for 1 hour, until completely cool.

Heat the remaining 1 tablespoon olive oil in a medium saucepan over medium-low heat. Once shimmering, add the vegetable mixture and brown sugar and cook for 2 hours, stirring occasionally, making sure to scrape the bottom. When the mixture has reduced by one-fourth and is dark in color, remove from the heat and let cool. Season with salt and pepper to taste, then stir in the chopped egg.

The vegetarian chopped liver will keep in the refrigerator in an airtight container for up to 3 or 4 days.

Romanian Eggplant Salad

MAKES 6 TO 8 SERVINGS

2 large eggplants
1 tablespoon extra-virgin olive oil
1 tablespoon kosher salt, plus more to taste
¼ teaspoon freshly ground black pepper, plus more to taste
½ small red onion, chopped
1 green bell pepper, chopped
3 cloves garlic, minced

Eggplant is a common ingredient in Sephardic cooking. In fact, the berry (it's a berry!) was once known as the *Jew's apple*, since Jews helped transport the eggplant from Spain to Italy and the rest of the Mediterranean in the fifteenth century. Ashkenazim, like other Europeans, mostly ignored the eggplant, except in Turkish-controlled areas like Romania, from whence this standby comes. It's a favorite of our longtime slicer Alina Sheffi, a Romanian-by-way-of-Israel who has been with us for nearly thirty years. As Alina tells it, when she walked in and saw the salad, she immediately felt at home. Even today, when we need a taste tester for eggplant salad, it's Alina who we must satisfy. A good side for vegetarians, the smokiness of the eggplant and the acidity of the peppers make for a refreshing bite.

Preheat the oven to 450°F. Line a baking sheet with parchment.

Cut the eggplants in half lengthwise and lay face up on the lined baking sheet. Rub lightly all over with olive oil, about a teaspoon, and season generously with the salt and pepper. Flip the eggplant so that the cut sides are facing down. Roast for about 40 minutes, until the eggplant is completely tender at the stem end and the skin is collapsing. Let cool completely. Peel and discard the skins. Place the eggplant pulp in a colander and let drain for 10 minutes.

While the eggplant is draining, heat the remaining olive oil in a large sauté pan over medium-high heat. Add the onion and green pepper and cook until the onions are translucent and beginning to take on a little color, about 7 minutes. Add the garlic, turn down the heat to medium, and sauté for 3 minutes longer.

Roughly chop the drained eggplant and mix it with the onion and pepper mixture in a large bowl. Combine well and season to taste with additional salt and pepper. Serve cold.

The Romanian eggplant salad will keep in the refrigerator in an airtight container for 3 days.

Health Salad

MAKES 4 SERVINGS

4 cups shredded cabbage
1 cup shredded carrot
½ cup chopped fresh dill
¼ cup apple cider vinegar
1 tablespoon white wine vinegar
1 tablespoon granulated sugar
1 teaspoon kosher salt
½ teaspoon freshly ground black pepper
½ cup pickled herring, chopped into small cubes

A historical salad, no longer extant, but one that might someday rise again, this is a traditional appetizing dish made to order. It begins with a simple coleslaw-y salad, then enhanced with herring selected by the customer from the case. Bracing, refreshing, and yes, healthy, this salad has sustained many a customer in search of a lighter bite over the years.

Toss together the cabbage, carrot, and dill in a large mixing bowl.

In a small bowl, whisk together the apple cider vinegar, white wine vinegar, sugar, salt, and black pepper until the sugar and salt are dissolved.

Add the dressing to the cabbage mixture and toss to coat. Allow the salad to marinate at room temperature for at least 15 to 20 minutes.

When ready to serve, gently fold the herring into the salad.

The health salad can be kept in an airtight container in the refrigerator for up to 5 days.

Cabbage Salad

MAKES 10 SERVINGS

FOR THE PICKLED CABBAGE

1¼ cups granulated sugar
2¼ cups white vinegar
1 head green cabbage
½ small white onion, thinly sliced
2 stalks celery, thinly sliced
3 tablespoons kosher salt
½ head red cabbage
Juice of ½ lemon

FOR THE VINEGAR SAUCE

¼ cup plus 2 tablespoons vegetable oil
2 tablespoons white vinegar
2 tablespoons granulated sugar
1½ teaspoons kosher salt
¼ teaspoon freshly ground black pepper

Cheap, hardy, and full of nutrients, the leaves and stalks of cabbage—or its precursor colewort—have fed Jews (and other peasants) for millennia. From stuffing it (SEE PAGES 190 and 193) to souping it, Jewish cooks have proved themselves adept interpreters of the haimish green. Here, pickling acts not just a method of preservation but a way of creating flavor. This quickly fermented vinegar-forward coleslaw, which customers often ask to have added to their bagel sandwiches, is a good example of how the sharp flavors of pickling can be found across the array of appetizing, and how the cabbage continues to nourish and sustain us.

PREPARE CABBAGE

Bring 2½ quarts water to boil in a small pot, then remove from the heat. Add the sugar and stir to dissolve. Add the vinegar, stir, then set aside to cool fully to room temperature.

Meanwhile, halve the green cabbage, remove the core, and thinly slice. Combine the cabbage, onion, and celery in a colander. Sprinkle with the salt and let sit for 20 minutes.

Meanwhile, in a separate bowl, core the red cabbage, thinly slice, and add the lemon juice. Toss to distribute evenly. Tightly cover and let stand overnight at room temperature.

MAKE SAUCE

Whisk together the oil, vinegar, sugar, salt, and pepper until emulsified. The vinegar sauce will keep in the refrigerator for 4 weeks.

TO ASSEMBLE

Drain the red cabbage in a large strainer over the sink. Follow that with the green cabbage and its pickling liquid. Transfer all the cabbage to a large bowl, add the vinegar sauce, and stir until evenly mixed.

The cabbage salad will keep, covered in the refrigerator, for 5 to 7 days.

New Potato Salad

MAKES 6 SERVINGS

FOR THE VINAIGRETTE
2 tablespoons red wine vinegar
2 teaspoons Dijon mustard
2 teaspoons lemon juice
½ teaspoon kosher salt
½ teaspoon freshly ground black pepper
½ cup extra-virgin olive oil

FOR THE SALAD
2 pounds red bliss potatoes
¼ cup diced celery
¼ cup minced red onion
3 tablespoons capers
2 tablespoons chopped fresh parsley
2 tablespoons chopped fresh dill
Kosher salt and fresh ground black pepper to taste

Along with the cabbage, the potato—a more recent addition to the Ashkenazi repertoire—might be our humblest and most constant companion. From it, we make latkes (PAGE 163), potato kugels (PAGE 213), pierogies, knishes (PAGE 159), dumplings and, of course, salads. For years we called this dish German potato salad. But that label was never fully accurate. Though certainly not the mayonnaise-heavy American style, ours never (obviously) contained bacon or bacon fat, signature elements of what has come to be thought of as German potato salad. And so, now, the new name: New Potato Salad.

Mix together the vinegar, mustard, lemon juice, salt, and pepper in a small bowl until incorporated. Slowly add the olive oil, whisking constantly, until the mixture emulsifies. Set the vinaigrette aside.

Bring a large pot of salted water to a boil. Meanwhile, clean and scrub the potatoes, then slice to a little less than ¼ inch thick. Add to the boiling water and cook for 9 to 10 minutes, until fork-tender. Drain the potatoes well and place in a large mixing bowl to cool slightly.

Add the vinaigrette and mix until the potatoes are coated. Once completely cool, add the celery, onion, capers, parsley, and dill. Season again with salt and pepper and serve.

The potato salad will keep in the refrigerator for 3 to 5 days.

Egg Salad

MAKES 4 SERVINGS

6 large eggs, hard-boiled (below) and peeled
⅓ cup mayonnaise
¼ cup finely diced celery (about 1 stalk)
¼ cup minced Spanish onion
½ teaspoon kosher salt
¼ teaspoon white pepper

It's hard to say why our egg salad is so popular. Frankly, the recipe is extremely straightforward and simple. But we make it in small batches and, because it turns over quickly, it's always fresh. Perhaps the most perfect way to eat the egg salad is on our challah, where the soft texture and the parallel egginess of the bread complement the delicate salad. The egg salad sando—highly popular with our Japanese clientele—is one of our most often ordered "off menu" items.

Chop the eggs into ¼-inch pieces and place in a large mixing bowl. Add the mayonnaise, celery, onion, salt, and pepper and stir gently with a rubber spatula.

The egg salad will keep in the refrigerator in an airtight container for 3 days.

HOW TO HARD-BOIL AN EGG

There's no shame in not knowing. Only in not asking.

Bring at least 2 quarts of water to a boil in a small pot. Carefully place 1 to 8 room-temperature eggs in the boiling water and allow the water to return to a low boil. Lower the temp to medium and cook at a gentle boil for 9 to 10 minutes. The whites should be set and the yolks should be firm but not hard—which, sadly, you'll only find out later. Remove the eggs and place in a bowl of ice water, allowing them to cool fully in the ice bath.

Once cool, peel by gently cracking an egg on a hard surface then rolling it in your hands. Gently peel off the shards of the shell, making sure to remove the thin membrane.

If you are hard-boiling more than 8 eggs at once, increase the size of your pot and ice bath and be sure to wait to start the timer only once the water has returned to a full boil. This can take 30 seconds to 1 minute.

HOW TO ASSEMBLE A PLATTER

Af yenems simkhe hot men a gutn apetit.
One brings a good appetite to someone else's special occasion.
YIDDISH PROVERB

Generously laden with gently placed slices of smoked fish, a platter is and will always be the ideal presentation of appetizing. A platter represents community, for it is rarely for one. A platter encourages experimentation, because chubs, some sturgeon, whitefish—they don't seem as daunting when just a taste is possible. A platter represents free will, for it is made to allow each nosher to assemble a plate to his or her liking. Free will is joyously exercised too in the *creation* of a platter. But, after one hundred years, we have thoughts.

When building a platter, a substrate is key, especially if the platter, as platters often do, will sit for a time. A leafy green like lettuce or Swiss chard is ideal. Apart from beautifying the presentation, this bottom layer serves as an oil catch, so as to avoid the sight of unseemly pooling. Aesthetically, one needn't be a color theorist to appreciate how, against a vibrant green, the rosy hues of smoked salmon and the near golden flesh of whitefish is as pretty as a Matisse.

Once the substrate has been laid, the fish must be placed. The quantity of fish is the single most important factor in the construction of a platter. This is not a mystical calculation. It is just math. Generally speaking, we recommend four to five slices (about four ounces) of smoked fish per person. How that amount is reached—whether through sturgeon, sable, salmon, whitefish, or trout—is up to you, but we always include twice the amount of smoked salmon per person as we do with other fish (so 1 ounce sable, 1 ounce sturgeon, but 2 ounces smoked salmon).

To lay the platter, harmoniously distribute the slices of fish in an equidistant manner. Garnishes, which we will get to later, should act as barriers between the different sorts of fish. Between the sable and Gaspe, for example, a fan of tomato can stand guard. Sometimes these barriers can be fish too. Often, for brises, shivas, and other life events, a whitefish is wanted. A fileted whitefish, laid out horizontally, is both visually striking and serves to demarcate the space. On Rosh Hashanah, the head of the year, not only is a whitefish called for, but a fish head as well. (As the prayer goes, "May we be the head and not the tail.")

Some people choose to create pinwheels or other intricate shapes of smoked fish. For years we did too, painstakingly folding the salmon into triangular shapes whose grain (fat lines) were perfectly aligned. But these days we prefer a more impressionistic approach. When placing the fish on the platter, think of loose brushstrokes. Grasping the fish from the thickest part, gently drape the fish into loose piles, maintaining as much air as possible between the layers. When taken from the platter, the fish should resolve itself into sheets. (This is more important for smoked salmon than sable or sturgeon, which are denser, drier, and flatter-fleshed fish.) Dense compact clumps of fish, in addition to being unsightly, are more difficult to make into well-balanced bites.

As for what best accompanies the fish, it is hard to go wrong. Capers (from caperberries to non-pareilles), olives, dill, chives, roes—these are among the many garnishes for a platter. (Lemon wedges, goyische, will not be found on our platters.) The more salient aspect of an accompaniment isn't what it is, but how it is presented. If it is to lie on the platter itself, the accompaniment must be self-contained and not prone to pooling. Liquids, brines, and juices are not your friend. Pickles, therefore, are not an ideal accompaniment to lay directly on a platter. (For this reason, too, if serving herring, it should be placed in a separate bowl.) Ramekins have never had higher callings than to be used to contain platter fixings. Invest in a few ramekins. They are small, versatile, and charming additions to the kitchen array.

In terms of what *can* rest on a platter, thinly sliced raw onions are fine too, but must not be allowed to touch the proximal appetizing. Like an allium Midas, anything they touch turns to onion. Tomatoes, sliced similarly thin, are a good, and perhaps even necessary, choice, but they should be placed at sufficient distance from the fish so as not to leak their juice. It is entirely within keeping of the spirit of an appetizing platter, if space is a consideration, to form a layer of tomatoes, onion, and dill, fanned out. These are like the Three Sisters of appetizing; their tastes complement each other and commingling is as natural as the sunrise.

Now that we have addressed the platter, let us broaden our discussion to the spread. The *spread* comprises not just the platter—the fish and its accompaniments—but the larger offerings of noshing. The tablescape, if you will. The broader array can include fish and fish-adjacent ingredients like spreads and salads not suitable for a platter—herring, hot smoke / cold smoke, whitefish salad, egg salad, etc. Cream cheese, which is a nonnegotiable, should be offered in at least two expressions: plain and scallion. However, opinions about cream cheese are tightly held and widely varied, so we suggest offering up to four options.

The final necessary element is bread. Breads provide the platform on which to schmear, a vessel for the fish, a vehicle for cream cheese. As bagel bakers and bialy makers, our preferences are clear. Bagels: always halved completely, bottom and top kept paired, and never pre-toasted (lest the bagels harden with time). And bialys: either kept whole or carefully halved, with the onion filling resting on the bottom half. However, the spread is yours. Crackers, shissel rye toasts, or matzo work as well.

Just as important as knowing how to create a platter is knowing how to consume it. Here the rules are much simpler: There is no wrong way to enjoy a platter. Except, of course, enjoying too much of it. Be neither shy nor greedy. You are not the only one who enjoys smoked fish, but you deserve it as well.

MY NAME IS HERMAN VARGAS. I started working at Russ & Daughters when I was sixteen, way back in 1980. I came to the United States from the Dominican Republic when I was fourteen, settling into the Lower East Side. When I started working at Russ & Daughters, most of the slicers were old-timers. Slicing thin wasn't so important because none of them could do it well. But here I was, barely able to speak English, competing for customers. I was so paranoid that someone would say, "What does this guy know about smoked salmon or about Jewish food?" I made sure I was always researching. I became obsessed. And I started to develop real relationships with the customers because I wanted to be accepted. I had no idea, when I was sixteen, that I would stay at Russ & Daughters for forty years, or that I would become part of its soul. But I happily have and it has become part of my soul too. **HERMAN VARGAS, FORMER LONG-TIME EMPLOYEE AND MANAGER AT RUSS & DAUGHTERS FOR FORTY-TWO YEARS**

BAGEL SA

NDWICHES

Like man's existence in the universe, bagel sandwiches seem like they've been around for a long time, but historically they are a very recent phenomenon. Appetizing has traditionally been food you ate at home, food meant for platters. Were sandwiches made? Certainly, but they weren't sold. In its original ecosystem, Russ & Daughters sold just one component of a bagel sandwich while neighboring bakeries like Moishe's and Tannenbaum's—to name just two on the same block of Houston Street—offered bagels. Surely our customers made bagel sandwiches, but we did not make bagel sandwiches for them. The distinction was important.

During Mark's era that began to change. An informal arrangement with Ben's Dairy and Moishe's Bake Shop—by which we would sell bagels only on the weekends when Moishe's was closed and Ben's wouldn't sell fish—broke down. The result liberated us to sell bagels when we so desired. Once all the elements were united under one roof, to not make a sandwich but rather to remand sandwich-making to off-site premises seemed preposterous.

Today bagel sandwiches make a good portion of our business at the store. Like all sandwiches, they are portable (important when there's no place to sit) and they are affordable. Most important, they are delicious. Now that we make our own sandwiches, we have developed strong opinions about how sandwiches should be made, opinions you'll find below. We have also created our own combinations that we feel best showcase the smoked fish that remains and shall forever remain the star of the sandwich.

A CLASSIC WITH THE WORKS

THE CLASSIC WITH THE WORKS is the closest thing to a mascot we have. For reference and for the uninitiated, the Classic is thinly sliced cold-smoked salmon and plain cream cheese. When we say the Works, we generally mean capers, tomato, and onion. That these are on a bagel goes without saying. On a busy day, we sell about five hundred of them. And though many of our customers order some variation of the Classic with the Works—holding the capers or opting for a cream cheese variant or ordering any one of our own alternative combinations—the Classic with the Works has become the standard.

Though as an institution Russ & Daughters has become closely aligned with bagels laden with cream cheese and lox, if you take a moment to contemplate the ingredients that constitute the Works, the unlikeliness of their combination becomes clear.

Bagels, okay. Bagels, as discussed, are as embedded in the history of the Lower East Side as the F train under Delancey. But cream cheese has no roots in the shtetl milieu from which the kosher traditions of appetizing come. Nor do capers, the small pickled immature flowers from a Mediterranean bush, which are the exclamation points of the Works. Tomatoes do make cameos in Jewish cuisine, but mostly of the Sephardic variety. Perhaps only onions—cheap to grow and, importantly, easy to store—have roots in the Old World. How did they all come to meet on the common ground of a bagel? Forget the melting pot; the American metaphor food is an everything bagel with lox, cream cheese, and the Works. For these disparate elements have been thrown together and they have stayed together due to the simple fact that, when executed properly, a Classic with the Works is the closest thing to perfect man has yet to make.

THE BAGEL: Not all of the sandwiches at Russ & Daughters are made with bagels. We give customers the option of bialy, rye, or pumpernickel. But, when it comes to the Classic with the Works, the bagel is the first among equals. We make our own bagels, on average 5,000 a day between our two bakeries. We favor a smaller, traditional New York style bagel of about five ounces. Not too sweet. Not too soft. This has become a rarity in a universe where bagels are the size of Saturn's rings, large doughy soft sweet things that are more akin to a circular loaf of bread than a bagel proper.

The reason a smaller bagel is better is two-fold: First is the ratio of glossy, crispy, miraculous crust to chewy, tender, yielding center. Second is the ratio between bagel and lox. We could use a larger bagel at the store for our bagel and lox, but it would require the use of so much lox it would be prohibitively expensive. And though precious, a bagel and lox with the Works should always be affordable.

Using a five-ounce bagel means one need not futz with it much. Cut in half, the bagel is a perfect staging ground for what follows. If, however, you are using a prodigal bagel of six or even seven ounces, a) you have our apologies, and b) there are two ways to modify the bagel. The first is scooping, tearing out the soft interior of the bagel to form a sort of moat. The reason for doing this is to maintain the inside-outside ratio of soft crumb to harder crust. The second approach is to cut the bagel not into halves but into three pieces, reserving a narrow tranche in the center—not coincidentally of about an ounce in weight—which solves the same problem. Of course, if the bagel is the proper bagel size, none of this is needed.

CREAM CHEESE: Modern cream cheese is an American invention. It was born only in 1875, making it a baby in cheese years, when a New York grocery concern by the name of Park & Tilford asked dairyman William A. Lawrence from Upstate New York to make an extra creamy version of Neufchâtel, an unripened cream-enriched cheese from Normandy, France, that was popular in Europe. Lawrence did, called it cream cheese, and it sold mildly well. A few years later, a cheese broker named Alvah Reynolds, a sort of Gordon Gecko of mid-nineteenth-century dairy marketing, convinced Lawrence to call his product Philadelphia Cream Cheese. In the pre-cheesesteak era, the rural land adjacent to Philadelphia was best known for its dairy. Sure enough, Philadelphia Cream Cheese went gangbusters. Over the years, the company changed hands many times. Today it's part of the $26 billion monolith known as Kraft Heinz.

Our cream cheese, on the other hand, comes from a small dairy in California that uses the milk of grass-fed cattle. Like other cheeses close to nature, ours varies with the season and the lifecycle of the grasses upon which the cattle feast. Regardless, our all-natural cream cheese is more tangy than the industrial cream cheese and less plasticine, thanks to the absence of gums and preservatives.

The application of cream cheese on a bagel neatly illustrates the law of diminishing returns. More is not necessarily better. Too much cream cheese threatens not only to overwhelm both the texture and taste of the other elements but also undermines the structural integrity of the sandwich such that it squishes. For our bagels, an ounce and a half of cream cheese, evenly distributed on the top and bottom halves, works best.

CAPERS: Capers, or more accurately, the pickled immature flower buds of the caper bush, are a late addition to the Works. They are small, salty, piquant flavor grenades. In early lox and schmears, they might have been seen as extraneous since the salmon was generally not cold-smoked but salted, so salty in fact that it needed the softening of cream cheese to mellow it. Beyond that, capers, though frequent contributors to the Greek and Sicilian Italian cuisine, are not part of the Eastern European canon. But, starting in the 1980s, capers began appearing on classic sandwiches of the Lower East Side and, well, they work. There are many different sizes of capers, from seven millimeter non-pareilles to gargantuan grusas. They come packed in salt, vinegar, or water. We use the smallest we can, which are the non-pareilles, importing them specially from Turkey. Capers are deceptively powerful and can easily overpower the sandwich's subtler elements. A Classic with the Works needs but five to seven capers. But where does one place the capers? This has been a matter of great debate among the slicers behind the counter. David Jacques, who has been slicing for decades, swears by gently pressing the capers into the cream cheese on the bottom layer. Capers are great escapers, he reasons, so anchoring them in the cream cheese prevents their roll.

TOMATOES: The presence of tomato should be tasted but not felt. It is there to impart its sweetness

IS A BAGEL AND LOX A SANDWICH? Bagel and lox sandwich is a tautology. It's like saying ATM machine. A tourist would say bagel and lox sandwich. New Yorkers say bagel and lox. It's New York vernacular. So, in conclusion, yes, it is a sandwich, just don't say it.

to the sandwich, which means the tomatoes must be well ripened. A well ripened tomato is, however, squishy. Therefore, we seek to cover the area of the sandwich with as few slices as possible with the slices being as thin as possible. (Not that we would know this, but a thinly sliced tomato also negates any toughness due to unripeness.)

SMOKED SALMON: Unless a customer specifies otherwise, we usually use Gaspe Nova, a mildly smoked, fatty, well-mannered smoked salmon, strong enough to hold its own against the array of flavors, but not so overpowering it chews up the scenery. No matter what kind of smoked salmon you go for, as has been previously discussed (PAGE 72), it is best sliced thin. The two ounces of smoked salmon, therefore, that we use for our Classic should be sliced into two or three one-to-two-millimeter slices, then gently draped atop the cream cheese on the bottom layer with as much tenderness and care as a quilt on a sleeping child. Thin, here and as always, is of vital importance, for even an additional millimeter can impart to the salmon a less than pleasing chewy mouthfeel.

ONIONS: Like capers, onions are an element best used with restraint. An element offering a bracing pop of flavor and pleasing crunchy texture, you'll want the thinnest slice of onion possible, cut cross-wise with its rings fluffed and distributed atop the tomato. Over the years, there has been much dispute as to whether red or yellow onions are better in the Works. We have, for reasons both aesthetic and gustatory, settled on red. Onions are the penultimate layer of the sandwich and the final layer of so-called interior ingredients. After they have been placed on the sandwich, carefully place the top half of the bagel—which should have already been cream cheese'd—atop the sandwich.

CUTTING THE SANDWICH: Unlike King Solomon's disputed baby, a bagel sandwich must be cut in half to be best enjoyed. And yet this seemingly minor act can be treacherous. All one's painstaking work of assembly can be ruined with heedless slicing. The culprits are often dull knives and heavy hands. Exerting undue downward pressure—by either the improper placement of the gripping hand or a general aggression of the knife-wielding hand—can lead to squishing, a malign phenomenon with serious structural consequences. Over years, our slicers have perfected a technique that safeguards the glorious arrangement of the Works.

Gently place a serrated knife's blade atop the bagel to be cut. Over the spine of the knife's blade, cup your other hand, palm down. Now grip the sides of the bagel with your thumb and fingers, allowing enough clearance for the blade to move freely. Using the gripping hand to render the bagel immobile, cut the sandwich completely in half with as little downward pressure as possible. Conscientiously check to ensure that no unintended unsevered bagel connects the two halves.

A NOTE ON SERVING: Like any other sandwich, a Classic with the Works begins to decay the moment it is made. This is the wondrous interplay of formation and dissolution that marks all life. It is also the reason that the sandwich should be served and, importantly, eaten as soon as possible. This is true if it is served open-faced or closed. At the store, and for the sake of practicality, we serve ours closed, wrapped in two layers, one of plastic wrap and a sturdier waxed paper outside of it. And yet we have often seen customers rip open this carefully wrapped package to devour the bagel before they leave the store. And we approve of this heartily. If, God forbid, you cannot eat your bagel immediately after it's assembled, you can refrigerate it for safekeeping. Yet this chilling somewhat dulls the symphonic melody of flavor and texture—so again, just to reiterate, it is best to eat a Classic with the Works immediately.

A Classic with the Works

MAKES 1 SANDWICH

1 bagel of your choice
2 tablespoons cream cheese
1 tablespoon capers
2 ounces sliced smoked salmon
2 thin slices tomato
2 thin slices red onion
1 sprig fresh dill

Cut the bagel in half.

Smear the cream cheese on the top and the bottom half of bagel.

Gently press the capers into the cream cheese on the bottom half of the bagel.

Gently drape the smoked salmon on the bottom half of the bagel.

Stack the tomato and onions onto the smoked salmon.

Feather the sprig of dill atop the tomato and onions.

Top with other half of the bagel. Gently cut in half, making sure not to exert undue downward pressure.

Enjoy.

Daughters' Delight

MAKES 1 SANDWICH

1 bagel of your choice
2 tablespoons cream cheese
1 tablespoon capers
2 ounces thinly sliced Gaspe Nova
2 thin slices red onion (optional)
2 thin slices tomato (optional)
2 ounces salmon roe

Our sandwich suggestions—of which Daughters' Delight is one of the most popular—are a way for us to introduce delicious but perhaps hitherto uncombined elements of appetizing. The genesis of this combination, for instance, was the introduction of salmon roe to the otherwise classic Nova and cream cheese bagel. Like little exclamation marks, the roe adds bursts of flavor and texture, well earning its name as a delight.

Slice the bagel.

Spread the cream cheese on both halves of the bagel.

Gently press the capers into the cream cheese on the bottom half of the bagel.

Gently lay the Nova atop the capers on the bottom half.

Add the red onion and tomato, if using, atop the Nova.

Spread the salmon roe on the top half.

Assemble the halves and slice.

Enjoy.

Pastrami Russ

MAKES 1 SANDWICH

1 pretzel bagel
1 slice muenster cheese
½ tablespoon unsalted butter
Mustard Mix (recipe below)
3 thin slices half-sour pickles (store-bought or PAGE 109)
2 ounces thinly sliced pastrami-cured smoked salmon

MAKES 2 CUPS OR 1 PINT MUSTARD MIX

½ cup spicy deli mustard
½ cup Dijon mustard
1 cup whole grain mustard

We are, as has been noticed, down the street from Katz's Delicatessen, perhaps the best deli in the world and famous for their incredible-gargantuan corned beef and pastrami sandwiches. Delicious but, obviously, not for us. The Pastrami Russ is R&D's homage to the Reuben, with our pastrami-spiced lox stepping in for traditional pastrami. It's not quite as heavy and certainly not as towering as the original, but it makes for a delightfully light(ish) nosh.

Slice bagel in half.

Heat an oven to 350°F.

Place cheese on top half of the bagel; spread butter on the bottom. Heat the bagel for 2 minutes or so in the oven until the cheese is melted and the bagel warm.

Spread 1 tablespoon mustard mix on the bottom of the bagel, then layer on the pastrami-cured smoked salmon and pickles. Close with the cheese-covered top and slice in half.

Enjoy.

MAKE MUSTARD MIX

Mix together the mustards until incorporated.

Mustard mix will last 2 weeks in the refrigerator.

Super Heebster

MAKES 1 SANDWICH

1 bagel of your choice

2 tablespoons horseradish cream cheese

¼ cup Whitefish & Baked Salmon Salad (PAGE 87)

1 tablespoon wasabi-infused flying fish roe

When Josh was working the counter, people would often come in and say, "Josh, make me something." This sandwich is what he'd make them and they were pleased, not simply because of the flavors—the lush whitefish salad with the hint of spice from wasabi roe and tartness from horseradish cream cheese—but because they thought they had invented it.

Slice and toast the bagel.

Spread the horseradish cream cheese on the bottom half of the bagel, careful to cover the entire surface.

Schmear the whitefish and baked salmon salad on the top half.

Spread the wasabi roe on the top of the whitefish and baked salmon salad.

Top with other half of the bagel.

Gently slice the sandwich in half.

Enjoy.

Fancy Delancey

MAKES 1 SANDWICH

1 bagel of your choice
2 tablespoons horseradish cream cheese
2 ounces thinly sliced smoked yellowfin tuna
2 ounces wasabi-infused flying fish roe
2 thin slices red onion
2 thin slices tomato
1 generous teaspon capers (approximately 10)

This sandwich was invented by our longtime slicer-turned-manager, Herman Vargas, as a way to introduce our customers to the pleasures of smoked yellowfin tuna. Judging from its popularity—it's one of our bestsellers—we'd say Herman was successful.

Slice the bagel.

Schmear the horseradish cream cheese on both halves, careful to cover the entire area of the bagel.

Lay the smoked yellowfin tuna on the bottom half of the bagel.

Spread the wasabi roe on the top half, careful not to burst eggs.

Add the onion, tomato, and capers.

Assemble the two halves and carefully slice (collecting any roe that may have tumbled out).

Enjoy.

...rcy 5-4880   ESTABLISHED SIN...

...USS & DAUGHTER...

NEW YORK CITY, N. Y.

...ENS OF LAKE STURG...

...izing - Smoked Fish - Caviar - Bagels & B...

...pen
...Y DAY   Famous Fo
                                                QUALITY & SE
...Delivery   **RETAIL & RESTAURANT**

NATIONWIDE SHI...

ORIGINAL TINS Caviar has always arrived from far-off lands in these picturesque 2 kg original tins (OTs). Our collection traces the history of caviar production, including now-banned Iranian caviar and wild Beluga.

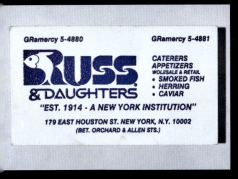

BUSINESS CARD Our first business cards were introduced in the late 1970s by Mark Russ Federman. We still have the same phone numbers, though we changed our motto to "Appetizing Since 1914" in the late aughts.

THE MONUMENT Legendary designer and cofounder of *New York* magazine, Milton Glaser (1929–2020) was a longtime supporter of Russ & Daughters. Inspired by his 1968 illustration (PAGE 4), in 2010 he made this sculpture for us and called it The Monument.

SHOPPING BAG From this humble paper bag (c. 1960s) and its uneven hand-set type we have drawn inspiration for many of our printed products today from bags to T-shirts. From the collection of Calvin Trillin, the bag is currently on display at Russ & Daughters Cafe.

SELTZER BOTTLES Since time immemorial, we have gotten our seltzer delivered weekly in these glass siphons from Walter the Seltzer Guy, one of the last remaining seltzermongers in New York.

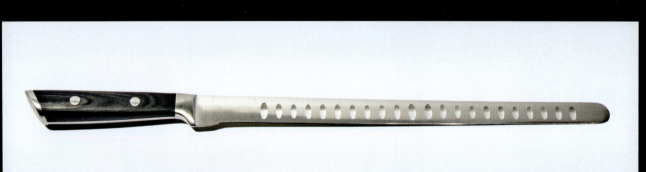

SLICING KNIFE The excellence of our slices isn't in our knives but in the slicers themselves. Nevertheless, we customize ours, honing ham slicers until they are long and narrow with flexibility in the blade. We have three sets of knives in rotation. Each is professionally sharpened once or twice a week, but honed throughout the day.

ANALOGUE SCALE For generations this very scale (left) was in use at the counter of the store. Though we retired it in the 1980s, it nevertheless remains in the shop, a silent symbol of equipoise.

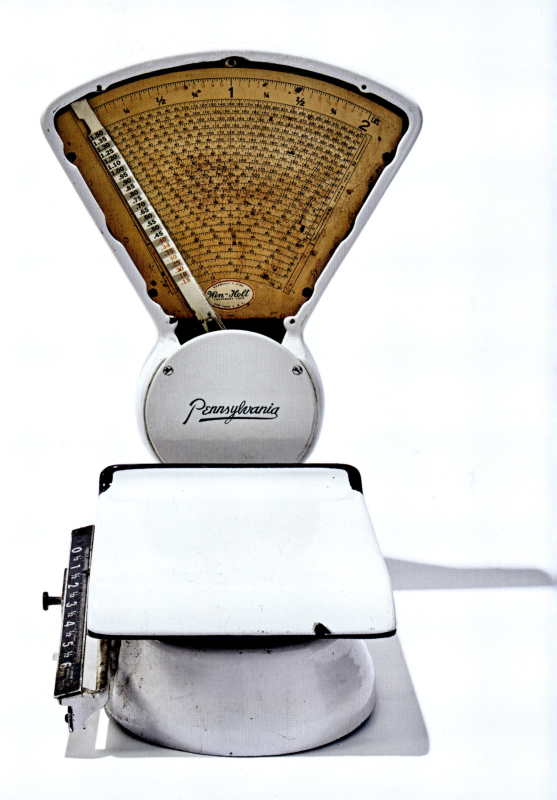

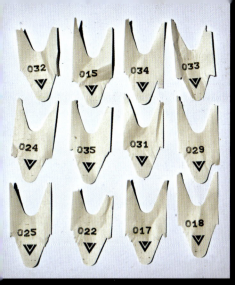

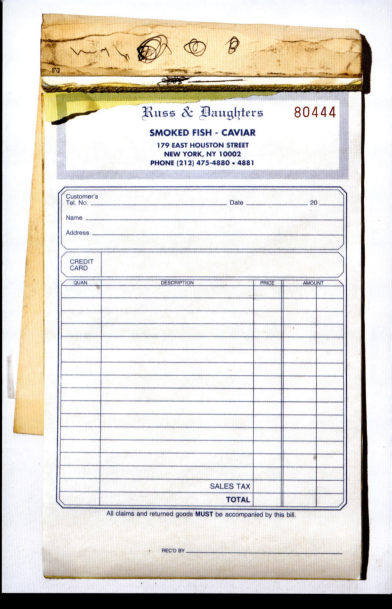

TAKE A NUMBER Order had always been hard to come by in the store (PAGE 37) until Mark instituted a ticketing system. Enter. Grab a ticket. Wait. Even this, though, hasn't stopped *mishegoss* as some impatient customers claim phantom numbers or attempt to reuse discarded tickets.

ORDER PAD Until 2008, we used these carbon copy ordering pads for phone orders, keeping the duplicates in the basement below the shop. When regular customers called, we'd have to go dig through the boxes and try to decipher the scrawl from the years previous.

APPLE PEELER AND CORER Used for many years to prepare the apples that were an ingredient in our chopped herring, today Joel Russ's apple peeler and corer is in the permanent collection of the Museum of the City of New York.

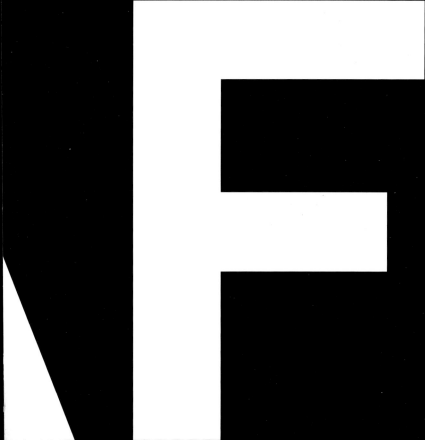

For nearly one hundred years, the entire footprint of Russ & Daughters consisted of our store on 179 East Houston Street. Within those four walls—technically three with a wall of windows—the customs of commerce ran along well-established, timeworn lines. Of course they changed over time, but the basic patterns and rhythms remained remarkably consistent.

In 2012, after six years of quietly retooling the logistical underpinnings of the operation in ways imperceptible to our customers but essential to the smooth running of the store, we began to contemplate our next step. We—along with anyone who has stepped into the store—have been struck by the obvious fact that there is nowhere to sit down. There is nowhere to eat, nowhere to gather on our premises. Sometimes there's hardly room to stand. Historically this made sense. Appetizing is the food of gatherings, food meant for a spread and a spread meant for a domestic table: kitchen, living room, shul. But as our clientele shifted and their needs evolved, the fact that we could not offer tables and chairs of our own became a *shanda*. We had only to turn our eyes right outside our door to see. Customers, bearing their herring, bagel sandwiches, and whitefish salads, branched out from 179 to the pair of benches in front of the store or to the park across the street, or fled to their vehicles. Sometimes it seemed that in every car parked on our block, a driver hungrily devoured a tray of appetizing, their plastic bag torn open like a bib, their container propped on the steering wheel. Silently they kvelled. But such isolation and diaspora is not what our ancestors had wanted for us. What if, instead of a car or a park bench, we had a restaurant to call our own?

As far as dreams go, a Russ & Daughters restaurant seemed risky to the point of wild. Neither one of us had any experience working in, let alone running, restaurants, a notoriously tricky industry. Nor could we wear our history lightly. Russ & Daughters is a touchstone for thousands of people, precisely because we have not (appreciably) changed. Even if we succeeded in bringing Russ & Daughters into an entirely different format, a restaurant might alienate our longtime customers. We didn't want to be the first in four generations to fail. As we asked our customers—many of whom are restaurateurs and chefs—their advice was mixed. Many flatly said the idea was *meshuge*. We had a good thing going. Why change it? Even the more enthusiastic among them warned that operating a restaurant was a risky business, one in which success was a rarity. But, they counseled, if we did decide to open a restaurant, we should stay true to who we were.

SLICING SALMON

We explored the city, looking at spaces, from the Lower East Side to the Upper East Side and all points between. Eventually we decided on a 5,000-square-foot storefront in Chelsea. Thankfully, the night before we signed the lease, we spoke on the phone. "You know, this just doesn't feel right," we said, in near unison. The Lower East Side had given birth to Russ & Daughters and it was in the Lower East Side that we should remain. A few weeks later, we found a small empty storefront three blocks away from the store, at 127 Orchard. The space was abandoned, the floors a mess, and the ceiling collapsed, but in our *kishkes* (guts), we knew it was our future home. The landlord, a customer, understood we weren't kidding when we said we wanted a hundred year lease. (We didn't get that, but we're also not going anywhere.)

He had only one stipulation before we closed the deal. He wanted to make sure he would be able to call in a Yom Kippur break fast order every year. So it was.

Like nearly every other building on the Lower East Side, 127 Orchard had been a tenement. And, like nearly every other building in the neighborhood, it had led multiple lives. Until the 1930s, the space was actually two tenements. A Methodist church, whose stated mission was to convert the Jews of the Lower East Side, occupied the Allen Street side; the Orchard Street side was home to a rotating cast of shops, selling *schmattas*, ties, sportswear. Eventually, in a beautiful karmic curlicue, the church left, to be replaced by a synagogue, Tifereth Israel. In the 1930s, the two spaces were combined and, like many other spaces in the Lower East Side, was occupied by a succession of small retail concerns. But for years before us, it had sat vacant.

Now we had a space, but what to do with it? Obviously, the restaurant would be a departure from the original appetizing store, but by how much and what would be the variance? The Cafe was really the first time we had exported our DNA, so designing it was a useful exercise in identifying exactly what were the inimitable Russ & Daughters characteristics. What could we have—or did we have to have—in the Cafe for it to be recognizably *us*? We began with a visual dictionary of the Russ & Daughters vocabulary. The black-and-white lightboxes, first installed in Joel's first renovation in 1949, with the names of our offerings painted by hand in clean type; neat lines of products lining metallic shelves; a two-tone white-and-chrome color scheme; signature white coats worn by counter staff; hexagonal white-and-black tiles on the floor, reminiscent of the store's mid-century renovation. Most important, perhaps, the appetizing counter as almost an altarpiece, with its treasury of smoked fish and a wooden working board on which sides of fish are laid.

On the walls we hung family photographs—Grandpa Russ with his daughters in their resplendent hatwear; Anne, white coated and serious, behind the counter; Mark, having just taken over, proudly holding a whitefish—but intentionally didn't label them. We wanted our customers to look at Ida, Hattie, and Anne and feel as if they could be part of *their* family too. In fact, working with the designer-builders Nico Arze and Matthew Maddy, we designed the Cafe to re-create as best we could the feeling of an intergenerational family gathering. We wanted spaces for strollers and for armchairs—like the one Great-Grandpa Joel sat in—for the *alte kakers* as they awaited their tables. (Space concerns, sadly, doomed that idea.) But we did our best to emphasize larger booths that can accommodate six people and a communal table that can handle an even bigger *mishpocha*. We added to the walls works of art we've collected through the years like proud parents: a wooden statue of a fish swimming through a bagel from legendary graphic designer Milton Glaser, a watercolor of the fish counter by Marcellus Hall, sketches of scores of customers and employees by the late inveterate sketcher Jason Polan, an original Russ & Daughters shopping bag Calvin Trillin had found in his home, stashed away in a drawer for forty years.

The Cafe would have not only seats and booths—relatively straightforward—but a bar too. We wanted it to be a place where people could gather not just during the day but also at night. Who knows what our ancestors would have made of a Russ & Daughters bar? (Mark wasn't a drinker, Herbie preferred cigars, and Joel drank homemade cherry slivovitz, but only on occasion.) We opted for a nine-seat white stone countertop with bar stools that splits the difference between soda fountain and a cocktail bar, for that was what we would become.

As for the menu—the recipes you'll find in this section—we felt ourselves interpreters rather than inventors. What would appetizing look like in a restaurant? Of course we would have platters showcasing our smoked and cured fish in situ. We would have bagel sandwiches, though here presented

deconstructed so you can assemble your own. Eggs were a given since their creaminess has long been known to complement the saltiness and smokiness of traditional appetizing. In the small pantheon of plated appetizing, lox, eggs, and onions is a classic. So is, for that matter, matzo brei, the rare occurrence of matzo being eaten outside of Passover. Other noshes, near-canonical dishes like kasha varnishkas, potato knishes, and latkes, were nonnegotiable. And though appetizing dwells in the imagination as daytime food, dinner was what we considered the hidden gem. Not only was it less crowded—we were crowded from day one—but it was when we could experiment with modern interpretations of Ashkenazi cuisine. We worked with a terrific mixologist named Yana Volfson to create a cocktail program that put an R&D twist on the classics. As it has for the last hundred years, our guiding philosophy was that if we were going to do something we were going to do it the right way. That might be a knish or challah French toast; or it might be an egg cream or a martini. Regardless, we'd do it the Russ & Daughters way, the haimish way.

We had of course expanded our staff since we took over, but the Cafe offered us the opportunity—demanded, really—that we bring on an entirely new cohort. This was the largest onboarding into the Russ & Daughters family since we opened in 1914. But, because this was a new restaurant, from general managers to cooks to servers and porters, we were all in this together. We gave lessons on family history, on appetizing, on the neighborhood itself, on what it means to be haimish. One porter from the Bronx was among the many who immediately and intuitively understood. "It means to treat everyone on the same level," he said. He was right.

Opening a restaurant in New York City is not for the faint of heart. But after months of construction, anxious waiting to get the gas turned on, and nerve-racking inspections from the health department, we opened our doors in May 2014. We were, thankfully, busy from day one. The hungry world was, of course, curious what we might do after a century. Service was remarkably smooth but our concerns weren't. Only after some old-timer customers from the shop came in and, taking us aside, told us we had done a good thing and, though they hadn't been able to imagine it before, that Russ & Daughters should have a Cafe and that the Cafe should look like this was obvious, did our worry subside.

For the first years of the Cafe's life we opened at 8 a.m. and closed at 10 p.m., seven days a week. Though the menu remained constant through all three meals—the pleasure of eggs and caviar at 7:30 p.m. should not be underestimated—dinner gave our chefs an opportunity to develop new recipes which we ran as dinner specials. Like everything we did, these were an amalgamation of the new and the old. Many relied on classic Ashkenazi fare, giving us a chance to ease out beyond our traditional appetizing offerings. Other recipes, like the Kippered Mac & Cheese and Shissel Chicken Cutlets, were avenues through which we could recontextualize our products in new and delicious ways.

When the pandemic forced us to shutter the restaurant in March 2020, we turned the space into a fulfillment center for our ballooning online business. When we finally reopened in July 2022, we decided to limit our hours to breakfast and lunch. Surprisingly we still do a brisk business in cocktails as well as house sodas and shrubs. These limited hours allow us to host parties and gatherings, such as our annual Second Seder (SEE PAGE 206) in the space.

Happily, the Russ & Daughters Cafe is on its way to becoming a Lower East Side institution, just as the store did exactly a century before the restaurant opened its doors. For us, it's tremendously gratifying to see the Russ & Daughters neon sign glowing on Allen Street with the same timeworn, welcoming glow of a place that's been there forever and isn't going away anytime soon.

NOSHES

& SALADS

Potato Knishes

MAKES 1 DOZEN KNISHES

FOR THE FILLING

3 medium russet potatoes (about 1½ pounds), peeled and cut into chunks

3 tablespoons vegetable oil

1 large Spanish onion, finely chopped

2 teaspoons onion powder

1 teaspoon kosher salt, plus more as needed

FOR THE DOUGH

2¼ cups all-purpose flour, plus more for rolling and shaping

½ cup vegetable oil

¼ cup water, plus more as needed

1 large egg

½ teaspoon baking powder

1 teaspoon kosher salt

½ teaspoon white vinegar

Once the knish was the king of the Lower East Side. A filling dish of ancient origin among poor Ukrainian Jews, the knish arrived on the Lower East Side with the influx of immigrants in the late 1800s. A knish offers affordable and soul-warming sustenance in the form of mashed potatoes and onions garbed in a golden dough. Great wars were fought over the knish—or at least, modest skirmishes across Rivington Street—by opposing knish-mongers. Like the bagel—and the Jewry of the Lower East Side—eventually the knish went mainstream. Also like the bagel, many versions abounded. The street cart knish is large and leaden. The stadium knish is larger still. Our version returns the knish to its more natural proportions. These aren't gut-busting bricks of carbs, but rather ethereal—OK, semi-ethereal—handheld dumplings filled with an airy onion-potato mixture.

MAKE THE FILLING

Bring a medium pot of water to a boil over high heat. Add the potatoes and cook, stirring occasionally, until tender, about 20 minutes. Drain through a colander, then return the potatoes to the pot and use a potato masher or sturdy fork to mash until completely smooth.

Meanwhile, heat the oil in a medium sauté pan set over medium-low heat. Add the onion and cook, stirring often, until soft and golden, 15 to 20 minutes. Let cool.

Add the cooled onions to the mashed potatoes along with the onion powder and salt, and stir to combine. Taste and add more salt, if needed.

Use a ¼-cup measuring cup to form 12 portions of the mashed potato mixture and place on a large, parchment-lined baking sheet. Cover with plastic wrap and refrigerate for at least 2 hours, or up to overnight.

MAKE THE DOUGH

Combine the flour, oil, water, egg, baking powder, salt, and vinegar in the bowl of a stand mixer fitted with the dough hook. Mix on low speed, scraping down the sides of the bowl as necessary, to form a dough, 7 to 10 minutes. The dough will feel relatively oily at this stage. Cover the mixer bowl and let the dough rest for 30 minutes.

On a well-floured surface, using a floured rolling pin, roll the dough into an ⅛-inch-thick rectangle about 12 by 16 inches.

Use a sharp knife to cut the dough into twelve 4-inch squares. (There will be excess dough. Discard it or save it for another use.)

CONTINUED →

TO ASSEMBLE AND BAKE

Preheat the oven to 400°F and line a large baking sheet with parchment paper.

For each knish, place one portion of the filling in the center of a square. Fold two opposite corners of the dough up and over the filling, pinching the corners together to seal (use a little water to act as a glue, if needed). Repeat with the opposite two corners to form a little parcel, and place the knish on the lined baking sheet.

Bake the knishes, rotating the baking sheet back-to-front halfway through, until golden brown, 25 to 30 minutes. Transfer the knishes to a wire rack to cool. Serve slightly warm or at room temperature.

Store leftovers, well wrapped, in the freezer for up to 6 months. Reheat briefly in an oven or toaster oven.

Everything Spiced Almonds

MAKES 5 CUPS, 8 TO 10 SERVINGS

1 large egg white
1 tablespoon extra-virgin olive oil
1 tablespoon Worcestershire sauce
2½ teaspoons brown sugar
2 teaspoons garlic powder
1 teaspoon Aleppo pepper powder
1 teaspoon onion powder
1¾ teaspoons kosher salt
1 pound raw whole almonds
¼ cup Everything Spice Mix (PAGE 271)

Bar nuts are not, perhaps, a traditional nosh. But they fit the description, a cheerful little something to snack on. And how could we resist the everything spice as we had, well, everything already on hand for our everything bagels. Addictive, easy to prepare, and long-lasting, these are one of our most popular bar snack specials at the Cafe, where they pair especially well with a Smoked Martini (PAGE 255.)

Preheat the oven to 350°F. Line a baking sheet with parchment.

In a bowl, whisk together the egg white, olive oil, Worcestershire, brown sugar, garlic powder, Aleppo pepper, onion powder, and salt until uniform.

Add the almonds and toss until coated. Add the everything spice and toss again until the nuts are coated with the spice.

Spread the nuts evenly on the lined baking sheet and bake for 12 to 15 minutes, stirring the nuts once, until lightly browned and crispy.

The almonds will keep in an airtight container at room temperature for 2 weeks.

Potato Latkes

MAKES 12 LATKES

2½ pounds russet potatoes, peeled
1 medium Spanish onion, peeled
2 large eggs
½ cup finely chopped scallions
¼ cup matzo meal
3 tablespoons unsalted butter, melted
2 teaspoons kosher salt
½ teaspoon ground black pepper
½ teaspoon baking powder
3 cups canola oil, for frying
Salmon roe and crème fraîche, for serving, optional
Applesauce and sour cream, for serving, optional

The latke, a fried potato pancake, comes swaddled in myth: We eat the latke on Chanukah because that's what the Hebrews did millennia ago. We eat the latke on Chanukah as a celebration of ancient miraculous oil. What makes a latke delicious is your grandmother's grated knuckle. Worse yet, a latke should be eaten only on Chanukah. No doubt these traditions were passed down with rabbinic authority but, as it turns out, none are true.

First of all, Chanukah celebrates the Hasmoneans, who didn't eat potatoes. They were grain-growing people. The potato latke is actually a derivation of a medieval Spanish-Italian-Jewish delicacy, made originally of fried cheese called *cassola*. Much later, as the cassola moved north and slowly became Ashkenazi, potatoes supplanted cheese. Secondly, Eastern European Jews use schmaltz, not oil, to fry. Thirdly, about the knuckles, no, that's gross. Maybe true, but gross.

But the greatest falsehood is that latkes are to be enjoyed on Chanukah *only*. Like bagels, latkes are and should be everyday food. At Russ & Daughters, we go through about eight hundred on a slow day. (We make forty thousand during Chanukah.) Our latke-making is still laborious. The secret to a perfect latke is to find the right amount of the starchy potato liquid so the patty coheres but is not dry. This is done by squeezing out excess liquid and adding only the starch back to the grated potatoes. This process relies on the somatic knowledge of bubbes. This, not their knuckles, is their greatest contribution. Secondly, one must be generous with the thickness. Latkes are not smashburgers. They need to have some height, lest they disintegrate when loaded with topping. (A thick latke, cut in half, also makes a wonderful "bun" for an egg sandwich. See Lower Sunny Side, on the following page.)

Coarsely grate the potatoes using a box grater, then do the same with the onion.

Place the grated potatoes and onion in a fine-mesh strainer set over a large mixing bowl. Gently press the mixture to remove as much liquid as possible, making sure it drains into the bowl below. Let the mixture sit for 3 to 5 minutes as it continues to drain. Pour off the excess liquid in the bowl, making sure to leave the starchy paste at the bottom.

Add the drained potato and onion mixture to the bowl with the starch. Add the eggs, scallions, matzo meal, melted butter, salt, pepper, and baking powder. Mix thoroughly with your hands.

CONTINUED →

Heat ½ tablespoon canola oil in a large skillet over medium heat until shimmering.

Form 12 latkes by gently shaping ¼-cup portions of the potato mixture into patties about 3 inches wide and 1 inch thick.

In batches if necessary, brown the latkes in the oil until golden brown, about 2 minutes per side, adding oil to the pan as needed. Transfer the finished latkes to a paper towel.

Use a paper towel to wipe the skillet clean. Add the remaining oil and heat over medium-high heat to 375°F. Working in batches without crowding, deep-fry the latkes for an additional 4 to 5 minutes, until golden crisp, turning once halfway through. Line a baking sheet or rack with paper towels. As the latkes fry, transfer to the paper towels and season lightly with salt. Serve immediately with salmon roe and crème fraîche, *or* with applesauce and sour cream, *or* (our preference) with both.

Latkes can keep in the refrigerator for up to 4 days. To reheat, place on baking tray in a 350°F oven for approximately 10 minutes, until they are heated throughout.

MAKES 1 SERVING

1 tablespoon clarified butter (PAGE 184)
2 large eggs
1½ ounces thinly sliced Gaspe Nova
2 Latkes

LOWER SUNNY SIDE

Heat a sauté pan over medium-high heat. Add the clarified butter and warm until bubbling. Break the eggs directly into the pan, being careful not to disturb the yolks, and lower the heat to medium. Cook until the whites are set and the yolks still runny, about 2 minutes. Tilt the pan and baste the tops of the eggs with the clarified butter to cook the egg white that coats the yolks.

Layer slices of Gaspe Nova over each latke, then top with a sunny-side-up egg. Serve immediately.

Kasha Varnishkas

MAKES 4 SERVINGS

1 cup kasha groats
2 large eggs, whisked
1½ teaspoons kosher salt
½ teaspoon freshly ground black pepper
5 tablespoons unsalted butter
2 cups water
2 cups (¼ pound) farfalle
¼ cup Caramelized Onions (PAGE 183)
2 cups chicken stock
2 teaspoons chopped fresh parsley

For many of us, there is no more comforting or satisfying experience than eating toasted buckwheat groats, or *kasha*, mixed with pasta, studded with caramelized onions, and coated in butter. Earthy and yet also luxurious, with notes of nuttiness, a bowl of kasha varnishkas is simply a bowl of home. Whether you eat yours in the morning with a soft-boiled egg on top, which when broken yields a golden yolk, or on a cold winter night to warm yourself, kasha varnishkas will sustain you, as it has Ashkenazi Jews for centuries, from the shtetlach of Odessa to the kitchens of North America. Part of its haimish appeal is how simple it is to make and how forgiving the recipe is. Don't sweat the measurements too much. The most important thing is to avoid mushy kasha; the key to maintain its texture and bite is to mix it with eggs before boiling. If possible, use kasha groats from Ukraine, which are among the best in the world. This we learned the hard way after the Russian invasion of 2022 disrupted supply chains (among many other true horrors). For a period of months we used non-Ukrainian groats and the kasha was just not the same.

In a large mixing bowl, mix together the kasha groats, eggs, ½ teaspoon of the salt, and the pepper. Heat a medium pot over medium heat. Add the kasha mixture and cook for 2 to 3 minutes, stirring to break up the grains and scrape the pot. Add 1 tablespoon of the butter and stir to distribute evenly. Cook the kasha for an additional minute in the butter, continuing to stir. Add the water and the remaining 1 teaspoon salt. Scrape the bottom of the pan, cover, and lower the heat to a simmer. Cook on low, stirring occasionally to break up any clumps, for 15 to 20 minutes, until the water is almost completely absorbed. Remove from the heat, fluff the kasha with a fork, and set aside to steam with the lid on.

Meanwhile, bring a large pot of salted water to a boil and cook the farfalle until al dente, about 10 minutes. Drain.

In a large Dutch oven, melt 2 tablespoons of the butter, add the caramelized onions, and stir to warm. Add the cooked groats, toss with the butter and onion, and heat together for 2 minutes. Add the farfalle and chicken stock and bring to a boil over medium-high heat. Lower the heat slightly, reduce to a medium boil, and cook, stirring and scraping the bottom of the pan until the stock has reduced by three-fourths, about 15 minutes. Remove from the heat and add the remaining 2 tablespoons butter in a few pieces, folding and tossing to emulsify the butter into the kasha. Adjust seasoning to taste, garnish with parsley, and serve.

The kasha varnishkas can be refrigerated in an airtight container for up to 4 days or frozen for up to 1 month.

Chopped Salad

MAKES 4 SERVINGS

FOR THE BUTTERMILK DRESSING

¼ cup sour cream

¼ cup mayonnaise

¼ cup buttermilk

2 tablespoons white vinegar

1 tablespoon lemon juice

½ teaspoon garlic powder

1½ teaspoons kosher salt

½ teaspoon freshly ground black pepper

FOR THE SALAD

16 ounces mixed greens, such as lettuce, arugula, and/or spinach, washed and dried

1 green apple, cored and diced

1 red beet, cooked, peeled, and diced

1 avocado, halved, pitted, and diced

2 large eggs, hard-boiled (PAGE 118), yolks and whites separated and diced

½ sheet matzo, broken into chunks

2 ounces smoked whitefish

Was there avocado in the shtetl or arugula in the tenement? Probably not. This chopped salad is an example of how we try to bridge the gap between the traditional offerings of appetizing and a more modern touch. How do we take something as omnipresent and, in a way, acultural as a chopped salad and make it ours? Well, it depends on what you chop. Here we've drawn from the well of tradition—matzo, apple, beet, eggs, whitefish—and the stable of the modern salad for what is, essentially, a rainbow of texture and flavor. Ordered in neat lines, each element adds its own character: the crispness of apple, the crunchiness of matzo, the softness of hard-boiled egg, the smokiness of whitefish, the earthiness of beets, the creaminess of avocado, all atop a bed of greens dressed with a tart buttermilk dressing. There's nothing traditional here but there is something compelling and uniquely Russ & Daughtersian.

MAKE DRESSING

In a small mixing bowl, whisk the sour cream and mayonnaise until smooth. Add the buttermilk and vinegar and mix well until the dressing is creamy and well combined.

Add the lemon juice, garlic powder, salt, and pepper. Taste and adjust seasoning according to your preference. Set aside.

The dressing can be kept in the refrigerator for 3 to 4 days.

TO ASSEMBLE

Toss the mixed greens with 1 to 2 tablespoons of the buttermilk dressing to coat them lightly.

To serve, place the greens down first on a large plate. Arrange rows of the apple, beet, and avocado on top. Then arrange rows of egg whites and yolks, matzo, and smoked whitefish. Drizzle a bit more of the buttermilk dressing over the rows and serve.

Red & Golden Beet Salad

MAKES 4 SERVINGS

FOR THE YOGURT GOAT CHEESE DRESSING

¼ cup Greek yogurt
¼ cup soft goat cheese
3 tablespoons milk
1 tablespoon lemon juice
Kosher salt and freshly ground black pepper to taste

FOR THE SHERRY VINAIGRETTE

2 tablespoons sherry vinegar
1 tablespoon Dijon mustard
¼ teaspoon garlic powder
½ teaspoon granulated sugar
3 tablespoons canola oil
1 tablespoon extra-virgin olive oil
Kosher salt and freshly ground black pepper to taste

FOR THE PUMPERNICKEL CROUTONS

Four ½-inch-thick slices pumpernickel bread, homemade (PAGE 293) or store-bought
1 tablespoon extra-virgin olive oil
Kosher salt and freshly ground black pepper to taste

FOR THE SALAD

½ pound baby golden beets (4 to 8 beets)
½ pound baby red beets (4 to 8 beets)
½ cup whole walnuts
6 to 8 ounces cleaned baby watercress
2 sprigs fresh dill, picked

Though versions of the beet and goat cheese salad proliferate in various fine dining forms—Foam! Gelee! Essence!—what could be more haimish than combining beets (cheap, nutritious) and cheese from a goat (beloved animal of poor farmers everywhere, a Chagallian muse.) This salad, borne from the very real need at the Cafe to complement our smoked fish with a healthy alternative, combines a modern version of the salad and the time-honored Ashkenazi tradition of pairing dairy and beets, as evinced in borscht. The addition of pumpernickel croutons and a zingy dressing adds kicks of texture and acid. It also makes a great base—if you absolutely cannot live without cured or smoked fish (we get it)—for pickled herring or kippered salmon.

MAKE DRESSING

Mix all ingredients in a medium mixing bowl together until uniform in consistency.

MAKE VINAIGRETTE

Whisk the vinegar, mustard, garlic powder, and sugar in a small bowl. Combine the two oils and slowly drizzle in while whisking until an emulsion forms. Season to taste with salt and pepper.

MAKE CROUTONS

Preheat the oven to 350°F.

Remove the crusts from the bread and cut the bread into ½-inch cubes. Place in a bowl and drizzle with the olive oil, tossing to coat evenly. Sprinkle with salt and pepper and toss again.

Spread the cubes on a baking sheet and bake, tossing every 5 minutes, for 10 to 15 minutes. They should be slightly darker and crispy. Transfer to a piece of paper towel to cool.

The croutons can be stored 5 to 7 days in an airtight container at room temperature.

ROAST BEETS

Preheat the oven to 375°F.

Rinse and trim the tops off all the beets. Wrap the beets all together in aluminum foil and roast directly on the oven rack for 50 minutes. Remove from the oven and allow to cool slightly. While still warm, peel the beets, cut in half and set aside.

CONTINUED →

ASSEMBLE

While the beets are cooling, lower the oven temperature to 350°F. Spread the walnuts evenly on a baking sheet and toast in the oven for 10 to 12 minutes, stirring occasionally, until lightly toasted. Set aside to cool.

To serve, in a bowl, toss the watercress with sherry vinaigrette to taste. Spread ½ to ¾ cup goat cheese dressing on a plate. Place the greens atop the dressing then evenly distribute the red and gold beets, croutons, toasted walnuts, and dill. Serve immediately.

EGGS

Eggs Benny

MAKES 2 SERVINGS

FOR THE HOLLANDAISE SAUCE
1 cup (8 ounces) clarified butter (PAGE 184)
4 large egg yolks
1 teaspoon water
¾ teaspoon fresh lemon juice, plus more as needed
1 pinch kosher salt
1 pinch cayenne pepper

FOR THE EGGS
8 ounces baby spinach, washed and trimmed
1 tablespoon white vinegar
4 large eggs
2 teaspoons clarified butter (PAGE 184)

Two 1½-inch-thick slices challah bread, lightly toasted
4 thin slices (1½ to 2 ounces) Gaspe Nova

Our Eggs Benny is not an eggs Benedict (trayf, ptooey!); it's an eggs Florentine. But it's *really* not an eggs Florentine either. It's an Eggs Benny. That's Benny as in Ben Waxman, a beloved denizen and merchant of the Lower East Side who passed in 2016. Benny owned a sporting goods store around the corner from the shop. In the 1970s, when the Lower East Side was emptying of its original Jewish inhabitants, Benny helped to found the Lower East Side Merchant's Association, a precursor to the LES Business Improvement District, an organization dedicated to advocating for small business owners like himself. Benny was a sweetheart, a longtime customer at the store, a friend of Mark's, and an old man by the time we opened the Cafe. When we showed him the menu, pointing to the Eggs Benny, and told him he was its namesake, he told us he felt like a rock star. To us, he always was.

MAKE HOLLANDAISE

Melt the clarified butter and hold it warm, roughly 130°F to 140°F.

Bring a small sauce pot of water to a boil, then lower the heat to a simmer. Meanwhile, whisk together the egg yolks, water, and lemon juice in a medium bowl to combine.

Make a bain marie by placing the bowl atop the simmering water, careful not to let the bottom of the bowl come in contact with the water. Whisk the yolks and juice vigorously, occasionally scraping the sides of the bowl so they don't scorch, until they are a pale yellow color and have tripled in volume. This is your sabayon, a basic component of Hollandaise. Slowly drizzle in the warm butter, continuously whisking, to emulsify. If the sauce becomes too thick before you have incorporated all of the butter, whisk in a teaspoon of lukewarm water at a time to thin it slightly before incorporating more butter. You may do this two or three times. When all of the butter has been incorporated, whisk the sauce for 1 or 2 minutes longer, until ribbons form when you lift the whisk from the bowl. Add an additional splash of lemon juice for acidity and the salt and cayenne to taste. Remove from the heat and keep warm.

Note: If your sauce breaks at any point during this process, you can make a new sabayon with one egg white and a tablespoon of water, then slowly whisk in the broken sauce as if it were the butter, along with any butter that had not been incorporated.

CONTINUED →

MAKE SPINACH

Prepare an ice bath by mixing equal parts ice and water in a large mixing bowl. In the same water you used for the bain marie, blanch the spinach for 30 to 40 seconds, until bright green. Then remove and place in the ice bath to arrest the cooking. Let cool for 2 minutes then thoroughly drain, wringing out as much water as possible.

Bring a medium sauce pot of water to a boil, add the white vinegar, and reduce the heat to a simmer.

MAKE EGGS

Crack each egg into a small strainer to strain out the thin portion of the white, then place each strained egg in a shallow dish. With a slotted spoon, swirl the water in a pot to create a vortex. Immediately lower one egg at a time into the center of the vortex, allowing 30 seconds for each egg to set up before adding the next. Once set, keep your first egg at 12 o'clock and each subsequent egg you drop in a clockwise fashion so that you can remove the eggs in the order they were dropped. Poach each for 3½ minutes, flipping them over halfway through. Remove each egg with a slotted spoon and place on a clean, lint-free kitchen towel (or paper towel) on a plate to remove excess moisture. Keep your poaching liquid to reheat your eggs for 30 to 60 seconds should they cool too much.

Heat a small sauté pan over medium heat. Add the clarified butter and spinach and heat until warm, 2 to 3 minutes.

TO ASSEMBLE

Equally divide the spinach and place atop each slice of challah. Layer two slices of Gaspe Nova on each slice of challah, then carefully slide on two poached eggs. Top with Hollandaise and serve immediately.

Nova & Cream Cheese Omelet

MAKES 1 OMELET

3 large eggs
1 tablespoon clarified butter (PAGE 184)
2 tablespoons of your favorite cream cheese, softened
2 ounces Gaspe Nova
½ teaspoon chopped fresh herbs (parsley, dill, chervil, or a combination)

When we say we are translators at the Cafe of the Russ & Daughters DNA, this omelet is what we mean. Not novel, hardly innovative, this omelet is simply another configuration of the classic flavors and ingredients we've been working with for years. And yet, when we look around the Cafe, the omelet is on nearly every table. Tucked inside fluffy eggs, the warm, slightly tangy cream cheese softens almost to a crème fraîche to coat the Nova, which is added at the very end. The result is a harmonious ode to appetizing, a new standard with old notes.

Preheat the oven to 400°F.

Whisk together the eggs in a small bowl.

Melt the clarified butter in a medium oven-safe pan over medium heat. Add the eggs to the pan and lower the heat to medium-low. Then, using a rubber spatula, pull the cooked eggs from the edge to the center of the pan, rocking the pan to distribute the uncooked egg to the edge. Once the eggs are about 60 percent set, gently tap the pan on the stove. (This encourages a smoother omelet.)

Spoon the cream cheese evenly onto the eggs, then transfer the pan to the oven for 3 minutes to finish cooking, until the eggs are solidified. Alternatively, cover the pan with a lid, lower the heat, and cook on the lowest setting for 5 minutes.

Add the Nova, and once the omelet is set, roll the omelet directly from the pan to a plate. Garnish with herbs and serve immediately.

Matzo Brei with Applesauce & Sour Cream

MAKES 3 TO 4 SERVINGS

4 to 5 sheets matzo
4 large eggs
¼ cup whole milk
¼ teaspoon kosher salt
¼ teaspoon freshly ground black pepper
2 tablespoons unsalted butter
¼ to ½ cup applesauce, for serving
¼ to ½ cup sour cream, for serving

Never has there been a more complicated or dramatic item on the Russ & Daughters Cafe menu than matzo brei. It seems simple: sheets of matzo, soaked in water, then dipped in egg and fried in butter. (*Brei* is Yiddish for fried.) Yet everyone, every single person who ordered it, had some hazy sense memory of matzo brei from their childhood, eaten on Passover mornings years ago. "Not the way my bubbe made it!" was a constant refrain and, frequently, the opening salvo of a long comparison between our version and their bubbe's. No matter how delicious ours was—and it was delicious—we knew we could never beat Bubbe. And so the simplest dish on the Cafe menu became the most contested. Eventually, we had to remove the matzo brei from the menu for our own sanity. You can still order it, but you need to ask for it and the brei comes with a disclaimer that we make the wet savory version, though you'll find both sweet and savory versions here. We think they're delicious. And if you don't like them, you don't like them. Apologies to Bubbe.

Prepare the matzo by breaking the sheets into small pieces and placing them in a bowl. Pour warm water over the matzo and let sit for 1 to 2 minutes, until it softens. Drain off the excess liquid.

In a separate bowl, beat the eggs with the milk until well mixed. Add the salt and pepper and whisk to incorporate.

Add the softened matzo to the egg mixture and gently mix to combine, allowing the matzo to soak up the liquid. Let sit for a few minutes to allow the matzo to fully absorb as much liquid as possible. In a large skillet, melt the butter over medium heat. Add the matzo mixture, spreading it out to cover the pan in an even layer. Let the mixture cook, pressing down gently with a spatula to help the matzo to cook evenly, for 2 to 3 minutes, until the bottom is golden brown. Carefully flip the matzo brei over in sections, like a pancake, to cook the other side for an additional 2 to 3 minutes, until golden brown.

Transfer the matzo to a plate and serve immediately, topping with applesauce and sour cream.

VARIATIONS Sweet: Instead of salt and pepper, add 1½ tablespoons sugar and ¼ teaspoon ground cinnamon to the egg mixture before cooking. Savory: In addition to the salt and pepper, add ¼ cup sautéed onions or finely chopped herbs, like chives or parsley, to the egg mixture before cooking.

Soft Scrambled Eggs with Caviar

MAKES 4 SERVINGS

12 large eggs
¼ teaspoon kosher salt
4 tablespoons clarified butter (PAGE 184)
2 tablespoons chilled unsalted butter, cubed
125 grams of your favorite caviar
1 loaf challah, thinly sliced and lightly toasted

We debated whether this recipe should in the egg section of the book or the caviar section. (Ontological debates have always been a Jewish pastime.) We opted to place it with the omelets, in part to emphasize that caviar need not always be so precious and intimidating. But it also shows that the eggs—from chicken and sturgeon, respectively—share equal billing in this dish. To achieve the necessary creaminess and prerequisite softness that makes scrambled eggs the ideal accompaniment to briny caviar, you need patience and finesse. Working slowly over a gentle heat, you must constantly break up the curds of the eggs while allowing the cold cubes of butter to work their way into the egg mixture. It takes some practice, but when presented with the finished product, each luxurious bite as much about texture as it is about taste, all that patience is rewarded.

Whisk the eggs in a large bowl until the yolks and whites are fully incorporated. Add the salt.

Bring a medium pot of water to boil over medium-high heat. Place a slightly smaller stainless steel bowl over the water, making sure the bottom of the bowl does not touch the surface of the water. Lower the heat slightly to maintain a low boil in the pot.

Add the clarified butter to the bowl and swirl to coat the bowl. Add the eggs and, using a rubber spatula, constantly scrape the sides of the bowl. Once the eggs reach the consistency of cottage cheese—about 5½ minutes—remove the bowl from the heat, add 2 tablespoons chilled butter, and gently fold until incorporated using the residual heat from the eggs. Divide evenly between four shallow dishes or bowls.

Top each serving with a quenelle (PAGE 101) of caviar and serve with toasted challah bread.

Lox, Eggs & Onions (LEO)

MAKES 4 SERVINGS

12 large eggs
Kosher salt, to taste
4 tablespoons clarified butter (see next page)
2 cups Caramelized Onions (recipe below)
6 ounces smoked salmon, Gaspe Nova preferred
8 slices Shissel Rye (PAGE 290), toasted

The LEO is to Jewry what the BEC is to goyim: breakfast nonpareil. This classic relies on the silkiness of the smoked salmon, the creaminess of eggs, and the sweetness of caramelized onions to welcome you to the day. There's little mystery to how it's made, however it is important to not overcook both the eggs and the lox, which is added to the pan with just enough time to warm through, but not so much that it becomes cooked (which would rob it of its texture.) We find LEO—and its cousin SEO (made with sturgeon)—is best eaten with a few slices from our caraway-forward traditional rye bread.

In a medium bowl, whisk the eggs with a pinch of salt. Set aside.

Heat 2 tablespoons of the clarified butter in a medium nonstick skillet over medium heat. Add the onions and stir until warm. Add the remaining 2 tablespoons clarified butter followed by the eggs and, using a rubber spatula, scrape the bottom and sides of the pan, gently folding so large curds form and turning down the heat to medium-low after about 30 seconds. When the eggs are 80 percent cooked, add the smoked salmon and gently fold into the eggs. As soon as the eggs have reached your desired consistency, transfer to a plate. Serve immediately with shissel rye.

Caramelized Onions

MAKES 2 CUPS

1 tablespoon extra-virgin olive oil
1 tablespoon unsalted butter
2 large Spanish onions (or 2 pounds yellow onions), peeled and thinly sliced
Kosher salt and freshly ground black pepper to taste

Onions, bracing and tear-inducing raw, are sweet and comforting once their sugars are caramelized by cooking. In their gentler form, they have become staples in many of our egg preparations. In the early morning hours before we open, the Cafe's kitchen is full of delicious smells of caramelized onions. At home, we suggest working in smaller batches, though cooking a lot doesn't hurt as caramelized onions are versatile. They can be used to add some sweetness to your favorite bagel sandwich or as a topping for, frankly, nearly anything.

Equally divide the olive oil and butter between two large sauté pans and place over medium-low heat. Once foaming, equally divide the sliced onions between the pans and spread out evenly.

CONTINUED →

Cook over medium-low heat, stirring occasionally to prevent burning, until the onions are a deep golden brown and reduced by three-fourths in volume, about 45 minutes.

Season with salt while sweating. (If you like, combine the two pans' worth of onions once their volume has lessened.) Season the caramelized onions again with a pinch of salt and pepper to taste and remove from the heat.

The onions will keep, covered in the refrigerator, for up to 5 days.

Clarified Butter

MAKES 12 OUNCES

1 pound (4 sticks) unsalted butter

The step of clarifying butter, a process by which the milk solids and water content are separated from the butterfat, increases the smoke point of the butter and results in a cleaner flavor in whatever you're cooking. The process takes some time but is relatively simple and, because clarified butter has a long shelf life, you won't have to do it often. However, if even this is too much, you can use ghee, which is clarified butter originating in Indian cuisine and typically available at most grocery stores.

Cut the butter into small, uniform pieces. Place the pieces in a heavy-bottomed saucepan and start melting over low to medium heat. Allow it to come to a gentle simmer and continue cooking over medium heat until it begins to foam and then crackle.

At this point the milk solids will begin to separate from the fat. As the milk solids separate, use a spoon to gently skim the foam off the top. Continue cooking as the remaining milk solids fall to the bottom of the pan and begin turning golden brown. Once all of the remaining solids have turned golden brown and settled, 15 to 20 minutes, remove the pan from the heat.

Carefully pour the clarified butter through a fine-mesh strainer, a few layers of cheesecloth, or a coffee filter, into a clean, dry container.

Let the clarified butter cool to room temperature. It will solidify slightly as it cools. Once cool, cover the container with a lid and store in a cool, dark place. Clarified butter has a long shelf life, up to 6 months, and doesn't need refrigeration.

DINNER

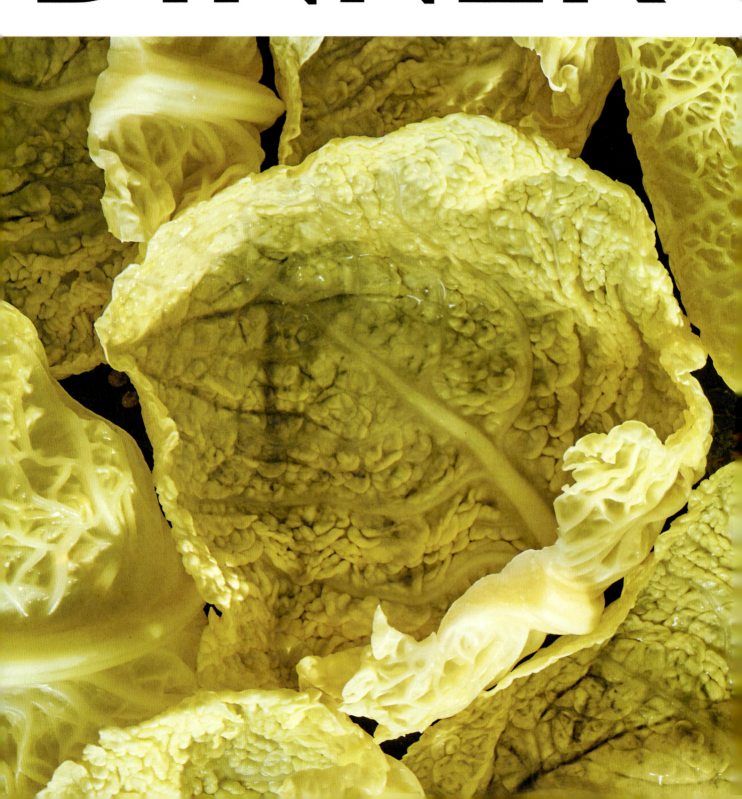

PECIALS

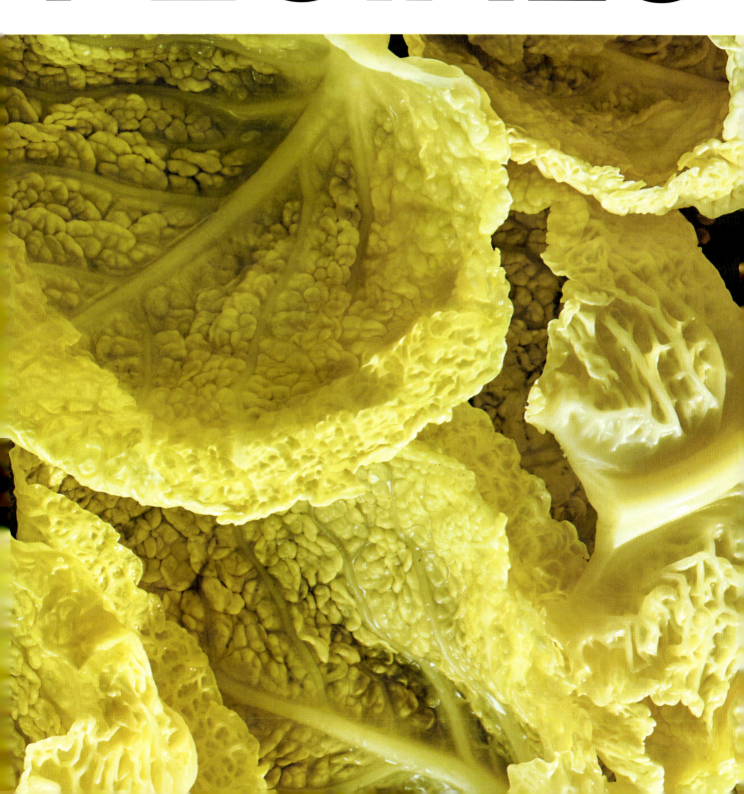

Aunt Ida's Stuffed Cabbage

MAKES 14 TO 16 STUFFED CABBAGE ROLLS

FOR THE CABBAGE
2 large heads green cabbage

FOR THE FILLING
2 pounds ground beef (80 percent lean)
1 medium yellow onion, finely chopped
½ cup uncooked white rice
2 large eggs
½ cup ketchup
2 teaspoons kosher salt
½ teaspoon freshly ground black pepper

FOR THE SAUCE
1 tablespoon neutral oil
2 medium yellow onions, sliced
42½ ounces canned diced tomatoes (one 28-ounce can and one 14½-ounce can)
2 tablespoons tomato paste
½ cup packed dark brown sugar
½ cup dark raisins, preferably Thompson raisins
½ cup ketchup
2 tablespoons apple cider vinegar
1 teaspoon kosher salt
½ teaspoon freshly ground pepper

Aunt Ida, the most headstrong of the Russ daughters, left the business to run her own appetizing shop in Massapequa before becoming an antiques dealer, so she didn't leave Russ & Daughters with much in the way of culinary legacy. But she was famous for her stuffed cabbage, at least at Russ family gatherings. This isn't a Cafe special so much as it is just special to us as a family. It's so special in fact, that though the original version had been lost to the sands of time, we were determined to track it down. First Niki reached out to Ida's son Marty Pulvers, a pipe monger living in California, with the slim hope that he had written down the recipe. He hadn't. So she turned for help from her friends at the American Jewish Historical Society and their library of Jewish cookbooks. Triangulating sense memory and historical accuracy, she settled on this sweet-and-sour version of stuffed cabbage, studded with raisins, typical for a Hungarian iteration. It was delightful fresh and even better the second day, just as we remembered it. After much transcontinental back and forth with Marty, it was agreed that this one comes very close to the original moist, sweet, and memorable recipe and that Ida would be proud.

Preheat the oven to 350°F.

Bring a large stockpot of salted water to a boil over high heat.

Meanwhile, prepare the cabbages by removing the hard stalk at the base with a paring knife. Using tongs, carefully place one head of cabbage in the boiling water and use tongs or a plate to keep cabbage submerged. Cook until the leaves are pliable and outer leaves start to fall off, 10 to 15 minutes. Remove the cabbage and let drain in a colander. Repeat with second cabbage.

When the cabbages are cool enough to handle, carefully peel off one leaf at a time. You need 16 outer leaves. Once you reach the small, white, harder leaves of the interior, set those aside to line the pot later. As you remove each leaf, use a paring knife to remove the hard stem at its base with a narrow V-cut. Place the trimmed leaves on a paper towel–lined baking sheet.

MAKE FILLING

Mix the ground beef, onion, rice, eggs, ketchup, salt, and pepper together in a mixing bowl.

Line the bottom of a 9 by 13-inch casserole dish or large Dutch oven with a layer of the reserved interior cabbage leaves and pieces.

On a work surface, form a loose oval shape with about ⅓ cup of the ground beef mixture. (Do not pack it too hard or the rice won't cook evenly.) Place the mixture in the middle of the cabbage leaf with the stem base closest to you, roll the bottom of the leaf over the mixture just once, then fold in the sides until they are touching. Carefully roll the leaf forward one rotation so the whole mixture is covered and the folded edges are inside the stuffed cabbage. Use a paring knife to remove excess leaf, and place the cabbage, fold side down, in the bottom of a wide Dutch oven or casserole dish. Repeat until all the filling has been used.

MAKE SAUCE

Heat the oil in a large saucepan over medium heat. Add the sliced onion and cook, stirring occasionally, until shimmering, 5 minutes. Add the tomatoes, tomato paste, brown sugar, raisins, ketchup, and apple cider vinegar. Season to taste with the salt and pepper. Bring to a boil, then lower the heat and simmer for 15 minutes, until slightly reduced. Taste the sauce and adjust with salt, pepper, and vinegar if needed, for sweet and sour balance.

TO COOK

Pour the sauce evenly over the cabbage in the casserole dish. Cover—either with aluminum foil or a lid—and bake for 1½ hours. Remove the cover and bake for an additional 30 minutes; the dish may still look a bit liquid-y, this will settle into a sauce as it cools. Let cool in baking dish for at least 15 minutes to let juices settle before serving. Remove the cabbage rolls one by one from the casserole and put on a platter or plate, spooning some of the sauce over the cabbage.

Vegetarian Stuffed Cabbage

MAKES ABOUT 10 STUFFED CABBAGE ROLLS

FOR THE CABBAGE
2 large heads savoy cabbage

FOR THE RICE FILLING
2 tablespoons extra-virgin olive oil
1 cup diced yellow onion
Kosher salt
1 cup sliced trimmed shiitake mushrooms (2 ounces)
1½ tablespoons pine nuts
2 cloves garlic, smashed and minced
½ teaspoon picked fresh thyme
½ teaspoon fennel seeds
½ cup basmati rice, rinsed and drained
¼ cup white wine
2 cups water (or chicken stock)
1½ teaspoons chopped fresh parsley

Ingredients continued

Jews have been stuffing cabbage since the sixteenth century and stewing the leaves for even longer. Affordable, easy to grow, replenishable, and nutritious, cabbage was an important—perhaps the most important—vegetable in the shtetl garden. There are as many recipes for stuffed cabbage as there are diasporic pantries. (See Aunt Ida's Stuffed Cabbage, PAGE 190). Many are made for holidays and special occasions. This one relies on rice, a tradition that comes to us from Middle Eastern and Romanian Jewry. (Jews from the north use bread or barley.) These Levantine flavors are carried through in the herbaceous filling (pine nuts, thyme, shiitakes) and appear again, outside of the cabbage, in the umami-rich mushroom sauce. As a nod to our long history as mushroom vendors—and because they endow a meaty, earthy flavor to the dish—we've doubled down on the mushrooms in both the stuffing and the sauce.

Bring a large pot of salted water to a boil over high heat. Meanwhile, prepare the cabbages by removing the hard stalk at the base with a paring knife and any outer leaves.

Using tongs, carefully place one head of cabbage into the boiling water and place a heavy ceramic plate on top to keep the cabbage submerged. Cook until the leaves are pliable, 10 to 15 minutes. Remove the cabbage and let drain in a colander. Repeat with the second cabbage.

When the cabbages are cool enough to handle, carefully peel off one leaf at a time. You need about ten large outer leaves. Once you reach the small, white, and harder leaves of the interior, set those aside. As you remove each leaf, use a paring knife to remove the hard stem at its base with a narrow V-cut.

Place the trimmed leaves on a paper towel–lined baking sheet.

MAKE RICE FILLING

Heat 1 tablespoon of the olive oil in a small pot over medium-high heat. Once shimmering, add the onion with a pinch of salt and cook, stirring occasionally, until soft and translucent, about 3 minutes.

Add the remaining 1 tablespoon olive oil, the mushrooms, and a pinch of salt and continue cooking, stirring occasionally, until golden, about 2 minutes. Add the pine nuts and cook until just beginning to brown, about 30 seconds. Add the garlic, thyme, and fennel seeds and cook until aromatic, about 30 seconds more. Next add the rice and ¾ teaspoon salt and stir for 5 minutes, or until the rice begins to toast.

CONTINUED →

Deglaze the pan with the white wine, then reduce the liquid until it is almost dry, about 30 seconds. Add the water (or chicken stock) and parsley. Bring to a simmer then reduce the heat to the lowest setting. Cover with a heavy lid and cook for 20 to 25 minutes, until the liquid is mostly absorbed. Set aside to cool slightly.

FOR THE MUSHROOM SAUCE

3 tablespoons extra-virgin olive oil
2 cups sliced shiitake mushrooms (4 ounces)
Kosher salt
1 cup diced yellow onion
2 cloves garlic, smashed and minced
1 teaspoon picked fresh thyme leaves
⅓ cup white cooking wine
1 tablespoon all-purpose flour
1½ cups water (or chicken stock)
Freshly ground black pepper

TO ASSEMBLE

2 cups water (or chicken stock)
1 lemon, sliced into rounds
Chopped fresh parsley, for serving

MAKE MUSHROOM SAUCE

Heat 2 tablespoons of the olive oil in a medium saucepan over medium-high heat. Once the oil is shimmering, add the mushrooms with a pinch of salt, reduce the heat to medium, and sauté for 5 minutes. The mushrooms should still be soft, not crispy. With a slotted spoon, transfer the mushrooms to a plate and set aside.

Add the remaining 1 tablespoon oil to the pan as well as the onion and a pinch of salt. Sauté until soft and translucent, about 4 minutes. Add the garlic and thyme and cook until aromatic, about 1 minute.

Return three-fourths of the mushrooms to the pan. Increase the heat to high, then deglaze with the white wine, scraping up any bits from the bottom with a wooden spoon. Allow the mixture to reduce until the wine is almost fully evaporated, about 1 minute.

Reduce the heat to medium-low and sprinkle the flour over the mixture. Cook, stirring frequently, until the flour is toasted, about 30 seconds. Add the water (or chicken stock) in small amounts, stirring and allowing the liquid to simmer before adding more. Once all the stock has been added, reduce the heat to medium-low and simmer for 10 minutes.

Transfer the mixture to a food processor—or use an immersion blender in the pot—and blend the sauce until smooth; if too thick, add more water a tablespoon at a time. Return the sauce to the pot, along with the reserved mushrooms, and bring to a low simmer. Adjust seasoning with salt and pepper. Makes about 2 cups.

TO ASSEMBLE

Take one cabbage leaf and place with the stem base closest to you. Spoon about 2 ounces (the size of a ping-pong ball) of the rice filling onto the side of the leaf closer to you, leaving a little bit of space at the bottom. Roll the bottom of the leaf over the mixture just once, then fold in the sides until they are touching. Carefully roll the leaf forward one rotation so the whole mixture is covered and the folded edges are inside the stuffed cabbage. Use a paring knife to remove excess leaf and place the cabbage, fold side down, in the bottom of a wide Dutch oven. Repeat with the remaining cabbage leaves and filling, packing all the stuffed cabbages tightly.

To cook, pour the water (or chicken stock) over the stuffed cabbage. Lay about 5 lemon slices over the top of the cabbage. Gently lay a heavy ceramic plate on top of the cabbage rolls to keep them from unwrapping. Bring the pot to a simmer over medium-high heat, then lower to the lowest setting. Cover and cook for 30 minutes, until the cabbage is tender.

Remove the plate and lemon slices. Carefully move the stuffed cabbage to a plate and drain off the remaining liquid in pot. Pour the mushroom sauce on top of the stuffed cabbage and garnish with parsley.

Pickled Carrots with Cumin & Caraway

MAKES 2 PINTS

- 1 teaspoon cumin seeds
- 1 teaspoon caraway seeds
- 1 cup distilled white vinegar
- 1 cup water
- 2 tablespoons granulated sugar
- 1 tablespoon kosher salt
- 2 cloves garlic, minced
- ½ teaspoon red pepper flakes, optional
- 1 pound carrots, peeled and sliced into thin rounds or sticks

The humble carrot doesn't appear as often as you might imagine in the food of Eastern European Jewry. It most often appears during Passover, in dishes like tsimmes and in soups. But in Sephardic cuisine, from which this preparation comes, the carrot—fresh, pickled, or cooked—is a mainstay. We're fierce champions of the sour and half-sour pickles, but when we opened the Cafe, we wanted to expand our pickled larder—and add a pop of color to a sometimes quite beige table—by adding carrot. Here we pair the acidity of the pickled carrots with the slight bitter flavor of caraway and its twin, cumin, which looks similar but imparts a warming nutty flavor.

Place the cumin and caraway seeds in a dry skillet and toast over medium heat, stirring frequently, for 1 to 2 minutes, until fragrant. Transfer to a plate.

Prepare the brine by combining the white vinegar, water, sugar, and salt in a small saucepan. Bring the mixture to a boil, stirring to dissolve the sugar and salt. Once boiling, remove the pan from heat and let the brine cool slightly, about 10 minutes. Stir in the toasted cumin and caraway seeds, garlic, and the red pepper flakes if you're using them. Allow the brine to cool to room temperature.

Place the carrot slices or sticks snugly into two sterilized pint jars (PAGE 109). Pour the cooled brine over the carrots, making sure they are fully submerged. Leave some headspace at the top of the jars.

Seal the jars tightly and place in the refrigerator. Allow the carrots to pickle for at least 24 hours before tasting. The longer they sit, the more flavorful they will become.

Store in an airtight container in the refrigerator for up to 1 month.

Chicken Paprikash

SERVES 4

2 tablespoons Hungarian paprika

1 teaspoon garlic powder

1 teaspoon onion powder

¾ teaspoon ground cumin

¾ teaspoon Aleppo pepper powder

4 chicken legs, thigh and drumstick attached (3½ pounds)

Kosher salt

2 tablespoons canola oil

1 tablespoon unsalted butter

1 large Spanish onion, thinly sliced

3 cloves garlic, minced

1 tablespoon all-purpose flour

1 cup chicken stock

1 (28-ounce) can crushed tomatoes

¼ cup sour cream, optional

Chicken paprikash, the Hungarian classic, is not easy to find on restaurant menus. Not only are Hungarian restaurants few and far between, but the dish itself is so homey that it seems better suited for private preparation than in a professional kitchen. But what is our Cafe if not an extended home for our customers? When we decided to offer dinner specials, Mark said, "You know what you should make? Chicken paprikash." He was understandably nostalgic for eating it as a kid, and that was reason enough for us. Chicken paprikash embodies Ashkenazi home cooking. Even Josh, when he left the ashram to visit his father, grew up eating it. And what is not to love about paprikash, as comforting a dish as you'll find in Jewish cuisine (where the competition is stiff)? As in all paprikashes, this one showcases paprika, the Hungarian pepper—here mild but available hot too—and a fair amount of onion, slowly cooked down with the spice mixture and tomatoes, until yielding and soft.

Preheat the oven to 350°F.

Combine the paprika, garlic powder, onion powder, cumin, and Aleppo pepper and set aside.

Pat the chicken dry and season with salt to taste. Heat the canola oil and butter in a Dutch oven over medium heat until the butter is foaming. Working in two batches, add the chicken, skin side down, and sear for 5 to 7 minutes, until golden. Flip and cook for an additional 5 to 7 minutes, until golden on the second side. Transfer the chicken to a plate and set aside.

Add the sliced onion to the pan and cook, stirring occasionally, for 7 minutes, until developing some color. Add the garlic and cook for another 2 to 3 minutes, until softened. Add the spice mix to the onions, stir to coat evenly, and cook very briefly, less than 30 seconds, until the spices are lightly toasted. Sprinkle the flour over the onion mix, then stir to coat evenly and soak up any fats. Cook very briefly, just 10 to 15 seconds, scraping the bottom so as not to scorch.

Add the chicken stock, scrape the bottom of the pan, and bring to a simmer. Add the crushed tomatoes, combine, and bring to a simmer. Cook 1 minute, then whisk in the sour cream, if using. Season with salt.

Add the chicken legs, cover with the sauce, and return to a simmer if necessary. Cover with the lid and place in the oven to bake for 15 minutes. Lower the temperature to 325°F and bake an additional 40 minutes, or until the chicken is tender. Let rest 10 minutes before serving.

A HUN IZ GUT TSU ESN ZELBANAND: IKH UN DI HUN. Chicken is good to eat in pairs: me and the chicken. YIDDISH PROVERB

Kippered Salmon Mac & Cheese

**MAKES ONE 9×13" PAN,
10 TO 12 SERVINGS**

1 pound bow tie pasta

½ cup (1 stick) plus 2 tablespoons unsalted butter, plus more softened butter for the baking dish

½ cup all-purpose white flour

4 cups (2 pints) half-and-half*

1 cup scallion cream cheese

1½ cups shredded Muenster cheese (about 5 ounces)

1½ cups shredded mozzarella cheese (about 5 ounces)

¾ cup panko breadcrumbs

Kosher salt and fresh ground black pepper to taste

½ pound kippered salmon

---

*For the half-and-half, you can substitute 2 cups whole milk plus 2 cups heavy cream. Or, for a slightly less-rich version, use 4 cups whole milk.

When we first opened the Cafe, the question arose about how much to incorporate our core products in this new venture and how. After a fair amount of experimentation, we opted for the most straightforward approach. Our traditional appetizing appears on platters; our baked goods in their proper place. But generally, there is not much newfangled on the menu. This is in part because cooking with cold-smoked fish—like lox, sable, and sturgeon—ruins their silky texture. It would be like watching an IMAX movie on a cell phone. Kippered salmon, however, which is already hot-smoked, is more amenable. Here the smokiness of the kippered salmon sits atop a decadent mac and cheese. Think of it like a less trayf-y spin on bacon mac and cheese.

Preheat the oven to 350°F. Grease a 9 by 13-inch broiler-safe baking dish with butter and set aside.

Bring a large pot of salted water to boil. Once boiling, add the pasta and cook for 2 minutes less than the package directs for al dente. Reserve 1 cup of the water, drain the pasta, and set aside.

In a large, heavy-bottomed sauce pot, make the roux by melting the ½ cup butter over medium heat. When foam subsides, add the flour, whisking or stirring with a rubber spatula to combine. Cook, stirring, until toasted smelling and lightly golden in color, 2 to 3 minutes.

Add 2 cups of the half-and-half and stir with a rubber spatula or whisk, scraping the bottom of the pot and cooking briefly to combine. Add the remaining 2 cups half-and-half and bring to a simmer, whisking constantly so as not to scorch the bottom of the pan. Continue to cook, whisking, until bubbles form and the mixture is thickened and smooth. Whisk or stir in the scallion cream cheese, then add the shredded cheeses in batches, folding or whisking until smooth and uniform. Season to taste with salt and pepper. Remove from the heat.

Fold the nearly cooked pasta into the cheese sauce and mix well. If the sauce is very thick, you can add a few spoonfuls of reserved pasta water to loosen the consistency a little. Transfer to the prepared baking dish. Bake uncovered until golden and bubbling around the edges, 25 to 30 minutes.

Meanwhile, melt the remaining 2 tablespoons butter, add the panko, and toss to evenly distribute. Season with salt and pepper.

Evenly top the mac and cheese with flakes of kippered salmon followed by an even layer of the buttered breadcrumbs. Place under broiler on low briefly, until golden and bubbling, 30 seconds to 2 minutes.

Shissel Chicken Cutlets with Tartar Sauce

MAKES 2 SERVINGS

½ cup all-purpose flour
2 large eggs
2 cups Shissel Rye Breadcrumbs (PAGE 291)
2 skinless boneless chicken breasts with the wing's drumette attached, sometimes called airline chicken breasts
Neutral oil, for shallow frying
2 ounces arugula, washed and dried
2 tablespoons extra-virgin olive oil
Juice from ¼ lemon
Kosher salt and fresh ground black pepper to taste
Lemon wedges, for serving
Tartar Sauce (see below), for serving

Our shissel rye is bracingly and perhaps unusually strong. It is as rye should be. We lean into the rye flour, rye sour, black nigella seeds, and caraway seeds. The rye breadcrumbs here are, as one might imagine, just as assertive and offer a unique breading for a chicken cutlet. Think of this as an Ashkenazi Milanese, a breast pounded thin, breaded, and fried until golden—but with chutzpah. We serve this at the Cafe with a ramekin of our homemade tartar sauce and a simple arugula salad to cut through the pleasing intensity of the chicken and its rye coating.

Preheat the oven to 375°F.

Place the flour in one bowl. Break the eggs and whisk together in a second, and put the rye breadcrumbs in a third.

Pound each breast and drumette into ¼-inch thickness, leaving the bone attached. Season each side lightly with salt. Working one at a time, dredge each breast in the flour, then the egg, and finally the breadcrumbs.

Heat ½ inch oil in a heavy-bottomed skillet over medium heat until it shimmers. Add one breast to the pan, and cook, flipping once, until deeply golden, 2 to 3 minutes per side. Remove the chicken breast to a rimmed baking sheet with a wire rack and season with salt and pepper. Repeat with the second breast. Transfer the rack to the oven, and bake until cooked through, about 5 minutes. Let cool slightly.

In another small bowl, toss the arugula with the olive oil and lemon juice and season to taste with salt and pepper.

Equally divide the arugula between two plates. Add the chicken breasts, top with a wedge of lemon, and serve with the tartar sauce on the side.

MAKES 1¼ CUPS

1 cup mayonnaise
2 tablespoons chopped shallot
1 tablespoon chopped cornichons
1 tablespoon capers, chopped
1 tablespoon fresh lemon juice
1 tablespoon chopped fresh dill
1 pinch cayenne pepper

TARTAR SAUCE

Mix all the ingredients together. Serve or refrigerate for up to 2 days.

Roasted Cauliflower with Garlic Labneh

MAKES 4 TO 6 SIDE-DISH SERVINGS

FOR THE GARLIC LABNEH
14 cloves garlic, peeled
2 cups extra-virgin olive oil (or more if needed)
2 cups labneh
Kosher salt

FOR THE ROASTED CAULIFLOWER
1 head cauliflower (about 2 pounds), stem and outer leaves removed, cut into small florets
Kosher salt and fresh ground black pepper to taste
1 tablespoon minced fresh parsley

Though Russ & Daughters belongs to the world of Eastern European Jewry, only a fool would ignore the vast and delicious culinary traditions of the Sephardim. That's the origin of this side dish. The garlic is a nice accompaniment to vegetable and meat dishes, while the garlic oil can replace olive oil in other recipes for some extra depth. The garlic labneh is lovely with some fresh pita, but don't forget to drizzle on some extra garlic oil. If you're serving a larger group, the garlic labneh is enough to accommodate two heads of cauliflower.

MAKE GARLIC LABNEH
In a small saucepan, combine the garlic and 2 cups olive oil (or enough to fully submerge the cloves of garlic). Slowly heat the mixture over medium-low heat until you begin to see bubbles rising. Reduce the heat to the lowest setting and let simmer for 30 to 35 minutes, until the garlic is fragrant and evenly golden brown. Let the garlic cool in the oil until it reaches room temperature.

Remove the garlic cloves from the oil and squish them through a small sieve to create 2 to 3 tablespoons paste. (Alternately, you can smoosh them with the side of a knife into a paste, but remove the tough ends of each clove before you do.) In a bowl, combine the garlic paste, labneh, and ⅓ cup oil from the garlic confit. Whisk until smooth and all the oil and garlic paste are incorporated into the labneh. Season with salt. (Makes 2¼ cups garlic-confit labneh.)

ROAST CAULIFLOWER
Preheat the oven to 400°F.

Toss the cauliflower in a bowl with salt, pepper, and 2 to 3 tablespoons of the olive oil from the garlic confit. Spread the cauliflower in one layer on a baking sheet.

Roast the cauliflower for 35 to 40 minutes, stirring halfway through. The cauliflower should be beginning to brown and fully tender throughout.

TO SERVE
Spread a generous amount (about 1 cup) of the garlic labneh on a large serving plate. Pile the roasted cauliflower on top of the sauce and drizzle with an additional tablespoon of garlic oil. Garnish with minced parsley and serve.

Labneh can be stored for 5 to 7 days in an airtight container in the refrigerator. Garlic oil will last 2 to 3 weeks at room temperature.

PASSOVE

R SEDER

For as long as we can remember, Russ & Daughters has swollen during the holidays. Lines have formed. Numbers taken, appetizing dispensed. Our offerings, after all, are made for gatherings and holidays when many gather. During these periods, our kitchens and bakery go into overdrive. Not only are we provisioning thousands of families with our usual fare, but we're also making our holiday special. On Chanukah, we do a brisk business in golden crisp latkes. During Passover, gefilte fish flies from the case and tsimmes departs in quarts and liters. On Rosh Hashanah, honey cake signals—and aspires to—a sweet New Year. And on Yom Kippur, a line forms in the predawn darkness along East Houston as customers get an early start on their break fast spreads.

For decades we were content to send our customers home with appetizing on their own. We knew it would feed families and friends across the country. But when we opened the Cafe in 2014, suddenly we had a space to host our own friends and family. In April 2015 we debuted our Second Seder. Traditionally, there are two seders to mark the Passover holiday, a holdover from when diasporic Jews didn't get the bulletin as to what night the rabbinical court deemed the first. (In Israel, there is only one seder.) In modern times, however, the second seder is often the friends' seder. For us it was a chance for longtime customers and friends to celebrate together at the Cafe. We printed special placemats that doubled as seder plates. We made a menu featuring some of our classics (hot smoke / cold smoke, sours, matzo ball soup) and specials, including a succulent brisket, flourless chocolate cake, and coconut macaroons. And we made sure there were plenty of cocktails. This was both a ceremonial seder and a party.

That first Second Seder—dubbed the First Annual Second Seder much like Joel first named his business J. Russ National Appetizing: a name that was also an aspiration—was hosted by the performance artist Laurie Anderson, who brought her storytelling prowess to Exodus. Suzanne Vega sang an acapella version of her song "Tom's Diner," retitled—for just one night—"Russ & Daughters Diner." (Note: We never fill coffee only halfway.) Since then, we've followed some permutation of formula, magical evenings centered around a theme (Civil Rights, Common Ground, Resistance). Like any tradition, each year has been both the same and different. With only a few exceptions, Andy Bachman, a dear family friend and rabbi, has been our spiritual and storytelling emcee ever since the beginning. Music has filled the space. We've had a remarkable lineup of artists, such as Lorin Sklamberg, Elvis Costello, Daniel Kohn, Freestyle Love Supreme, and Eléanor Biezunski, to name a few.

Many of our guests know each other; many are strangers when they arrive. They come by car, foot, train, and plane, from around the corner and across the country. No matter from where or how they arrive, they're family when they leave. In the night of the Lower East Side, the Cafe glows with camaraderie and communion and the doors are left ajar for Elijah.

Though just a baby tradition in the timeline of Russ & Daughters—and just a blink of an eye in the history of the Jewish peoples—nevertheless the Second Seder has become a touchstone for us, a way to reaffirm our connection to the Jewish American experience.

RUSS & DAUGHTERS HAS A CENTRAL ROLE in New York Jewish identity. When Niki and Josh opened the cafe, people's excitement was palpable. If the counter on Houston was a community of people standing, enjoying a particular kind of New York Jewishness, rooted in family, history, the Lower East Side, and great food, the cafe was a place to sit down and relish in it. Deciding to do the seder was very much a no-brainer. Given the nature of the family's relationship to the Jewish religion, we knew it would be free-form: a wild ride, with a lot of singing and conversation, making the message of Passover both rooted in history and the world today. What I share is that we are a people, a family, a nation, we have a variety of expressions of Jewishness: text, music, culinary. There are multiple dimensions to Jewish identity. It doesn't have to be a religious ceremony for it to be deeply and profoundly Jewish. ANDY BACHMAN, RABBI

RUSS & DAUGHTERS

THE FIRST ANNUAL SECOND SEDER

LAURIE ANDERSON AND FRIENDS

April 5, 2015

NOSHES

HOT SMOKE/COLD SMOKE
KIPPERED (BAKED) & SCOTTISH SMOKED SALMON SPREAD

CHOPPED LIVER
CHOPPED CHICKEN LIVER, PICKLED RED ONION

SOURS
PICKLED VEGETABLES & PICKLES FROM THE BARREL

DINNER

MATZO BALL SOUP
CHICKEN, VEGETABLES, MATZO BALL

SALMON & WHITEFISH GEFILTE FISH
FRESH GRATED HORSERADISH

BRISKET
BEEF BRISKET, CARAMELIZED ONION, POTATO, SPINACH, ROASTED CARROTS

DESSERT

FLOURLESS CHOCOLATE CAKE

ALMOND MACAROON COOKIES

$10 COCKTAILS

KARPAS
HORSERADISH-INFUSED POTATO VODKA, COINTREAU, LEMON JUICE, PARSLEY

MAROR
HORSERADISH-INFUSED POTATO VODKA, VERMOUTH, FORMULA ANTICA, ANGOSTURA BITTERS, BABY BEET

CHAROSET
BULLEIT BOURBON, HOUSE-MADE APPLE & CINNAMON SYRUP, LEMON JUICE, MANZANILLA SHERRY

WINE & CHAMPAGNE
LOUREIRO, APHROS 9/36
DOYARD BRUT 17/80

REDS
Cabernet Franc, SEBASTIEN DAVID 10/40
Poulsard, DOMAINE PIGNIER 13/52
PINOT NOIR, SILAS 16/62

Second Seder PROGRAM

WELCOME by LAURIE ANDERSON

KADESH with JUDITH BERKSON

ORCHATZ (WASH)

KARPAS with ANNIE OHAYON

YACHATZ
Crack in the Wall, SONG, SUZANNE VEGA

MAGID
The Four Questions, YIDDISH, BASYA SCHECHTER
The Four Questions, TRADITIONAL, JUDITH BERKSON
The Story of the Four Daughters, LAURIE ANDERSON
The Liberation Narrative, LAURIE ANDERSON
"Let My People Go", LAURIE ANDERSON with JUDITH BERKSON
The Plagues, LAURIE ANDERSON
"Exodus", STORY, ROMA BARAN
"Taitch," SONG, BASYA SCHECHTER
MUSIC, SUZANNE VEGA
DAYENU

RACHTZAH (WASH)

MOTZI/MATZAH/MAROR/KORECH
blessings by ANNIE OHAYON

SHULCHAN ORECH
DINNER

TZAFUN
"Chocolate", A POEM BY PAUL MILLS

FINDING THE AFIKOMEN (DESSERT)

BARECH
PRAISE SONG by LAURIE ANDERSON

NIRTZAH
UN CABRITO Y QUIEN SOPIESE

BETZAH - Egg

MAROR - Bitter Herbs

ZEROA - Shank Bone

RUSS & DAUGHTERS

Tsimmes

MAKES 4 QUARTS, 8 TO 10 SERVINGS

1 cup pitted prunes, cut in half
1 cup Turkish apricots, cut in half
1 cup dried apple rings, cut in half
½ cup golden raisins
4 large carrots, peeled, halved lengthwise, and sliced into ⅓-inch half-moons
2 pounds sweet potatoes, peeled and cut into ½-inch dice
¼ cup orange juice
¼ cup packed brown sugar
1½ teaspoons ground cinnamon
Grated zest of 2 lemons

As they do for charoset, every child—and all those with a sweet tooth and a young heart—reaches for the tsimmes at the Passover and Rosh Hashanah tables. *Tsimmes* is a general term from *zuomuose*, Middle High German for "side dish," but in the modern world has come to mean a glazed carrot stew studded with fruit and bathed with honey and brown sugar. (The sweetness is what corrals it into the Rosh Hashanah canon.) There are near endless variations of tsimmes: with or without meat (ours is without, naturally) and with root vegetables ranging from parsnips to turnips to rutabagas. During the holidays we make ours by mixing carrots and sweet potatoes while leaning heavily into our inventory of the dried fruits that line the front window of the shop for pops of flavor and texture.

Bring 4 quarts of water to boil in a large stockpot. In a large bowl, mix together all the dried fruit then cover with the boiling water. Cover tightly with tin foil and let sit overnight, or for up to 48 hours. Drain the rehydrated fruit and place in a large bowl.

Preheat the oven to 350°F. Grease a medium baking pan.

Bring a large pot of lightly salted water to a boil. Add the carrots and sweet potatoes and cook until tender, 10 to 12 minutes. Drain the carrots and potatoes and toss into the fruit mixture. Add the orange juice, brown sugar, cinnamon, and lemon zest and gently mix.

Pour the mixture onto the greased baking pan and bake for 1 hour 20 minutes, stirring the mixture every 20 minutes or so. Remove from the oven, cover with aluminum foil and seal, then return to the oven for an additional 20 minutes. Serve immediately.

Tsimmes can be kept covered in the refrigerator for 1 week.

Charoset

**MAKES ABOUT 4 CUPS,
6 TO 8 SERVINGS**

¾ cup walnuts halves
2 medium Gala or Fuji apples, peeled, cored, and roughly chopped
1 Granny Smith apple, peeled, cored, and roughly chopped
½ cup golden raisins
1½ teaspoons brown sugar
1 teaspoon freshly grated ginger
¾ teaspoon ground cinnamon
¼ cup kosher-for-Passover Concord grape wine, preferably Manischewitz Extra Heavy Malaga Wine
2 tablespoons lemon juice

The meaning of *charoset* has been the subject of much Talmudic debate. Between two matzo, it's the middle of a Hillel sandwich, named after the first-century sage. It is the dip for bitter herbs (*maror*), meant to symbolize the bitterness of slavery. It also symbolizes the mortar Israelites used to make bricks in Egypt and/or the sweet-smelling tree under which Israelite women gave birth. Often, unfortunately, charoset resembles most mortar: pasty and not sweet. Ours departs from the traditional late-Ashkenazi recipe of apples, sugar, wine, nuts, and spices with the addition of ginger and lemon juice to add a brightness. It's so good that lots of people—including us—make extra to enjoy in the days after the seder—straight, on top of yogurt for breakfast, or however else they can think of. (The wine and lemon are great natural preservatives.)

Preheat the oven to 350°F. Spread the walnuts evenly on a baking sheet and toast in the oven for 8 to 10 minutes, stirring occasionally, until lightly roasted. Let cool slightly, then roughly chop.

In a large bowl, mix together the walnuts, apples, raisins, sugar, ginger, and cinnamon. Add the wine and lemon juice and mix all the ingredients well. Store, covered, in the refrigerator overnight.

Serve chilled or at room temperature. Give it a toss before serving to redistribute the juices.

The charoset keeps in a covered container in the refrigerator for 1 week.

Salmon & Whitefish Gefilte Fish

MAKES 6 SERVINGS

1 teaspoon granulated sugar

1 teaspoon kosher salt

¼ teaspoon freshly ground black pepper

1 pound fresh salmon, skinned and boned

¼ pound fresh whitefish, skinned and boned

1 small white onion, cut into small dice (1 cup)

1 large egg

1½ tablespoons chopped fresh dill

1 cup matzo meal, coarsely ground

2 quarts homemade fish stock (recipe on following page) or high-quality store-bought

1 (½-ounce) packet gelatin

¼ to ½ cup red horseradish, to taste

Russ & Daughters sits in the historical nexus of gefilte fish–making in the United States and we have a responsibility to make the real stuff. Tales are told of carp—from which gefilte fish is made—kept in tenement bathtubs for maximum freshness. (There's even a very good children's book about gefilte fish called *Big Dreams, Small Fish* by Paula Cohen, a friend of Russ & Daughters who passed away just before her book came out.) Traditionally, gefilte fish was eaten among observant Jews on Shabbos, since deboning a fish counts as a forbidden action. (Cutting a boneless fish, not so much.) In the dark days of industrial gefilte of the mid-century, you couldn't blame anyone for eating it only once a year—on Passover—and even then only out of a sense of ancestral obligation. It took us years to land on a gefilte fish we find superlative, a gefilte fish not just of obligation but of delight. Our secret—if you can call it that—is not only that we use the highest quality whitefish we can but that we add salmon, which gives our gefilte fish both a pinkish hue and a slightly more robust flavor. It's light and fresh with a hint of dill and will make converts out of gefilte skeptics.

Mix together the sugar, salt, and pepper and set aside.

Using a very sharp knife, dice the salmon and whitefish into roughly ¼-inch pieces. Arrange them, spread out and not overlapping, on a baking sheet lined with parchment paper. Set the sheet in the freezer for 10 to 15 minutes to chill the fish while you prep the onions and measure the other ingredients. Set the blade and, if possible, the bowl of your food processor in the fridge to chill as well.

Once the fish is chilled, the pieces should be firm/frozen on the very exterior, but still thawed and somewhat malleable at the center. If you accidentally freeze your fish, set it on the counter for a minute or two to thaw slightly before beginning the process. Working quickly, evenly distribute one-third of the chilled fish in the bowl of a food processor, along with some onion. Add another layer of fish, then a layer of onion, repeating until all the contents are in the bowl. Pulse the fish and onions in short bursts, pausing occasionally to scrape the bowl and lightly toss the ingredients, especially at the beginning. Pulse until the mixture is uniform and the consistency of crumbled ground meat. Be careful to work quickly, don't let things get too warm, and don't overprocess. You are not looking for fish paste.

Transfer the minced fish and onion to a large mixing bowl. Add the egg, mixing to combine, followed by the chopped dill, mixing again to distribute, followed by the sugar, salt, and pepper mixture, mixing once again to fully combine.

CONTINUED →

Finally, add the matzo meal and mix until combined. The mixture should be light and slightly springy.

Lay plastic wrap directly on top of the mixture and refrigerate for a minimum of 1 hour (or up to 12 hours) to allow the flavors to blend.

When ready to cook, bring the fish stock to a boil in a large stockpot over medium heat. Once the stock boils, reduce the heat to low and keep at a simmer.

Form the gefilte mixture into six oblong balls, 5 ounces each, by scooping with a large spoon and shaping with clean hands. Working in batches to make sure they don't touch, place the gefilte fish oblong balls in the simmering stock. Once they rise to the surface, cook for another 10 to 15 minutes, flipping them about halfway, then gently remove to a plate to cool slightly. Reserve the fish stock.

Strain the stock through a sieve or a cheesecloth to remove any solids. Return 4 cups to the stove and, if necessary, reheat until steaming (discard any remaining stock). Pour the warm stock into a large heatproof bowl and sprinkle the gelatin over the top, whisking to combine. Allow to cool to room temperature, 20 to 30 minutes, then place in the refrigerator until it develops a jelly-like consistency, about 4 hours.

Slice the gefilte fish and serve cold, with the fish jelly on the side and small dollops of horseradish.

FISH STOCK

MAKES 8½ CUPS

2½ pounds fish bones and heads (preferably from whitefish, pike, carp, or sablefish)
3 quarts water
2 stalks celery, cut in half
1 small carrot, cut into quarters
1 small white onion, peeled and cut into quarters
2 teaspoons granulated sugar
2 sprigs fresh parsley
2 to 3 whole peppercorns
2 teaspoons kosher salt
1 bay leaf

Rinse the fish heads and bones under cold running water. In a large stockpot, cover the fish heads and bones with cold water and bring to a boil for 5 minutes, then drain, discarding the liquid and scum. Return the heads and bones to the pot along with all the remaining ingredients and cover with fresh water. Bring to a boil over high heat. Reduce the heat to low and skim off the foam and oil that rises to the top. Simmer for 1 hour. Remove from the heat and strain the stock through a fine-mesh strainer. Discard the solids.

Let the stock sit in the refrigerator for 1 day before using.

The stock can keep in the refrigerator for 3 days or in the freezer for up to 2 months.

Potato Kugel

MAKES 8 TO 10 SERVINGS

¼ cup (½ stick) unsalted butter, plus more softened for baking dish

3 pounds russet potatoes, peeled

1 large Spanish onion, peeled

3 large eggs

1 cup matzo meal

2 teaspoons kosher salt

½ teaspoon freshly ground black pepper

½ teaspoon cream of tartar

The OG Jewish pudding, kugel comes in two variations: savory and sweet. This one is savory, a more direct descendant of the steamed puddings prepared by twelfth-century German housewives who placed a ball of bread batter (*kugel* means ball) atop steaming cholent as it cooked. The resultant pudding soaked up all the aromatics from the stew. In the modern times and with the advent of the oven, steaming gave way to baking, and butter, once expensive, is now accessible (and welcome). But the combination of starch, fat, eggs, and omnipresent onions are the signature flavors of kugel and they have remained constant. Since we serve this potato kugel at the seder we substitute matzo meal for bread, but the same characteristics that have endeared kugels to generations of Jews are here: the crisp hashbrown-like exterior and the soft, just-set custardy interior.

Preheat the oven to 400°F. Grease a 9 by 9-inch ceramic baking dish with softened butter. In a small saucepan (or microwave) melt the remaining butter.

Using a box grater, grate the potatoes and onion into a large mixing bowl. Add the melted butter, eggs, matzo meal, salt, pepper, and cream of tartar and mix thoroughly.

Pour the mixture into the greased baking dish and cover tightly with aluminum foil. Bake for 1 hour. Remove the foil and bake for an additional 15 to 20 minutes, until the top is golden brown and crispy and the center is set. Let cool slightly and serve.

To store, let the kugel fully cool, cover, and keep in the fridge for up to 3 days.

VER ES EST LANG KUGL, DERLEBT LANG. Whoever eats kugel a long time, will live a long time. YIDDISH PROVERB

Brisket

MAKES 6 TO 8 SERVINGS

FOR BRISKET RUB
MAKES SCANT ½ CUP

¼ cup kosher salt
1½ tablespoons ground black pepper
¼ teaspoon cayenne pepper
2 tablespoons onion powder
2 tablespoons garlic powder
1½ teaspoon ground cumin
1½ teaspoon ground coriander
1½ teaspoon smoked paprika

1 piece brisket, 4 to 5 pounds
Brisket Rub (recipe above)
2 tablespoons vegetable oil
2 to 3 stalks celery, chopped into large pieces
1 white onion, chopped into large pieces
2 to 3 carrots, peeled and chopped into large pieces
½ pound button mushrooms, cleaned and trimmed (halved if large)
10 cloves garlic, minced
2 teaspoons dried ginger
2 bay leaves
1 bunch fresh thyme
1 tablespoon kosher salt
1 tablespoon tomato paste
1 cup dry red wine
4 cups chicken stock
1 (15-ounce) can crushed tomatoes

Yes, we are aware. Brisket is meat and appetizing stores don't serve red meat. On the other hand, Russ & Daughters Cafe was never an appetizing store and wasn't meant to be one. It's a restaurant and restaurants do serve meat, delicious meat. When we first opened, our chef prepared a slow-and-low cooked brisket with 7UP and ketchup, a real grandmother version. Over the years, we've experimented with brisket recipes, from more traditional to very involved. Ultimately, the most haimish won out. It's easy to make and even easier to enjoy. After hours in the oven, the meat emerges glistening and bursting with flavor. For years now, this brisket has been the showstopper at our Second Seder, a good answer to "How is this night different than any other night?"

Make the brisket rub by combining all the ingredients together in a small bowl.

Using a small knife, trim any large pieces of fat from the brisket, leaving roughly ¼ inch where possible. Rub the entire brisket generously with the rub and let rest on the counter for 30 minutes.

Preheat the oven to 325°F.

Heat the oil in a large heavy Dutch oven (at least 5½ quarts) over medium heat. Add the brisket, fat side down, and sear on all sides, adjusting heat as needed to avoid burning, until browned, 15 to 18 minutes total.

Remove the brisket and let it rest on a cutting board. In the same Dutch oven, combine the celery, onion, carrots, mushrooms, garlic, ginger, bay leaves, thyme, and salt. Cook, stirring occasionally, until fragrant and beginning to soften, 6 to 8 minutes. (Add a small splash of water if the bottom of the pot is browning too much.) Add the tomato paste and cook, stirring, for 2 minutes. Add the red wine, stock, and crushed tomatoes. Using a wooden spoon, scrape the fond from the bottom of the pan and bring the mixture to a boil.

Return the brisket, fat side up, to the pan. Cover the pot, transfer to oven, and bake until the brisket is very tender (a fork should easily come out when pierced), 3 to 3½ hours. Remove from the oven, uncover, and let the brisket cool for 1 hour. Remove the brisket from the pot and slice into ½-inch pieces.

Strain the sauce from the pan into a pot and remove any fat that rises to the top. (Makes about 3½ cups strained, defatted sauce.)

Place the sliced brisket in an oven-safe serving vessel and cover with the strained sauce. Place back into the oven at 325° for 10 minutes to reheat, and serve.

Chocolate Toffee Matzo

MAKES 20 PIECES

5 whole matzo sheets, about half a 16-ounce box
1 cup (2 sticks) unsalted butter
1 cup packed plus 2 tablespoons brown sugar
¾ cup chopped dark chocolate
2 tablespoons Maldon salt

Like soccer in America, matzo is something we care about intensely at discrete periods of time and very little about in the interim. Unlike the World Cup, which takes place every four years, matzo's moment to shine is Passover. Though we utilize matzo in various forms all year-round—as part of our Matzo Ball Soup (PAGE 45) and fried with egg in our Matzo Brei (PAGE 178)—we burn through matzo at Passover. Because the process of making matzo is minutely described by the Talmud, we do not make our own. Rather we rely on Streit's, another fourth-generation family business, who for many years were our neighbors on the Lower East Side. Matzo, on its own, is a taste acquired over generations. But matzo, dipped in caramel, drizzled with chocolate, and sprinkled with sea salt, is a taste acquired at first bite.

Preheat the oven to 350°F. Line a 13 by 18-inch baking sheet with a piece of parchment paper, spray with noncook cooking spray, and set aside.

Lay the sheets of matzo on a cutting board and lightly score each with a bread knife bilaterally in both directions. Snap each cracker into four even pieces. You should have 20 roughly 3¼-inch squares.

Make your caramel by combining the butter and brown sugar in a small, very clean saucepan over low heat, stirring until melted and evenly incorporated. Continue to stir until the mixture comes to a simmer. Stop stirring and allow it to simmer for 5 minutes, then remove from the heat.

Carefully lay one matzo cracker in the caramel. Using a pair of tongs, carefully lift the cracker and lay the other side in the caramel. Still using the tongs, hold the cracker at an angle over the pot and shake off excess caramel, then lay the coated matzo on the prepared baking sheet. Repeat with the remaining matzo. Transfer to the oven and bake for 8 to 9 minutes, until golden brown. Let the matzo cool.

Melt the dark chocolate in a plastic container in the microwave in 20-second increments, stirring in between, until fully melted. Lightly drizzle the dark chocolate atop the cooled matzo. While the chocolate is still melted, sprinkle the matzo with Maldon salt. Wait until the chocolate hardens and enjoy.

The chocolate toffee matzo will keep in an airtight container at room temperature for 2 weeks.

Flourless Chocolate Cake

MAKES 8 TO 10 SERVINGS

FOR THE CAKE

12 ounces chopped 65 percent dark chocolate or baking wafers

6 tablespoons unsalted butter, plus more softened butter for the pan

1 teaspoon coffee extract

5 large eggs

¾ cup granulated sugar

FOR THE GANACHE

1 cup (8 ounces) chopped 65 percent dark chocolate or baking wafers (not chips)

½ cup heavy cream

¼ cup cocoa powder, for garnish

Some offerings in the Cafe, like the hamantaschen and latkes, started out as holiday-only specialties and were gradually extended throughout the year to become everyday offerings. Not so with the flourless chocolate cake. Because it is so decadent and so rich, we make it only for Passover. The presence of and clamor for this delicious cake reflects the fact that people look to us to provide a beginning-to-end holiday experience. A very small slice goes a very long way, especially when it's made even richer by crumbling Chocolate Toffee Matzo (PAGE 216) on top as a garnish.

Preheat the oven to 350°F with a rack in the center. Butter a 9 by 10-inch springform pan and line the bottom with parchment. Butter the parchment and up the sides of the pan. Wrap the outside bottom and sides of the pan with foil to keep any water from getting in. Place in a larger roasting pan (you'll use this to create a bain marie).

In the top of a double boiler over simmering water, gently melt the chocolate, butter, and coffee extract together. Set aside.

In the bowl of a stand mixer with the balloon whip attachment, whip the eggs and sugar together until pale yellow and roughly doubled in volume. Gradually fold the melted chocolate mixture into the egg and sugar mixture until completely combined. Pour the mixture into the prepared springform pan. Carefully add boiling water to the roasting pan to come about halfway up the sides of the cake pan.

Carefully transfer to the oven and bake for 35 to 40 minutes, until the cake's center is completely set. It should have a dull look to the top, not shiny, and an instant-read thermometer should register at least 200°F when inserted into the cake. Remove from the bain marie and let cool in the pan before extracting the cake.

MAKE GANACHE

Melt the chocolate and cream together in the top of the double boiler over simmering water. Pour the finished ganache over the completely cooled cake. You can choose to smooth the top or leave it rough. Once the ganache has cooled, dust the top of the cake with cocoa powder using a fine-mesh sieve.

The cake can be covered and stored in the fridge for up to 7 days.

Tip: Make sure to use a very sharp knife to slice the cake. Dip the knife in hot water in between each slice and clean the blade completely before attempting more slices.

Coconut Macaroons

MAKES 2 DOZEN

3 cups sweetened shredded coconut

¾ cup sweetened condensed milk

¼ cup coconut flour

1 teaspoon vanilla extract

2 large egg whites

¼ teaspoon kosher salt

¼ teaspoon cream of tartar

Some of what we eat during Passover is custom-made for Passover. Think tsimmes, charoset, and matzo. These are the symbolic foods of Pesach. Macaroons, on the other hand, came to the holiday through fortuitous convenience. The coconut macaroon, synonymous with Passover dessert and begged for at Hebrew schools across America, is the descendant of the Italian amaretti (and a distant cousin of the French macaron). Because it relies on egg whites, as opposed to prohibited leavening agents like flour, the macaroon was quickly embraced by Jews during Passover. Macaroons come in many flavors, from the far-fetched to the canonical, but coconut macaroons are, by far, the most common in the United States, thanks to shrewd shredded coconut macher Franklin Baker, who parlayed a boatload of Cuban coconuts in 1897 into an international coconut concern. We too began serving macaroons only at Pesach but, yielding to popular demand and thanks to the capacity of our bakery, we now offer them year-round. As opposed to canned macaroons—a *shanda*—ours are as fluffy as a pillow, as light as a cloud, and generously apportioned with shredded coconut.

Preheat the oven to 325°F. Line a large baking sheet with parchment paper or lightly grease it.

Combine the shredded coconut, condensed milk, coconut flour, and vanilla in a large mixing bowl and mix until well combined.

In a separate bowl, beat together the egg whites, salt, and cream of tartar until stiff peaks form. This will take a few minutes with an electric mixer on medium-high speed.

Gently fold the whipped egg whites into the coconut mixture until evenly incorporated. Be careful not to deflate the egg whites too much.

Using a spoon or a cookie scoop (about 1½ tablespoons), scoop out about 24 portions (each about the size of a ping-pong ball) of the coconut mixture and drop them onto the prepared baking sheet, leaving some space between each.

Bake for 20 to 25 minutes, until the macaroons are lightly golden brown on the outside. Allow the macaroons to cool on the baking sheet for a few minutes before transferring them to a wire rack to cool completely.

Store any leftover macaroons in an airtight container at room temperature for up to 1 week. They can also be frozen for 2 to 3 months.

VARIATION Chocolate-Covered Macaroons: Melt 12 ounces chopped 65 percent dark chocolate or baking wafers in a plastic container in the microwave in 20-second increments, stirring in between. Working one at a time, dip the tops of the macaroons into the chocolate and place on a parchment-lined baking sheet to cool.

SWEETS

Blintzes

MAKES 12 TO 14 BLINTZES, 6 SERVINGS

FOR THE CREPE BATTER
2 cups whole milk
4 large eggs
1⅓ cups all-purpose flour

FOR THE FILLING
1½ pounds farmer's cheese
½ cup granulated sugar
1 teaspoon pure vanilla extract
¼ teaspoon ground cinnamon

FOR THE BLUEBERRY COMPOTE
2 cups frozen blueberries
2 tablespoons water
¼ cup granulated sugar
½ teaspoon vanilla extract
Grated zest of 1 lemon (1 tablespoon)

TO COOK AND ASSEMBLE
6 to 7 tablespoons unsalted butter

Blintzes are a perfect example of why our Cafe menu has a section called *Sweet* rather than *Dessert*. Blintzes can, and should, be eaten any time of day—breakfast, afternoon snack, or at the end of a meal. Originally, in the Old World, blintzes were a recipe made for Shavuot, the holiday which celebrates both the end of the wheat harvest and the giving of the Ten Commandments on Mount Sinai. An Ashkenazi specialty, the word *blintz* is related to the Russian *blini* and means pancake. By the time they started appearing on the menus of dairy restaurants in the Lower East Side, blintzes had been shorn of their religious overtones. (We've been making them, for instance, for at least the last thirty years.) Who doesn't like a svelte silken pancake which holds soft sweet cheese in its embrace? Why wait an entire (lunar) year when you can eat them all the time? Savory blintzes, theoretically, also exist, frequently filled with mushrooms, but our family only knows them to be sweet, filled with sweetened farmer's cheese and topped with blueberry compote (though your favorite jam will also suffice).

MAKE DOUGH
Combine the milk, eggs, and flour in a blender and process until smooth, or mix by hand with a whisk until all clumps disappear. Strain the crepe batter through a fine-mesh strainer. Cover and refrigerate for at least 1 hour, or up to 1 day.

MAKE FILLING
Combine the farmer's cheese, sugar, vanilla, and cinnamon in a large bowl and mix with a large spoon or sturdy whisk until well combined. Cover and place in refrigerator. (Makes 3¼ cups.)

MAKE BLUEBERRY COMPOTE
Combine all the ingredients in a heavy-bottomed saucepan and stir to combine. Cook over medium heat for 10 minutes, or until the blueberries are just starting to burst. Reduce the heat to low and cook for an additional 5 minutes, until the mixture has reduced slightly. Let cool, then place in a clean jar. (Makes about 1 cup.)

The compote will keep in the refrigerator for up to 3 days.

COOK AND ASSEMBLE
Melt 4 tablespoons of the butter and reserve by your cooktop.

CONTINUED →

Brush a heavy 10-inch nonstick skillet with just enough butter to coat and place over medium heat. When hot, ladle in just enough crepe batter (about ¼ cup) to coat the bottom of the skillet. Tilt and swirl the skillet in a clockwise motion until the batter is evenly spread in a thin layer across the pan. Allow the crepe to cook undisturbed until it is set and a pale color with very little browning, 1 to 2 minutes. Use an offset or nonstick spatula to lift the edge of the crepe, then use your fingers to carefully flip the crepe and cook on other side for just 30 seconds to 1 minute. Place the cooked crepe on a flat plate.

Repeat the process, brushing the skillet with melted butter each time, to make about 12 crepes, stacking them on top of each other on the plate. Let cool to room temperature, then cover with plastic wrap and refrigerate until completely chilled, at least 1 hour, or up to 1 day.

Spoon 2 heaping tablespoons of the chilled filling into the center of one crepe. Fold over a third of the crepe from the right and a third of the crepe from the left and then roll the crepe up from the bottom burrito-style. Set on a plate or tray seam side down and refrigerate, covered, for at least 1 hour.

After the blintzes have rested and set-up in the refrigerator, melt 1 tablespoon butter in a nonstick skillet over medium heat. Working in batches, place the blintzes in the pan, seam side down, making sure they do not touch, and brown gently on one side for 2 minutes. Flip and cook another 2 minutes to brown the other side. Lower the heat to low if the blintzes are browning too quickly. Repeat with the remaining butter to brown all the blintzes.

Serve the blintzes immediately (or rewarm from room temperature for 10 to 15 minutes in a 250°F oven) with the blueberry compote.

Noodle Kugel

MAKES ONE 8" OR 9" SQUARE KUGEL, 8 TO 10 SERVINGS

½ cup golden raisins
8 ounces (5 cups) dry wide egg noodles
8 ounces (1 cup) plain farmer's cheese
8 ounces (1 cup) cream cheese
2 cups sour cream
6 large eggs
¼ cup (½ stick) unsalted butter, melted and cooled
1 teaspoon vanilla extract
1 tablespoon kosher salt
½ cup granulated sugar

Custardy, creamy, and sweet, noodle kugel—also called *lokshen kugel*—has barreled into the Jewish American canon. A quick glance at the ingredients below confirms this is not a dish for the faint of heart—or the intolerant of lactose. Dairy is the hero here, forming the sweet custard in which the egg noodles are suspended. There are, of course, as in all kugels, both savory and sweet versions. The savory was often served hot on Friday and cold on Saturday. This sweet version competes with Babka French Toast (PAGE 231) and Challah Bread Pudding (PAGE 311) for wobbly delicious decadence.

Preheat the oven to 325°F. Place the raisins in a small bowl and cover with hot water.

Meanwhile, bring a large pot of water to boil. Add the egg noodles and cook until tender, 5 to 6 minutes. Drain the noodles and set aside.

Combine the farmer's cheese, cream cheese, sour cream, eggs, melted butter, vanilla extract, and salt in a blender and blend until smooth.

Drain the raisins and toss with the cooked noodles. Place in an 8- or 9-inch square baking dish. Pour the cheese mixture over the noodles, then sprinkle the sugar evenly over the kugel.

Place in the oven, with a baking sheet on the rack below to catch any overflow, and bake for 45 to 50 minutes, until the kugel is set in the middle. Let cool slightly before serving.

Noodle kugel can be stored in the refrigerator for 3 to 5 days.

Lemon Sorbet with Poppy Seeds

MAKES ABOUT 6 CUPS FROZEN SORBET (5 CUPS BASE)

1½ cups water
2 cups granulated sugar
1 teaspoon powdered pectin, such as Sure-Jell original
2 tablespoons triple sec
2 cups fresh lemon juice
1 tablespoon poppy seeds

Poppy seeds, at least in Ashkenazi cuisine, find their highest expression atop bagels and as a paste (called *mohn* in Yiddish) in hamantaschen and other pastries. Their flavor is delicate, nutty, and sweet. Outside of that they are, we think, strangely underutilized. (Except by Hungarians, who make a range of delicious baked goods with poppy seed paste.) Most often they are paired with lemon, whose bright acidity zings off the earthier poppy seeds. There are lemon–poppy seed vinaigrettes and lemon–poppy seed pound cakes and lemon–poppy seed cookies. Why not a lemon–poppy seed sorbet? And, if so, then why not a touch of triple sec? As a rule, Jews don't do palate cleansers. We are a people of accumulation, of history, ours are not palates to be cleansed. However, lemon has always been part of the Russ & Daughters continuum. Grandma Anne used to wash her hands with squeezed lemon at the end of a day at the shop. As a nod to her, here, we use lemon sorbet as a cleanser to cut through the richness of smoked salmon.

Bring the water to simmer in a medium pot. Add the sugar and pectin, stirring to dissolve. Remove from the heat, transfer to a nonreactive bowl, and cool slightly, about 10 minutes. Stir in the triple sec, lemon juice, and poppy seeds. Cool to room temperature. Cover and refrigerate for at least 4 hours, or until the mixture is 40°F to 43°F degrees.

Once the mixture is completely chilled, process it in your ice cream machine according to the manufacturer's instructions. Transfer to a large airtight container and freeze at least 2 hours before serving. The sorbet keeps in the freezer for a month.

Ice Creams

MAKES 1¾ QUARTS (7 CUPS) ICE CREAM (ABOUT 5 CUPS CUSTARD BASE)

FOR THE CUSTARD BASE
2 cups whole milk
¾ cup granulated sugar
1 teaspoon kosher salt
8 large egg yolks
2 cups heavy cream
Flavoring of choice (see below)

HALVAH FLAVORING
½ pound marble halvah, crumbled

BLACK & WHITE COOKIE FLAVORING
4 Black & White Cookies (PAGE 303), 12 ounces, crumbled

CARAMEL APPLE FLAVORING
4 Granny Smith apples (1½ pounds), peeled, cored, and diced (4 cups)
⅓ cup granulated sugar
Water
3 tablespoons unsalted butter
1 tablespoon heavy cream
1 teaspoon vanilla extract
1 teaspoon ground cinnamon

For obvious reasons, ice cream has not been part of the traditional appetizing canon. First, it melts. Second, 75 percent of Ashkenazi Jews are lactose-intolerant. But, that's nothing a little Lactaid can't help.

When we opened the Cafe, we wanted to incorporate some of our signature flavors into ice cream, which we had never been able to do at the store. We started with halvah, which we knew we wanted on the menu in some form. Simply crumbling it into a rich ice cream base, it turns out, was the answer. From there, we broadened our mix-ins to incorporate the vaguely Rosh Hashanahian caramel apple and the classic black & white cookie. We serve them as single scoops and in various other configurations, as in between two slices of babka (PAGE 305) as a sandwich.

MAKE CUSTARD BASE
Combine the milk, sugar, and salt and in a medium saucepan. Bring to a simmer over medium heat, just until small bubbles start to form around the edge of the saucepan. Remove from the heat.

In a bowl, whisk the egg yolks, then slowly whisk in 1 cup of the hot milk mixture to temper the eggs. Once the mixture is warm to the touch, slowly pour the eggs back into the saucepan. Cook over medium-low heat, stirring constantly with a wooden spoon, until it reaches about 170°F, 3 to 4 minutes. It should have the consistency of heavy cream and be thick enough to retain a line drawn across the back of the spoon with your finger.

Pour the heavy cream into a large bowl, then slowly whisk in the custard mixture. Mix well, lay a piece of plastic wrap directly on top of the custard, and cool to room temperature. Chill in the refrigerator overnight, or until the custard reaches 40°F to 43°F. The custard base will keep in the refrigerator for up to 3 days.

FOR THE ICE CREAMS
Process the completely chilled mixture in an ice cream maker according to the manufacturer's instructions, stirring in the flavoring (see options at left) in the last 3 minutes of churning. Transfer to a large airtight container and freeze for at least 2 hours before serving.

Ice cream can be kept, frozen obviously, in the freezer for up to 1 month.

MAKE CARAMEL APPLE FLAVORING

Heat a large nonstick pan over medium heat. Add the apples and cook, stirring occasionally, until they begin to caramelize, 10 to 15 minutes. Add a splash of water to deglaze and continue cooking, deglazing with a small amount of water as necessary, until the apples are golden and soft and begin to lose their form, 15 to 20 minutes more. Remove from the heat and set aside.

Meanwhile, make a caramel sauce: In a very clean small sauce pot, sprinkle the sugar in an even layer and cover it with just enough water to completely saturate the sugar (about 2 tablespoons). Make sure there are no sugar crystals stuck to the sides of the pan (you can use a wet pastry brush to brush the crystals off the side of the pan if they form). Heat the sugar and water over medium-high heat, without stirring, and bring the mixture to a boil. Cook, swirling the pan occasionally but not stirring it, until the sugar turns a light amber and a candy thermometer registers between 340°F and 350°, about 10 minutes. Remove from the heat and immediately stir in the butter and then the cream (it will foam briefly) until the caramel takes on a lustrous texture.

Fold the applesauce into the caramel sauce, transfer to a nonreactive container, and cool to room temperature.

Stir the apple mixture, the vanilla extract, and the cinnamon into the custard base in the last 3 minutes of churning in the machine.

Blueberry Kasha Crumble

MAKES ONE 9" SQUARE DISH, 6 SERVINGS

FOR THE CRUMBLE
½ cup buckwheat flour
½ cup packed brown sugar
½ teaspoon kosher salt
½ cup (1 stick) cold unsalted butter
½ cup rolled oats
⅓ cup puffed kasha (see Note)

FOR THE BLUEBERRY FILLING
4 cups blueberries
Grated zest and juice of 1 lemon
⅓ cup granulated sugar
2 teaspoons cornstarch

Whipped cream, for serving

Is it the healthiest dessert in the world? No, no it is not. Is it the most decadent? Also no. Traditional? Not really. Innovative? Hardly. What blueberry kasha crumble is, however, is a perfect balance between savory and sweet. The buckwheat flour and kasha—often seen in Kasha Varnishkas (PAGE 167) but rarely as a sweet cameo as it is here—prevent the crumble from becoming cloying. An embarrassment of blueberries, made oozy by the oven, commingle with the crumble, and a dollop of whipped cream provides immeasurable pleasure.

MAKE DOUGH
Whisk together the buckwheat flour, brown sugar, and salt in a large bowl. Cut in the butter with a pastry cutter or your fingertips until evenly worked through. Add the oats and puffed kasha, stirring to combine.

MAKE FILLING
Gently mix together the blueberries, lemon zest and juice, sugar, and cornstarch in a large bowl and set aside.

TO ASSEMBLE AND BAKE
Preheat the oven to 375°F with a rack in the center.

Pour the blueberry filling into a 9-inch square (2½-quart) baking dish. It should reach halfway up the sides. Squeeze the crumble dough into clumps with your hands and scatter over the top of the filling.

Bake until browned and bubbling, 40 to 45 minutes. Let cool for 15 minutes, then serve with dollops of homemade whipped cream.

Note: Packaged puffed kasha is also called *puffed buckwheat*. If you can't find it, substitute rolled oats. The buckwheat flour will still bring the kasha flavor, it will just be more subtle.

Babka French Toast

MAKES 8 SERVINGS

1 Chocolate or Cinnamon Babka (PAGE 305), cut into 1½-inch slices

3 large eggs

1½ cups milk

2 tablespoons granulated sugar

1 tablespoon vanilla extract

1½ teaspoons kosher salt

4 tablespoons (½ stick) unsalted butter

Topping of choice

TOPPINGS FOR CHOCOLATE BABKA

1½ cups fresh berries

6 ounces (¾ cup) crème fraîche

TOPPINGS FOR CINNAMON BABKA

CANDIED WALNUTS

1½ cups shelled walnuts

3 cups water

½ cup granulated sugar

1½ tablespoons unsalted butter, softened

Kosher salt to taste

APPLE COMPOTE

3 large Granny Smith apples, peeled, cored, and roughly chopped

¼ cup granulated sugar

1 cinnamon stick

1 teaspoon vanilla extract

1 teaspoon kosher salt

Water as needed

When we opened the Cafe it seemed only natural to exploit the possibilities of babka in all its various iterations. Essentially a sweet challah with toppings already folded into it, we quickly found it makes for a decadent French toast, one of the most popular items on the menu, frequently split (and often fought over) by a table. Chocolate babka pairs well with fresh berries and crème fraîche, while the slightly more autumnal cinnamon babka is accompanied by candied walnuts and an apple compote. But either one is just as delicious with simply a pat of warm butter slowly melting into the warm French toast.

Slice the babka and lay the slices out on a rack to dry slightly. In a large bowl, whisk together the eggs, milk, sugar, vanilla extract, and salt. Submerge each slice of babka in the batter for a minute or two, flipping the slice halfway through, until the slice is totally saturated. Be careful not to leave it too long, or it will fall apart.

Heat the butter in skillet over medium-high heat. Once hot, cook the babka about 3 minutes a side, or until golden brown, making sure not to crowd the pan.

Transfer the French toast to a warm serving plate.

Shingle the French toast on a serving plate. For the chocolate babka, top with the berries and whipped cream. For the cinnamon babka, top with the candied walnuts and apple compote.

CONTINUED →

CANDIED WALNUTS

Preheat the oven to 350°F.

Spread the walnuts on a baking sheet and toast in the oven for 10 minutes, until lightly brown and toasted.

In a medium pot, bring the water to boil over high heat. Add ¼ cup of the sugar and stir to dissolve. Add the walnuts and boil for 3 minutes. Strain and set aside.

Toss the nuts in a bowl with the remaining ¼ cup sugar, the butter, and the salt. Transfer to the baking sheet and bake again for 12 to 14 minutes, stirring roughly halfway through, until they are dry and golden brown. They will become crispy as they cool.

APPLE COMPOTE

Combine the apples, sugar, cinnamon, and a splash of water in a large wide pot. Cook over high heat, stirring occasionally, until all the liquid has evaporated, 5 to 7 minutes. Continue cooking as the apples caramelize at the bottom of the pan. Deglaze the pan with another splash of water, scraping the bottom to mix the browned bits in with the apples. Repeat this process of deglazing and scraping until the apples are golden brown. This will take about 8 to 10 minutes.

Mix in the vanilla extract and salt. Then cool completely.

The apple compote will keep in the refrigerator for 5 days.

DRINKS

EGG CREAMS

THE EGG CREAM, the most New York of all refreshments, was born a few blocks away from Russ & Daughters at Louis Auster's candy store on 2nd Avenue and 7th Street. The year was 1890, and the Lower East Side was chockablock with dairy restaurants, candy shops, and soda fountains. Auster's original concoction, milk and seltzer, yielded a splendid raft of bubbles and the name—egg cream—which has befuddled imbibers ever since. Theories abound as to how the egg-less, cream-less beverage became known as an egg cream. Some think egg is a derivation of the Yiddish *echt* (meaning genuine or real); others posit egg cream comes from a mangle pronunciation of chocolat et crème, a similar Parisian beverage. Regardless of the etymology, Auster's drink was an immediate sensation and upon it he built an empire for his six sons. His egg cream grew even more iconic when, in 1895, he added a chocolate syrup manufactured by Herman Fox of H. Fox and Company in Brownsville, Brooklyn.

The fortunes of the egg cream rose and fell with the dairy restaurants of the Lower East Side, itself tied to the popularity of the Yiddish theatre. As the Yiddish Rialto, as 2nd Avenue was known, faded, so too did the popularity of the egg cream. But by then, the drink had been caught up in the American jet stream. We had been making egg creams for years at the store, but when we opened the Cafe, we knew we had the chance to delve deeper. At first, we experimented making our own chocolate syrup with high-quality couverture chocolate. But it became immediately clear: a chocolate egg cream is not a chocolate egg cream without Fox's U-Bet.

It is an unspoken rule of egg cream purveyors that they will claim their egg cream is the best egg cream. We are no different. However, our egg creams are the best in New York. The secret, such as it is for so simple a drink, is the temperature. Everything—the glass, the milk, and the seltzer—must be very cold for the proper foam to form; and an egg cream is not meant to be nursed but downed, before its foamy head dissipates.

Chocolate Egg Cream

MAKES 1 SERVING

2 ounces Fox's U-Bet chocolate syrup, very cold
4 ounces whole milk, very cold
Plain seltzer, very cold

Add the Fox's U-Bet to a tumbler, then the milk. Fill the glass three-fourths full with a slow stream of seltzer. Allow a moment for the fizzing to subside, then fill to the top.

Using a bar spoon, stir in a front-to-back (not circular) motion until the Fox's U-Bet, milk, and seltzer are combined. Serve immediately.

Buxar Egg Cream

MAKES 1 SERVING
2 ounces Buxar Syrup (BELOW)
4 ounces whole milk
Plain seltzer

Buxar, or bokser, is Yiddish for carob, a vaguely chocolate-like pod familiar to the children of hippies, who use carob as a healthy chocolate alternative, and Jews, who traditionally eat carob on Tu B'Shevat. Though not as toothsome as chocolate, buxar's taste nevertheless is nostalgic and dear.

Add the buxar syrup to a tumbler, then the milk. Fill the glass three-fourths full with a slow stream of seltzer. Allow a moment for the fizzing to subside, then fill to the top.

Using a bar spoon, stir in a front-to-back (not circular) motion until the syrup, milk, and seltzer are combined. Serve immediately.

MAKES 16 SERVINGS
3 cups carob molasses
1 cup Simple Syrup (PAGE 251)

BUXAR SYRUP

Combine the molasses and syrup in a container and whisk well. Buxar syrup will keep in the refrigerator for up to 3 to 5 weeks.

Malt Egg Cream

MAKES 1 SERVING
2 ounces Malt Syrup (BELOW)
4 ounces whole milk
Plain seltzer

The roasted toasted flavor of malted milk—made with evaporated milk powder, barley, and wheat flour—is familiar to all malted milk ball aficionados and anyone who has enjoyed a malted milkshake. Here, those flavors get an effervescent kick.

Add the malt syrup to a tumbler, then the milk. Fill the glass three-fourths full with a slow stream of seltzer. Allow a moment for the fizzing to subside, then fill to the top.

Using a bar spoon, stir in a front-to-back (not circular) motion until the syrup, milk, and seltzer are combined. Serve immediately.

MAKES 10 SERVINGS
2 cups granulated sugar
2 cups water
1⅓ cups malted milk powder

MALT SYRUP

Combine the sugar and water in a small sauce pot and bring to boil over high heat. Add the malted milk powder and whisk until the powder is completely dissolved and the syrup is clear. Remove from the heat and let cool.

The malt syrup keeps in the refrigerator for up to 2 to 3 weeks.

Fershnikit Egg Cream

MAKES 1 SERVING

2 ounces chilled chocolate whiskey

1 tablespoon Fox's U-Bet chocolate syrup

4 ounces whole milk

Plain seltzer

Egg creams are the drinks of youth and innocence. But they're perhaps even *more* enjoyable when mixed up with—*fershnikit* means drunk—a shot of chocolate whiskey. We use whiskey from Kings County Distillery, our neighbors at the Brooklyn Navy Yard and the oldest distillery in New York State. (But if you can't find chocolate whiskey, any whiskey will do.)

Add the whiskey and Fox's U-Bet to a tumbler, then add milk. Fill the glass three-fourths full with a slow stream of seltzer. Allow a moment for the fizzing to subside, then fill to the top.

Using a bar spoon, stir in a front-to-back (not circular) motion until the whiskey, syrup, milk, and seltzer are combined. Serve immediately.

Vanilla Egg Cream

MAKES 1 SERVING

2 ounces Vanilla Syrup (below)

4 ounces whole milk

Plain seltzer

Add the vanilla syrup to a tumbler, then the milk. Fill the glass three-fourths full with a slow stream of seltzer. Allow a moment for the fizzing to subside, then fill to the top.

Using a bar spoon, stir in a front-to-back (not circular) motion until the syrup, milk, and seltzer are combined. Serve immediately.

MAKES 1½ CUPS

1 vanilla bean

1 cup demerara sugar

1 cup hot water

VANILLA SYRUP

Split the vanilla bean lengthwise. Add the whole vanilla bean and seeds and the sugar to a small sauté pan. Add the hot water, bring the mix to a boil to dissolve the sugar, then cool and refrigerate. Allow the syrup to sit for at least 48 hours before using. Do not strain.

Keep in an airtight container in the refrigerator for up to 1 month.

SHRUBS

IT WAS SIMPLE STAR-CROSSED FATE, perhaps, that shrubs—a genre of vinegar and fruit drinks dating back to the Middle Ages—had never before been paired with appetizing. Both traditions rely on the edifying properties of vinegar. One for making pickles, the other to add a delightful and refreshing tartness to beverages. As for our commingling of the two, one day during a scorching humid summer day at the shop, one of our employees, looking to cool down, went into the walk-in refrigerator and poured herself some of the pinkish brine that was pickling our beets. She squeezed in some lemon and a bit of sugar. The drink was so good she passed it around to the other employees who, unsurprisingly, were equal parts grateful and refreshed. Only later, upon further research, did we realize we had re-created the ancient shrub. When we first started selling the beet and lemon shrub, it was not well known at all and you hardly ever saw it on menus. But now, we like to think we helped put shrubs back on the map.

Once we opened the Cafe, we let our shrub interest blossom to include other flavors: cherry, pineapple, mango, watermelon. Effervescent, bracing, with an equilibrium between sweetness and acidity, shrubs are easy to make, once you prepare the syrup.

Unless otherwise noted, make shrubs by combining 1½ ounces shrub base with 8 ounces seltzer. Serve cold over ice; or for an adult version, cold over ice with a shot of vodka.

Beet & Lemon Shrub Base

MAKES 2 QUARTS
1 cup lemon juice
1 cup Simple Syrup (PAGE 251)
2 cups Pickled Beet Juice (below)
4 cups water

Mix together all the ingredients and stir until combined.

The shrub will keep in the refrigerator for 7 days.

MAKES 1½ QUARTS
2 quarts water
2 large beets, peeled and diced
3 tablespoons distilled white vinegar
3 tablespoons granulated sugar
2 teaspoons kosher salt

PICKLED BEET JUICE

Bring the water to a boil in a large sauce pot. Add the beets and boil for 15 to 20 minutes, until fork-tender. Remove the pot from heat and stir in the vinegar, sugar, and salt until dissolved.

Transfer the entire mixture to a nonreactive container and refrigerate, covered, for 48 hours.

Strain the liquid, reserving the boiled beets for another use.

The beet juice will keep in the refrigerator for up to 2 weeks.

Pineapple Shrub Base

MAKES 3 CUPS

1 whole very ripe fresh pineapple, peeled, cored, and cut into large chunks
2 cups sherry vinegar
2 cups water
2 cups granulated sugar
2 leaves fresh sage, whole
2 sprigs fresh rosemary, whole

Combine the pineapple, sherry vinegar, and water in a large sauce pot and bring to a boil over medium-high heat. Reduce the heat and simmer for 1 hour. Cool to room temperature then refrigerate for 48 hours.

Strain the liquid through a fine-mesh sieve, pressing down on the fruit to extract as much liquid as possible. Place the strained syrup in a sauce pot and add the sugar. Bring to a simmer over medium heat, then simmer for 1 hour, or until reduced by 25 percent. Let cool, then add the sage and rosemary, allowing the herbs to infuse for another 24 hours. Strain.

The shrub will keep in the refrigerator for up to 2 weeks.

Mango Shrub Base

MAKES 3 CUPS

½ pound packed dried mangoes, roughly chopped
1 fresh ripe mango, peeled (pits included)
½ quart Champagne vinegar
2 cups water
3 tablespoons whole white peppercorns
1½ teaspoons dill seeds
1½ teaspoons coriander seeds
1½ teaspoons fennel seeds
3 cups granulated sugar
Grated zest and juice of 1 orange

Combine all the ingredients in a large pot and bring to a boil over high heat. Reduce the heat to medium and simmer for 1 hour, or until reduced by a quarter.

Transfer to a large nonreactive container and cool to room temperature. Cover with foil or a tight-fitting lid and let sit overnight at room temperature.

Strain to remove the solids, pressing down to extract as much liquid as possible.

The mango shrub will keep in the refrigerator for up to 4 weeks.

Cherry Shrub Base

MAKES 3 CUPS

1 pound dried cherries
4 cups granulated sugar
4 cups white balsamic vinegar
2 cups water
1 tablespoon Szechuan peppercorns
1 tablespoon star anise
1 tablespoon anise seeds

Combine all the ingredients in a sauce pot and bring to a boil over high heat. Reduce the heat to medium-low and simmer for 1½ hours. Let cool, then strain, pressing down on the fruit to extract as much liquid as possible.

The cherry shrub will keep in the refrigerator for up to 4 weeks.

SODAS

WE ALWAYS ENVISIONED the bar at the Cafe as an old-fashioned soda counter, where you happened to be able to nosh and enjoy some cocktails too. The soda counter tradition hails from roughly the same time frame as Russ & Daughters, beginning in the 1920s and peaking in the 1950s, in the same borough and with a similar sort of wholesomeness. Haimish but sophisticated. Like our shrubs, our sodas are based on homemade syrups mixed with seltzer. In the shop we carbonate our own. At home, we recommend Vintage seltzer, which has an aggressive bubble. But the most important things are that you choose *seltzer*, not sparkling water or club soda, and that it is extremely cold. Though the syrups are best made at scale and take a little bit of work, they last for a month and there's nothing better than a homemade soda. Unless otherwise noted, make sodas by combining 1½ ounces syrup and 6 ounces seltzer. Serve cold over ice or, for an adult version, cold over ice with a shot of vodka.

Coffee Syrup

MAKES 1½ CUPS

2 cups freshly ground coffee
2 cups granulated sugar
2 cups freshly brewed coffee

Mix all the ingredients in a large mixing bowl until dissolved and refrigerate overnight. The following day, transfer the mixture to a large saucepan and bring to a boil over high heat. Reduce the heat to medium-low and simmer for 1 hour, until reduced by half. Strain through a fine-mesh strainer and refrigerate.

The syrup will keep refrigerated for up to 1 month.

Lemon-Lime Syrup

MAKES 3 CUPS

Grated zest and juice of
 5 large lemons
Grated zest and juice of
 5 large limes
2 cups granulated sugar
1 cup water
1 tablespoon cardamom pods
1 tablespoon anise seeds
2 teaspoons dill seeds

Mix the lemon and lime zests with the sugar in a small bowl, cover, and refrigerate overnight.

In a small saucepan, mix the sugar-zest mixture, lemon and lime juices, and water and stir thoroughly until the sugar is dissolved. Bring to a simmer over medium heat. Remove from the heat and cool completely. Strain through a fine-mesh strainer.

In an airtight container, combine the mixture with the cardamom, anise, and dill and refrigerate for 24 hours. Strain once more through a fine-mesh strainer to remove the spices.

The syrup will keep in the refrigerator for up to 1 month.

To make the soda, mix 1 ounce syrup with 6 ounces seltzer and stir.

Jasmine Syrup

MAKES 2½ CUPS
2 cups water
2 cups granulated sugar
2 tablespoons jasmine pearl tea leaves
1 tablespoon fennel seeds
2 teaspoons anise seeds
2 teaspoons dill seeds

In a large saucepan, mix the water, sugar, and tea and bring to a simmer over medium heat. As soon as the mixture begins to simmer and the sugar is fully dissolved, turn off the heat and let steep for 30 minutes. Strain the mixture through a fine-mesh strainer and let cool completely.

Add the fennel, anise, and dill seeds and refrigerate, covered, overnight. Strain again the next day and store.

The syrup will keep in the refrigerator for 1 month.

JASMINE CUCUMBER SODA

MAKES 1 SERVING
4 slices cucumber
3 tablespoons fresh lime juice
2 tablespoons Jasmine Syrup (above)
Seltzer

Muddle the cucumber in a cocktail shaker then add the lime juice and jasmine syrup. Shake lightly and strain into a 10-ounce glass. Top with the seltzer.

Ginger Lavender Syrup

MAKES 3 CUPS
1 cup roughly chopped peeled fresh ginger
1 cup granulated sugar
1 quart water
2 teaspoons dried lavender

Blend the ginger and sugar in a blender or food processor until it has a coarse sandy texture. Mix the ginger-sugar mixture, water, and lavender in a small pot over medium heat until dissolved. Let sit for 24 hours, then strain and refrigerate.

The ginger lavender syrup will keep, tightly covered, in the refrigerator for 1 month.

Grape Syrup

MAKES 3 CUPS
1 (46-ounce) bottle Welch's grape juice
4 cups sugar
1 tablespoon ground timut pepper
1 tablespoon jasmine pearl tea leaves

Combine the grape juice and sugar in a saucepan and bring to a boil over medium heat. Simmer until the liquid is reduced to half of its original volume. Add the timut pepper and simmer over medium-low heat for 1 hour. Remove from the heat, add the tea, and let stand for 24 hours. Strain.

The grape syrup will keep in the refrigerator for 1 month.

COCKTAILS

ALCOHOL AND APPETIZING have always—and sometimes raucously—gone together. Nothing beats caviar and a martini. But generally speaking, what accompanied smoked fish, pickles, and black bread spread with schmaltz was clear hard liquor. A shot of slivovitz, a plum brandy; a bottle of vodka with two shot glasses. The cocktail, in the sense of a well-balanced and carefully considered combination of spirit and mixers, was uncommon. Though we're not a cocktail bar—let alone a cocktail den—cocktails are important to us at the Cafe. When we opened we devised a list that played off the classics while injecting a little shtetl chic. Of course, there will always be a round glass bottle of slivovitz behind the counter. But now that's just one option of many.

Lower East Side

MAKES 1 SERVING

3 (¼-inch-thick) slices of cucumber
2 ounces Tanqueray gin
¾ ounce lime juice
¾ ounce Simple Syrup (recipe below)
2 small sprigs fresh dill

The genesis of a cocktail can read at times as biblical. The Southside, hailing from Chicago and supposedly Al Capone's drink of choice, is basically a gin gimlet with mint that was made popular by New York's "21" Club. The Southside begat the Eastside, with the addition of cucumber. And the Eastside begat our own version, the Lower East Side, in which the classic Old World flavor of dill is substituted for the mint. It's a way for us to pay homage both to our cuisine and to our neighborhood and update a classic cocktail with a refreshing savory twist.

Fill a coupe glass with ice and set aside.

Muddle the cucumber in a cocktail shaker. Add the gin, lime juice, simple syrup, and sprigs of dill. Fill with ice and shake hard.

Pour the ice from the coupe. Strain the cocktail through a fine-mesh sieve into the chilled coupe and garnish with a dill leaf.

MAKES 1½ CUPS

1 cup granulated sugar
1 cup water

SIMPLE SYRUP

Combine the sugar and water in a small saucepan over medium heat. Stir until dissolved. Let cool.

The simple syrup keeps in the refrigerator up to 1 month.

Escubac Fizz

MAKES 1 SERVING

¾ ounce lemon juice
¾ ounce Ginger Lavender Syrup (PAGE 248)
¾ ounce Pickled Beet Juice (PAGE 242)
2 ounces Luksusowa vodka
¾ ounce Escubac
1 large egg white
Slice of raw beet, for garnish

The most classic fizz—that is, a cocktail with an acidic juice topped with soda water—is a gin fizz. When an egg white is added, for increased creaminess and a beautiful foamy head, it becomes a silver fizz. (Add a yolk and it's a golden fizz.) Here, instead of gin we use vodka and Escubac, an alcohol that sits at the intersection of a gin, an aquavit, and an herbal liquor. But the star is really the beet, which lends the drink not only its rubicund color but the earthy notes that pair so well with the delicate ginger lavender syrup.

Place the lemon juice, ginger lavender syrup, beet juice, vodka, Escubac, and egg white in a cocktail shaker and give a hard shake. Add ice and shake, gently this time, until the shaker is cold to the touch. Strain into a coupe glass and let the foam settle slightly before garnishing with a slice of raw beet and serving.

Heads & Tails

MAKES 1 SERVING

Spiced Salt (recipe below), for the rim
1½ ounces Espolòn Blanco tequila
½ ounce Del Maguey Vida mezcal
¼ Dolin dry vermouth
¾ ounce Lemon-Lime Syrup (PAGE 247)

Like the Naked and Famous of the twenty-first century, the Heads & Tails is a classic four-ingredient cocktail in which each element finds equilibrium with the other three. Riffing on the idea of heads and tails—being parts of the fish we eat at Rosh Hashanah, the "head" of the New Year—we feature mezcal, which comes from the head of agave plants. The smokiness of mezcal and the pop of spice from the salt also happen to be a beautiful complement to our smoked fish.

Rim a rocks glass with the spiced salt.

Combine the tequila, mezcal, vermouth, and lemon-lime syrup in a metal bar mixing canister, fill with ice, and then give a couple of hard shakes. Strain into the prepared glass.

SPICED SALT

MAKES ½ CUP

5 tablespoons kosher salt
1½ tablespoons granulated sugar
1 tablespoon freshly ground black pepper
½ tablespoon ground chipotle pepper

Combine all the ingredients and fold together so flavors are evenly distributed.

Schmoozer

MAKES 1 SERVING

1½ ounces Dickel rye whisky
½ ounce Linie aquavit
¼ ounce Demerara Syrup (below)
5 dashes Peychaud's bitters
3 dashes Angostura bitters
Herbsaint, for rinsing
Lemon twist

When he's not at work, one of Josh's favorite cocktails is the Sazerac. The Schmoozer is our version of that New Orleans classic, but substitutes the cognac with Linie aquavit, a Nordic potato-based liquor with notes of caraway and other herbaceous aromatics that echo some of our familiar flavors. It's like a Sazerac but more haimish.

Place ice in a rocks glass and set aside.

Combine the rye, aquavit, demerara syrup, and bitters in a mixing glass with ice. Give it an extended stir, about 20 seconds, until about an ounce of dilution has occurred.

Pour the ice from the rocks glass and rinse with the Herbsaint. Strain the cocktail into the chilled glass. Wring the lemon twist to release oils, slap the entire rim of the glass, then discard the twist.

MAKES 1½ CUPS

1 cup demerara sugar
1 cup water

DEMERARA SYRUP

Combine the sugar and water in a small saucepan over medium heat. Stir until dissolved. The simple syrup keeps in the refrigerator up to 1 month.

Smoked Martini

MAKES 1 SERVING

Laphroaig whisky, for rinsing
1 ounce Perry's Tot gin
½ ounce Belvedere vodka
½ ounce Cocchi Americano aperitif
½ ounce Lillet Blanc aperitif

At Russ & Daughters we traffic in smoke in all its forms: hot smokes, as in the kippered salmon; and cold smokes, as in our lox. But it wasn't until we opened the Cafe and created our cocktail list that we thought of peated smoke. This classic martini gets its smokiness from Laphroaig, a Scottish whisky from Islay, famous for the peat from its bogs. It's a beautiful echo from glass to platter.

Fill a coupe glass with ice and set aside to chill. Once chilled, pour out the ice and rinse with the Laphroaig, swirling the whisky in the glass until the sides are coated.

Combine the gin, vodka, and both aperitifs in a mixing glass with ice. Stir until about an ounce of dilution has occurred, about 30 seconds. Strain into the coupe and serve.

Maror Martini

MAKES 1 SERVING

1½ ounces Beefeater gin
½ ounce Escubac
½ ounce Cocchi Americano aperitif
½ ounce Cheverny Blanc or other dry white wine
1 sprig fresh parsley, for garnish

Maror refers to the five bitter herbs on a seder plate that symbolize the bitterness of slavery. Traditionally, parsley is not one of them. But making a classic day-into-night martini isn't exactly in the Haggadah either. This riff on an Eventide martini—traditionally gin and Cocchi Americano—features Escubac, a botanical-forward nonjunipered gin-like spirit, and Cheverny, a dry white wine from the Loire valley. It's mellow and complex. The parsley here, far from reminding us of any ancestral bitterness, is just a lovely garnish.

Pour the gin, Escubac, Cocchi Americano, and Cheverny in a mixing glass with ice cubes. Stir well. Strain into a chilled martini cocktail glass and garnish with the parsley.

Break Fast Martini

MAKES 1 SERVING

¾ ounce lemon juice
½ ounce Simple Syrup (PAGE 251)
1 teaspoon bitter orange jam
1 large egg white
2 ounces Beefeater gin
Pernod absinthe, for rinsing
Angostura bitters, for garnish

The breakfast martini is a classic cocktail, invented by Salvatore Calabrese in the mid-1990s at London's Lanesborough Hotel. More of a corpse reviver than a proper martini, the drink combines the sweetness of orange jam, the acidity of lemon juice, and the clean flavors of gin. Our Break Fast Martini uses Calabrese's classic as a base, but adds egg white foam. It's a perfect way to break the fast, or simply unwind.

Place ice in a coupe glass and set aside.

Combine the lemon juice, simple syrup, and orange jam in a cocktail shaker.

Place the egg white in the top half of a cocktail shaker. Add the gin to the juice mixture in the bottom half of the shaker.

Combine the two halves and give an extended dry shake, at least 30 seconds, until you feel the top of the canister lift a little from the egg whites expanding. Open the canister, add ice, and shake to chill.

Remove the ice from the chilled coupe and rinse the coupe with the absinthe. Strain the martini into the coupe. Garnish with three dots of Angostura bitters, then use a toothpick to make a fishtail design.

Bloody Mary

MAKES 1 SERVING

10 ounces tomato juice

1 tablespoon minced fresh horseradish

2 teaspoons apple cider vinegar

2 teaspoons lemon juice

2 teaspoons Worcestershire sauce

2 teaspoons freshly ground black pepper

¾ teaspoon kosher salt

1½ teaspoons freshly ground black pepper

2 ounces infused Luksusowa vodka (below)

1 sprig fresh dill, for garnish

1 stalk celery, for garnish

Appetizing is a breakfast tradition; drinking really shouldn't be. But a cocktail that nods toward the morning while edging closer to noon? Perfect. Our Bloody Marys are what we call *serialized*. They rely not on a singular bracing base but on one of four types of infused vodka for their flavor. Some of these flavors, like caraway and dill, are well known to the flavor palate of appetizing. Others, like fenugreek and smoked pepper, are simply delicious and complementary notes.

Combine all the ingredients in a tumbler and serve over ice in a highball glass. Garnish with the dill and celery.

Vodka Infusions

CARAWAY

¼ cup caraway seeds

DILL

8 large sprigs of dill, stems removed

FENUGREEK

¼ cup fenugreek seeds

SMOKED PEPPER

2 dried chipotle peppers

Infuse 1 quart Luksusowa vodka with one of the four infusions to the left for at least 24 hours, then strain. Flavors will intensify the longer they steep, so they may need to be diluted with plain vodka.

The infused vodka will keep in the refrigerator for 3 months.

In 2013, around the time we opened the Cafe, we began to realize our voracious appetite for baked goods could no longer be satisfied by outside suppliers. We powered through bagels, hoovered through bialys, and blasted through babka with the ferocity of a hungry city. Finding suppliers who lived up to our very demanding specifications was proving to be difficult. All that stood between us and our very own bakery was space, effort, time, work, money, and expertise. In other words, we could do it.

In the summer of 2015, we rented a 5,000-square-foot space in Bushwick, Brooklyn, as a temporary solution. We brought out of retirement one of the last old-school bagel makers—an Irish American former-cop-turned-bagelmeister named Jeff Baynon who used to run the legendary Columbia Bagels—to work with us as a consultant. Jeff held that intangible fingertip feeling for how to make bagels, holding the recipes and measurements in his head. For one very hot summer, Jeff showed us the ropes in a Bushwick basement. But the situation was untenable. The heat was scorching, the humidity was 100 percent, and we had already outgrown the site's production capabilities. We needed a real bakery and a long-term home.

On a long-neglected strip of the Brooklyn waterfront, a solution presented itself in the form of the Brooklyn Navy Yard. The Navy Yard was once one of the largest naval shipyards in America. Founded in 1801 by President John Adams, its dry docks and fabrication workshops built seminal American battleships, from wooden to ironclad to steel. During the height of its activity, in World War II, the Navy Yard employed nearly 70,000 people. Cavernous buildings, designed by the U.S. Army Corps of Engineers, held materiel from tanks to ammunitions. But in 1966 the facility was decommissioned, and the nearly three hundred acres languished in a diminished state for years. By the late '90s, however, new light industrial tenants began to move in. In 2004, Steiner Studios, a film studio, transformed a series of massive warehouses into soundstages. And by the time we were in the market for a spot for our bakery, the Navy Yard was looking to fill the nearly million-square-foot former navy warehouse called Building 77.

Through a customer, Hank Gutman, who happened to be the chairman of the Brooklyn Navy Yard Development Corporation, we were invited to take a tour of the raw space on a cold day in January 2015. What you see today—a sun-flooded elegant industrial corridor connecting Flushing Avenue to the interior of the Navy Yard and lined with food vendors and cozy places to sit—hardly resembles the building's original state. First of all, the building was designed without windows. (Cargo doesn't need sunlight.) As the BNYDC renovated the building, they removed 3 million pounds of concrete, installing windows on all sixteen floors. By the time we took a tour, the windows were installed but the vast floor stretching before us was unfinished. Everything

A BAG OF BAGELS ON THE COUNTER

was raw. A pair of monstrous gantry cranes hung from the ceiling, still ready after all these years to pluck supplies and cargo from railroad cars. To imagine that this could become the home of the new Russ & Daughters bakery took chutzpah. Just our portion—over 18,000 square feet—was daunting. It was much more space than we needed, either in the moment or for the foreseeable future. But we wanted a home for decades—generations, in fact—to come. We were confident we would grow into it.

We decided to build not just a working bakery from which we could centralize all our kitchens but also an appetizing counter to cater to Brooklynites, as well as neighbors in the Navy Yard. As soon as we could, we began to move in bakery equipment: huge mixers, each the size of an emu; a large bagel oven; a bagel former. And we built a steam-generating proofing box and a sheeter. We asked our friends at Let There Be Neon to construct another Russ & Daughters neon sign, and hired some fifty employees, some bakers, some packers, some slicers among them.

We opened the doors of the bakery in 2018. When you walk into Building 77, you'll see our double-story glass-walled bakery. You can, and many do, watch as our bakers prepare our babkas, bialys, rugelach, black & white cookies, and loaves of shissel rye, challah, and pumpernickel. And, of course, our bagels. For children, the hungry, and the discerning, watching a bagel being made is fascinating. Strips of dough enter the bagel former, emerging perfectly round and barreling down a chute like smoke rings. They're boiled in a vat of malted water, then fished out by our bakers and placed on wooden bagel boards. Here is where a plain bagel gets poppy seeded, or sesame'd or everything'd. The bagel boards are then placed in a rotating deck oven to bake the bagels, and then the bagels are flipped and baked a bit longer. They emerge in their variegated shades—a pale straw for plain, yellower for egg, mahogany for pumpernickel—to either be shuttled the few feet away, still hot, to the bins at the counter; or driven fifteen minutes to the stores in Manhattan; or cooled and packaged to be shipped around the country.

What the visitor doesn't see is that behind the bakery two full kitchens are working full-tilt, making the salads, schmears, latkes, and blintzes that will be distributed across the city and, in fact, the country. Behind these kitchens is more space, where pallets of babkas are neatly stacked, and care packages await shipping.

Finally we have a space to work, to grow, to stay. Scale isn't the indicator of artisanry. Care is. Even more, this, precisely this, is what our great-grandfather Joel Russ had in mind when, even as he was lugging his pushcart down Orchard Street, he called his business J. Russ National Appetizing.

BAGELS

& BIALYS

We are, and have always been, proud purveyors of smoked and cured fish. As it happens, smoked and cured fish these days is most popularly enjoyed between the slices of a bagel, accompanied by cream cheese, tomato, capers, onions, and other sundry accoutrements. So when we saw bagel makers closing and that the art of making these iconic breads was becoming endangered, we sprung into action. For if you must travel along a path made of bagels to reach the Promised Land of appetizing, then bagels are manifestly our concern. Our bakery started with the project of perfecting the bagel, and today we make 2,000 to 3,000 dozen of them in a normal week. Most of them perfect, we hope.

What makes a bagel a bagel are a few key characteristics. First, of course, the shape. It is a ring; it has a hole. This hole has been subject to intense scholarly debate for centuries. (Is the negative space a something or is it a nothing? Each has its implications.) This circular shape has also meant the bagel has been associated with life events from birth to bris to bar mitzvah to wedding to shiva. Life is a circle; a bagel is too. Now nosh.

But there are many circular breads, from the taralli of Puglia to the knäckebröd of Sweden. This leads us to the second essential characteristic of a bagel. A bagel is boiled before it is baked. The signature sheen on the surface of a good bagel is thanks to this pre-bake boil, which also retards the yeast development and helps the bagel keep its final form. A bagel is made of a tough dough, one high in gluten and low in moisture, which yields a perfect chew. A bagel is not soft like white bread; it is not bubbly like sourdough; it does not have the crumb of a baguette. A bagel is unique.

And finally, despite its mainstreaming into American culture, the bagel is Jewish. From its roots in Poland in the sixteenth century, the bagel has accompanied Jews through the peregrinations of their lives, from birth to death, from Old World to New World, from tenements to tennis clubs. The history of the bagel in America began in the cramped basements of the Lower East Side, where bakers worked fourteen-hour shifts seven days a week. It is tied inextricably to the labor movement, as bagel bakers won hard-earned rights through their collective action in the Bagel Bakers Union. Not to be too overheated about it, but the bagel has become the bready life preserver floating in the melting pot of America, connecting Jews and non-Jews over their shared love of this humble ring.

As for our bagel selection, we hew closely to the traditional flavors. You'll not find rainbow bagels or Parmesan bagels or blueberry, French toast, chocolate chip, or jalapeño bagels. In our minds, plain, poppy, sesame, everything, and onion bagels constitute the classic spread. We also make egg, cinnamon raisin, whole wheat, and pumpernickel bagels, but that is as far as we go.

Today, there are over five hundred bagel specialty stores in New York City and bagels are sold at thousands of more locations, from bodegas to coffee shops. A bagel is at all times proximate. Convenient, perhaps, but not comparable. A true authentic New York bagel is rarer now than at any time before. Our mission at Russ & Daughters is to help our customers reconnect to the authentic New York bagel, wherever they are.

So why go to the trouble of making bagels at home? Perhaps because the very reason that bagels, in some form, are so easily obtained means we have lost sight of the magic behind them. A bagel is not simply something that appears in a bin effortlessly or out of thin air. It is something made, a bread with a long history. Buy a bagel, and you may be pleased. Make a bagel, and you become part of bagel history, something that goes round and round and never ends. That, like the hole of a bagel, isn't nothing.

A NOTE: Bagel making at our bakery is a time-consuming and laborious process that necessitates a host of commercial equipment. It is impractical for all but the most obsessive home baker. Therefore, we've adapted and streamlined our bagel recipes here. So don't worry if the bagels don't look exactly like they do at our stores. Trust us, they are just as delicious.

Plain Bagels

MAKES 12 BAGELS

FOR THE DOUGH

2¼ teaspoons active dry yeast

2¼ cups warm water (between 90°F and 100°F)

6 to 6¼ cups bread flour

1 tablespoon kosher salt

2 tablespoons barley malt syrup*

Cornmeal for dusting baking sheet, optional

FOR THE BOIL AND BAKE

2 tablespoons barley malt syrup

Sesame seeds, poppy seeds, and Everything Spice Mix (see below), for topping, optional

FOR EVERYTHING SPICE MIX
YIELD 1 CUP

5 tablespoons sesame seeds

5 tablespoons poppy seeds

3 tablespoons dried minced onion

2 tablespoons dried minced garlic

1 tablespoon coarse salt (ideally pretzel salt)

---

*Barley malt syrup can usually be found in health food stores.

Stir together the yeast and warm water in the bowl of a stand mixer fitted with a dough hook. Let sit until bubbling and frothy, 3 to 5 minutes. Meanwhile, in a separate bowl, whisk together 6 cups of the bread flour and the salt.

Mix the barley malt syrup into the yeast mixture. Add the flour mixture and mix on low speed, adding up to ¼ cup additional flour as needed, until a supple, elastic dough forms, 7 to 10 minutes. (You might not need all of the additional flour.) Cover the bowl and let the dough rise until doubled in size, 1½ to 2 hours.

Gently deflate the dough by pressing on it to release the air pockets, and divide it into 12 equal portions, rolling each portion into a ball. Sprinkle a large baking sheet with cornmeal or line it with a clean dish towel, then lay the dough balls on top. Cover with a second dish towel and let rest for 10 minutes.

To form the bagels, roll each ball of dough into an approximately 8-inch-long rope. Wrap the rope around your hand so that the two ends meet, overlapping by about 1 inch, in your palm. Pinch the two ends together with your other hand, then roll the pinched end on the counter to seal the bagel into a circle.

Arrange the formed bagels back on the baking sheet, cover, and let rise for another 30 to 60 minutes; see "A Note on Proofing" on PAGE 273. (To test if the bagel has finished proofing, place one bagel in a bowl of lukewarm water. If it floats, it is ready.)

When proofing is complete, preheat the oven to 425°F and place racks in the upper and lower thirds of the oven. Bring 3 quarts of water to a boil in a large pot over high heat. Stir in the barley malt syrup.

Line two large baking sheets with parchment paper. Working in batches of four, gently add the formed bagels to the pot for 45 to 60 seconds, flipping about halfway through. Remove the bagels with a slotted spoon and arrange on the two baking sheets. If desired, sprinkle the bagels with sesame seeds or poppy seeds.

Bake the bagels, swapping the baking sheets top-to-bottom halfway through, until lightly golden brown and cooked through, 16 to 20 minutes.

Transfer the bagels to wire racks to cool before serving.

FOR EVERYTHING SPICE MIX

Mix together all the ingredients. Store in an airtight container, for up to 6 months.

BAGELS: HOW TO ROLL

① DIVIDE THE DOUGH

Gently deflate the dough by pressing on it to release the air pockets, and divide it into 12 equal portions, rolling each portion into a ball.

② ROLL THE DOUGH

To form the bagels, roll each ball of dough into an approximately 8" long rope.

③ **WRAP AND PINCH**
Wrap the rope around your hand so that the two ends meet, overlapping by about 1", in your palm. Pinch the two ends together with your other hand.

④ **SEAL THE BAGEL**
Roll the pinched end on the counter to seal the bagel into a circle.

A NOTE ON PROOFING: Proofing, a process in which the dough is left to rise in a warm humid area, is an important aspect in the development of the bagel. (Without proofing, you'll end up with a flagel.) At the bakery we have a proofing room, whose temperature and humidity is closely watched. But you can proof just as easily at home. To create a proofing zone in your oven, boil water in a pot and place in a turned-off oven. Place the baking sheet of formed bagels in the oven and allow to rise. The steam from the boiling water will create an optimal space for the bagels to proof.

Cinnamon Raisin Bagels

MAKES 12 BAGELS

FOR THE CINNAMON PASTE
1 tablespoon barley malt syrup*
2 teaspoons vegetable oil
¾ teaspoon ground cinnamon

FOR THE DOUGH
2¼ teaspoons active dry yeast
2 tablespoons granulated sugar
2¼ cups warm water (between 90°F and 100°F)
6 to 6½ cups bread flour
1 tablespoon kosher salt
2 tablespoons barley malt syrup
2 tablespoons vegetable oil
¾ cup raisins, soaked in water for 5 minutes and drained well
Cornmeal for dusting baking sheet, optional

FOR THE BOIL AND BAKE
2 tablespoons barley malt syrup

*
Barley malt syrup can usually be found in health food stores.

MAKE CINNAMON PASTE
Combine the barley malt syrup, vegetable oil, and cinnamon in a bowl and stir to form a smooth paste. Cover and set aside.

MAKE DOUGH
Stir together the yeast, sugar, and warm water in the bowl of a stand mixer fitted with a dough hook. Let sit until bubbling and frothy, 3 to 5 minutes. Meanwhile, in a separate bowl, whisk together 6 cups of the bread flour and the salt.

Mix the barley malt syrup and vegetable oil into the yeast mixture. Add the flour mixture and mix on low speed for 5 minutes.

Add the soaked and drained raisins and continue mixing, adding up to ½ cup additional flour as needed, until the raisins are well dispersed and a supple, elastic dough forms, 4 to 5 minutes. Add the cinnamon paste and mix until just swirled into the dough, about 1 minute. Cover the bowl and let the dough rise until doubled in size, 1½ to 2 hours.

Gently deflate the dough by pressing on it to release the air pockets, and divide it into 12 equal portions, rolling each portion into a ball. Sprinkle a large baking sheet with cornmeal or line it with a clean dish towel, then lay the dough balls on top. Cover with a second dish towel and let rest for 10 minutes.

To form the bagels, roll each ball of dough into an approximately 8-inch-long rope. Wrap the rope around your hand so that the two ends meet, overlapping by about 1 inch, in your palm. Pinch the two ends together with your other hand, then roll the pinched end on the counter to seal the bagel into a circle.

Arrange the formed bagels back on the baking sheet, cover, and let rise for another 30 to 60 minutes; see "A Note on Proofing" on previous page. (To test if the bagel has finished proofing, place one in a bowl of lukewarm water. If it floats, it is ready.)

Meanwhile, preheat the oven to 425°F and place racks in the upper and lower thirds of the oven. Bring 3 quarts water to a boil in a large pot over high heat. Stir in the barley malt syrup.

Line two large baking sheets with parchment paper. Working in batches of four, gently add the formed bagels to the pot for 45 to 60 seconds, flipping about halfway through. Remove the bagels with a slotted spoon and arrange on the baking sheets.

Bake the bagels, swapping the baking sheets top-to-bottom halfway through, until golden brown and cooked through, 16 to 20 minutes.

Transfer the bagels to wire racks to cool before serving.

Egg Bagels

MAKES 12 BAGELS

FOR THE DOUGH

2¼ teaspoons active dry yeast

2 cups warm water (between 90°F and 100°F)

6 to 6½ cups bread flour

1 teaspoon ground turmeric

1 tablespoon kosher salt

2 tablespoons barley malt syrup*

1 large egg and 1 large egg yolk

Cornmeal for dusting baking sheet, optional

FOR THE BOIL AND BAKE

2 tablespoons barley malt syrup

Sesame seeds, poppy seeds, and Everything Spice Mix (PAGE 271), for topping, optional

---

* Barley malt syrup can usually be found in health food stores.

Stir together the yeast and warm water in the bowl of a stand mixer fitted with a dough hook. Let sit until bubbling and frothy, 3 to 5 minutes. Meanwhile, in a separate bowl, whisk together 6 cups of the bread flour with the turmeric and salt.

Mix the barley malt syrup, egg, and egg yolk into the yeast mixture. Add the flour mixture and mix on low speed, adding up to ½ cup additional flour as needed, until a supple, elastic dough forms, 7 to 10 minutes. (You might not need all of the additional flour.) Cover the bowl and let the dough rise until doubled in size, 1½ to 2 hours.

Gently deflate the dough by pressing on it to release the air pockets, and divide it into 12 equal portions, rolling each portion into a ball. Sprinkle a large baking sheet with cornmeal or line it with a clean dish towel, then lay the dough balls on top. Cover with a second dish towel and let rest for 10 minutes.

To form the bagels, roll each ball of dough into an approximately 8-inch-long rope. Wrap the rope around your hand so that the two ends meet, overlapping by about 1 inch, in your palm. Pinch the two ends together with your other hand, then roll the pinched end on the counter to seal the bagel into a circle.

Arrange the formed bagels back on the baking sheet, cover, and let rise for another 30 to 60 minutes; see "A Note on Proofing" on PAGE 273. (To test if the bagel has finished proofing, place one bagel in a bowl of lukewarm water. If it floats, it is ready.)

Meanwhile, preheat the oven to 425°F and place racks in the upper and lower thirds of the oven. Bring 3 quarts water to a boil in a large pot over high heat. Stir in the barley malt syrup.

Line two large baking sheets with parchment paper. Working in batches of four, gently add the formed bagels to the pot for 45 to 60 seconds, flipping about halfway through.

Remove the bagels with a slotted spoon and arrange on the two baking sheets. If desired, sprinkle the bagels with sesame seeds, poppy seeds, or Everything Spice Mix.

Bake the bagels, swapping the baking sheets top-to-bottom halfway through, until golden and cooked through, 16 to 20 minutes.

Transfer the bagels to wire racks to cool before serving.

Pumpernickel Bagels

MAKES 12 BAGELS

FOR THE DOUGH

2¼ teaspoons active dry yeast

2¼ cups warm water (between 90°F and 100°F)

6 cups bread flour

½ to ¾ cup pumpernickel flour

2 tablespoons dried minced onion

1 tablespoon kosher salt

2 tablespoons barley malt syrup*

2 tablespoons vegetable oil

Cornmeal for dusting baking sheet, optional

FOR THE BOIL AND BAKE

2 tablespoons barley malt syrup

---

* Barley malt syrup can usually be found in health food stores.

Stir together the yeast and warm water in the bowl of a stand mixer fitted with a dough hook. Let sit until bubbling and frothy, 3 to 5 minutes. Meanwhile, in a separate bowl, whisk together the bread flour, ½ cup of the pumpernickel flour, the dried onion, and salt.

Mix the barley malt syrup and vegetable oil into the yeast mixture. Add the flour mixture and mix on low speed, adding up to ¼ cup additional pumpernickel flour as needed, until a supple, elastic dough forms, 7 to 10 minutes. (You might not need all of the additional flour.) Cover the bowl and let the dough rise until doubled in size, 1½ to 2 hours.

Gently deflate the dough by pressing on it to release the air pockets, and divide it into 12 equal portions, rolling each portion into a ball. Sprinkle a large baking sheet with cornmeal or line it with a clean dish towel, then lay the dough balls on top. Cover with a second dish towel and let rest for 10 minutes.

To form the bagels, roll each ball of dough into an approximately 8-inch-long rope. Wrap the rope around your hand so that the two ends meet, overlapping by about 1 inch, in your palm. Pinch the two ends together with your other hand, then roll the pinched end on the counter to seal the bagel into a circle.

Arrange the formed bagels back on the baking sheet, cover, and let rise for another 30 to 60 minutes; see "A Note on Proofing" on PAGE 273. (To test if the bagel has finished proofing, place one bagel in a bowl of lukewarm water. If it floats, it is ready.)

Meanwhile, preheat the oven to 425°F and place racks in the upper and lower thirds of the oven. Bring 3 quarts water to a boil in a large pot over high heat. Stir in the barley malt syrup.

Line two large baking sheets with parchment paper. Working in batches of four, gently add the formed bagels to the pot for 45 to 60 seconds, flipping about halfway through. Remove the bagels with a slotted spoon and arrange on the two baking sheets.

Bake the bagels, swapping the baking sheets top-to-bottom halfway through, until lightly golden brown and cooked through, 16 to 20 minutes.

Transfer the bagels to wire racks to cool before serving.

Whole Wheat Bagels

MAKES 12 BAGELS

FOR THE DOUGH

2¼ teaspoons active dry yeast

2¼ cups warm water (between 90°F and 100°F)

5 cups bread flour

1 to 1¼ cups whole wheat flour

1 tablespoon kosher salt

2 tablespoons barley malt syrup*

Cornmeal for dusting baking sheet, optional

FOR THE BOIL AND BAKE

2 tablespoons barley malt syrup

Sesame seeds, poppy seeds, and Everything Spice Mix (PAGE 271), for topping, optional

---

*Barley malt syrup can usually be found in health food stores.

Stir together the yeast and warm water in the bowl of a stand mixer fitted with a dough hook. Let sit until bubbling and frothy, 3 to 5 minutes. Meanwhile, in a separate bowl, whisk together the bread flour, 1 cup of the whole wheat flour, and the salt.

Mix the barley malt syrup into the yeast mixture. Add the flour mixture and mix on low speed, adding up to ¼ cup additional whole wheat flour as needed, until a supple, elastic dough forms, 7 to 10 minutes. (You might not need all of the additional flour.) Cover the bowl and let the dough rise until doubled in size, 1½ to 2 hours.

Gently deflate the dough by pressing on it to release the air pockets, and divide it into 12 equal portions, rolling each portion into a ball. Sprinkle a large baking sheet with cornmeal or line it with a clean dish towel, then lay the dough balls on top. Cover with a second dish towel and let rest for 10 minutes.

To form the bagels, roll each ball of dough into an approximately 8-inch-long rope. Wrap the rope around your hand so that the two ends meet, overlapping by about 1 inch, in your palm. Pinch the two ends together with your other hand, then roll the pinched end on the counter to seal the bagel into a circle.

Arrange the formed bagels back on the baking sheet, cover, and let rise for another 30 to 60 minutes; see "A Note on Proofing" on PAGE 273. (To test if the bagel has finished proofing, place one bagel in a bowl of lukewarm water. If it floats, it is ready.)

Meanwhile, preheat the oven to 425°F and place racks in the upper and lower thirds of the oven. Bring 3 quarts water to a boil in a large pot over high heat. Stir in the barley malt syrup.

Line two large baking sheets with parchment paper. Working in batches of four, gently add the formed bagels to the pot for 45 to 60 seconds, flipping about halfway through. Remove the bagels with a slotted spoon and arrange on the two baking sheets. If desired, sprinkle the bagels with sesame seeds, poppy seeds, or Everything Spice Mix.

Bake the bagels, swapping the baking sheets top-to-bottom halfway through, until golden brown and cooked through, 16 to 20 minutes.

Transfer the bagels to wire racks to cool before serving.

Bagel Chips

MAKES 15 TO 18 BAGEL CHIPS

3 bagels, preferably day-old
½ cup extra-virgin olive oil
2 tablespoons Everything Spice Mix (PAGE 271)

Preheat the oven to 350°F.

Slice the bagels into thin slices using a sharp serrated knife. The slices should be between ⅛ and ¼ inch thick.

Place the slices in a single layer on a baking sheet and brush with the olive oil on both sides. Sprinkle evenly with Everything Spice Mix.

Bake the bagel slices for 10 to 15 minutes, flipping halfway through, until the chips are golden brown and crispy. (The exact time depends on how fresh and how thick the bagels are.) Remove the bagel chips and let them cool.

Bagel chips will keep in an airtight container for 2 weeks.

Bialys

MAKES ABOUT 1 DOZEN BIALYS

FOR THE DOUGH

2¼ teaspoons active dry yeast
2¼ cups warm water (between 90°F and 100°F)
6 to 6½ cups bread flour
1 tablespoon kosher salt

FOR THE FILLING AND ASSEMBLY

2 tablespoons vegetable oil, plus more for greasing bowl
1½ Spanish onions, halved through the root and thinly sliced
1 teaspoon granulated sugar
2 teaspoons poppy seeds
¼ teaspoon kosher salt, plus more as needed
Cornmeal for baking sheets

Baked but not boiled, discus-shaped but hole-less, the bialy suffers from its perennial comparison to its cousin the bagel. But on its own terms, the bialy is worthy of veneration and, of course, noshing. The bialy comes from Bialystock, a town in northeastern Poland whose specialty, an onion-topped roll, was dubbed *kuchen* (little bread.) Famous in the region, the kuchen was known—outside of Bialystock, of course—as the *bialystoker kuchen*, the little bread from Bialystock. (Much the same way, in New York we call pizza *pizza*, but outside New York it's called *New York pizza*.) Over time, this little bread from Bialystock came to be known as a bialy. Along with many Bialystoker Jews, the bialy arrived in New York in the late 1800s, and for a time, rivaled the bagel's popularity. (The Bialystock diaspora can be seen in the Lower East Side's Bialystoker Place and Bialystoker Synagogue, and in Max Bialystock, the titular character of the movie [and later Broadway show] *The Producers*.) In Joel's era, bialys could be had on every corner on the Lower East Side. Over time, as Bialystokers in America moved up and out of the Lower East Side, the bialy's fortunes waned. By the 1970s, only one bialy bakery—Kossar's, founded by Bialystoker native Morris Kossar in 1936—was still extant. Our own bialys are, like our bagels, traditionally sized, and properly savory with a poppy seed–onion topping. Though it is possible to make a sandwich out of a bialy with careful slicing, they are perhaps best enjoyed toasted with a schmear of butter and a few slices of sturgeon on top.

Stir together the yeast and warm water in the bowl of a stand mixer fitted with a dough hook and let sit until bubbling and frothy, 3 to 5 minutes.

In a separate bowl, whisk together 6 cups of the bread flour and the salt. Add the flour mixture to the yeast mixture and mix on low speed, adding up to ½ cup additional flour as needed, until a supple, elastic dough forms, 7 to 10 minutes. (You might not need all of the additional flour.) Cover the bowl and let the dough rise until doubled in size, 1 to 2 hours.

MAKE FILLING

Heat the vegetable oil in a large frying pan set over medium heat. Add the onions and sugar and cook, stirring often, until softened and golden brown, 15 to 20 minutes. If the mixture starts to burn, nudge the heat down and stir in a teaspoon or two of water. Stir in the poppy seeds and salt, then remove from the heat. Taste and add more salt, if needed. Set aside to cool.

CONTINUED →

TO ASSEMBLE

Gently deflate the dough by pressing on it to release the air pockets, and divide it into 12 equal portions, rolling each portion into a ball. Arrange the balls on a lightly greased baking sheet and cover loosely with plastic wrap. Let the dough balls rise again until puffed, about 1 hour.

Preheat the oven to 450°F and sprinkle two large baking sheets with cornmeal. Working with one ball of dough at a time, pat it into an approximately 4-inch round. Use your fingers to press a small indentation in the center, then place the shaped bialy on one of the cornmeal-dusted baking sheets. Repeat with the remaining dough balls.

Spoon 1 rounded teaspoon of the filling into the center of each round. (Reserve any remaining filling for another use.)

Bake the bialys, swapping the baking sheets halfway through, until lightly golden brown and cooked through, 15 to 18 minutes.

Transfer the bialys to wire racks to cool before serving.

BREADS

Challah

MAKES 2 LOAVES

2¼ teaspoons active dry yeast
2 tablespoons granulated sugar
1 cup warm water (between 90°F and 100°F)
4 large eggs
¼ cup neutral vegetable oil, plus more for greasing bowl
4½ to 5 cups all-purpose flour
1¼ teaspoons kosher salt

Just as the Sabbath represents the queen of the Jewish week, challah represents the queen of Jewish bread. Even among Old World Ashkenazi peasants, who subsisted mostly on dark rye bread, white flour was used for baking challah. In the fifteenth century, taking a page from exuberant German bakers, Jews began to braid their loaves, in strands of three, four, six, or twelve. They began to add oil, a nod to how bread was baked in the Temple and, later, sugar, a reference perhaps to the sweetness of heaven-sent manna. Or, maybe, just maybe, the symbolism developed simultaneously or even ex post facto, because who doesn't absolutely adore as luxurious and fetching a loaf as a challah?

In the bowl of a stand mixer fitted with the dough hook, combine the yeast, sugar, and water and let sit until bubbling and frothy, 3 to 5 minutes.

Add three of the eggs and the oil and mix on low speed just to combine. Add 4½ cups of the flour and the salt and mix to form a wet and sticky dough. Continue mixing on low speed, scraping down the sides of the mixer bowl as necessary and adding up to ½ cup additional flour (you might not need all of it), to form a smooth, elastic ball of dough, 7 to 8 minutes.

Rub about 1 teaspoon oil around the bottom of a large bowl. Add the dough and turn to coat, then cover the bowl and let the dough rise until doubled in size, 1½ to 2 hours.

Transfer the dough to a lightly floured surface and divide in half. Working with one half of the dough at a time (keeping the other covered so it doesn't dry out), divide it into six equal portions. See following pages for braiding guide.

SECOND PROOF AND BAKE
Transfer the challah to a large, parchment-lined baking sheet and repeat the process with the second half of the dough. Lightly cover the loaves and let them rise for another 30 to 45 minutes.

Meanwhile, preheat oven to 350°F. Beat the remaining egg in a bowl and use a pastry brush to coat the loaves with a layer of egg wash. Wait a few minutes, then brush with a second coat of egg wash.

Bake, rotating the baking sheet back-to-front halfway through until the loaves are golden brown and cooked through, 25 to 30 minutes. Remove from the oven and let the challah rest for about 45 minutes before slicing.

CHALLAH: HOW TO BRAID

① Roll each portion of the dough into an approximately 12-inch-long rope. Arrange the ropes vertically, parallel to each other. Pinch the strands together at the top to seal and tuck the sealed end under itself.

② Take the two outer ropes and cross them over one another to switch places, crossing the rope from the left over the rope from the right.

③ Take the rope furthest to the right and cross it over to be in the middle. Then, take the second rope from the left and cross it all the way to the far right.

④ Take the farthest rope on the left and move it to the middle, then take the second rope from the right and cross it all the way to the left.

⑤ Repeat the pattern until you reach the end of the ropes, then pinch the bottom ends together and tuck them under the loaf.

At our bakery you can see our bakers braiding our six-strand challah at an amazing velocity, their hands a blur. That takes practice and repetition, so be patient. When you're braiding, remember you want the plaits to be tight against one another. Also, don't sweat it. A malformed loaf can be easily zhuzhed into form once the braiding is finished.

Shissel Rye

MAKES 1 LOAF

FOR THE RYE SOUR
½ cup dark rye flour
¼ cup dried minced onion
1 cup warm water (between 90°F and 100°F)

FOR THE DOUGH
2½ cups bread flour
½ cup dark rye flour
1 teaspoon instant dry yeast
¾ cup warm water (between 90°F and 100°F)
3 tablespoons whole charnushka (nigella seeds)
1 tablespoon whole caraway seeds
2 tablespoons vegetable oil, plus more for greasing bowl
1½ teaspoons kosher salt
Cornmeal for dusting

If challah is the bread for celebrations, for most Jews of the Old World—and a few wise ones here too—the everyday loaf is shissel rye. For millennia, rye, a grain, grew wild in the fields of Europe where it was often harvested alongside the more precious wheat. Dense, slightly sour with a tight crumb, bread made from rye was a shtetl staple and became synonymous with Jews in America. This was thanks to, among other factors, Levy's "You don't have to be Jewish to love Levy's real Jewish rye" ads, conceived by Judy Protas, one of the original Mad Women—not Mad Men—of advertising in the '60s and '70s.

There are a few different kinds of rye bread that range from chocolaty brown (pumpernickel, PAGE 293) to a pale straw color, depending on both the proportion of rye flour used and how that grain is treated. We make an über traditional Jewish rye loaf with caraway seeds called a shissel rye. (*Shissel*, in Yiddish, means dish or bowl.) Some so-called Jewish ryes, like the common deli rye, which is more like a white bread, are rye in name only, but ours is not. Since the ratio of rye flour to wheat flour is relatively high, what you get is a true rye-forward loaf with a signature flavor augmented by the slight licorice-y warm flavors of both caraway and charnushka (black caraway or black nigella) seeds.

MAKE RYE SOUR

In a small bowl, mix together the rye flour, dried onion, and warm water until fully incorporated. Cover and allow to sit at room temperature for at least 12 hours, or overnight. The rye sour keeps, covered, for up to 2 weeks in the refrigerator.

MAKE DOUGH

In the bowl of a stand mixer fitted with the dough hook attachment, add the bread flour, rye flour, ½ cup of the rye sour, the yeast, warm water, charnushka, caraway seeds, and vegetable oil. Let the mixture sit for 5 minutes without mixing.

Add the salt and mix on low speed until the dough forms into a springy ball, 8 to 10 minutes. Remove the dough and lightly grease the bowl with oil. Return the dough to the bowl, turn to coat it with oil, cover the bowl, and let rise for 1 hour.

Turn out the dough onto a lightly floured work surface and form into a round by cupping the dough in your hands and rotating it while exerting slight pressure with your palms. Sprinkle a baking sheet with cornmeal and place the loaf on top. Cover with a slightly damp dish towel and let rise in a warm spot for 1 hour. Alternatively, create a proofing zone in your oven by boiling a pot of water and placing it in the turned-off oven. Add the loaf to the oven where the steam from the boiling water will create optimal conditions for the loaf to proof.

Preheat the oven to 450°F and place a baking stone in the oven. (If you do not have a baking stone, you can bake directly on the baking sheet.)

Use a sharp knife to score the top of the loaf from left to right with a few straight lines, then slide the loaf onto the baking stone. Use a spray bottle to mist the loaf with water, then bake until golden brown and a thermometer inserted into the center of the loaf registers 195°F, 40 to 45 minutes.

Transfer the loaf to a wire rack to cool for at least 1 hour before slicing.

MAKES 2 CUPS OF SHISSEL RYE BREADCRUMBS

Remove the crusts from about 8 to 10 slices of bread, and cut into pieces.

Spread on a large baking sheet and let air-dry for 2 to 3 hours.

Transfer the pieces to a food processor and pulse until they are the texture of breadcrumbs.

Spread the crumbs back on the baking sheet and toast in a 300°F oven until fully dry, 8 to 10 minutes.

Let cool before using.

Pumpernickel

MAKES 1 LOAF

FOR THE PUMPERNICKEL SOUR

1 cup pumpernickel flour

⅓ cup dried minced onion

1¼ cups warm water (between 90°F and 100°F)

FOR THE DOUGH

2½ cups bread flour

1¾ cups pumpernickel flour, plus more if needed

Pumpernickel sour (see above)

1½ teaspoons instant dry yeast

1 cup warm water (between 90°F and 100°F)

2 tablespoons vegetable oil, plus more for greasing bowl

2 tablespoons molasses

1 tablespoon ground caraway seeds

1 tablespoon dried minced onion

1½ teaspoons kosher salt

Cornmeal for dusting

The darkest of our breads and the most flavorful, our pumpernickel relies on flour made with rye grains and their bran for both its deep color and intense flavor. Originally a German bread—*pumpernickel* means "farting demon," perhaps because it is not the easiest to digest—pumpernickel became synonymous with delicatessens here in America. However, even within the world of appetizing, pumpernickel has its place, especially as an accompaniment to something fatty like a schmear of butter and a layer of sturgeon, or with a nice piece of herring.

MAKE PUMPERNICKEL SOUR

In a small bowl, mix together the pumpernickel flour, dried onion, and warm water until fully incorporated. Cover and allow to sit at room temperature for at least 12 hours, or overnight. The pumpernickel sour keeps, covered, for up to 2 weeks in the refrigerator.

MAKE DOUGH

In the bowl of a stand mixer fitted with the dough hook attachment, add the bread flour, pumpernickel flour, ½ cup of the pumpernickel sour, and the yeast, warm water, oil, molasses, caraway, and dried onion. Let the mixture sit for 5 minutes without mixing.

Add the salt and mix on low speed until the dough forms a springy ball, 8 to 10 minutes. If it is too wet, add more pumpernickel flour, 1 tablespoon at a time, until the desired texture is reached. Remove the dough and lightly grease the bowl with oil. Return the dough to the bowl, turn to coat it with oil, cover the bowl, and let rise for 1 hour.

Turn out the dough onto a lightly floured work surface and form into an elongated oval, about 10 inches in length with slightly tapered ends. Sprinkle a baking sheet with cornmeal and place the loaf on top. Cover with a slightly damp dish towel and let rise in a warm spot for 1 hour. Alternatively, create a proofing zone in your oven by boiling a pot of water and placing it in the turned-off oven. Add the loaf to the oven where the steam from the boiling water will create optimal conditions for the loaf to proof.

Preheat the oven to 450°F and place a baking stone in the oven. (If you do not have a baking stone, you can bake directly on the baking sheet.)

Use a sharp knife to score the top of the loaf from left to right with a few straight lines, then slide the loaf onto the baking stone. Use a spray bottle to mist the loaf with water, then bake until golden brown and a thermometer inserted into the center of the loaf registers 195°F, 40 to 45 minutes.

Transfer the loaf to a wire rack to cool for at least 1 hour before slicing.

Marble Rye

MAKES 2 LOAVES

Because they have very similar densities and texture, shissel rye dough and pumpernickel dough can be fruitfully mixed with each other to form marble rye, another classic loaf of the Jewish American pantry. The result is visually appealing with a flavor, naturally, slightly more intense than regular shissel rye but not quite as rye-forward as pumpernickel.

To make marble rye bread, take one recipe of shissel rye dough and one recipe of pumpernickel dough. Divide each in half then roll into a 10-inch square, about ¾ inch thick. Place the shissel atop the pumpernickel dough and twist them together.

Divide the dough into halves and cover loosely on the workspace with plastic wrap.

Spread cornmeal on a large baking sheet or bread board. Transfer the loaves to the board and shape the loaves into rounds by cupping in your hands atop a bread board and rotating it while exerting slight pressure with your palms. Cover with a slightly damp dish towel and let rise in a warm spot for 1 hour. Alternatively, create a proofing zone in your oven by boiling a pot of water and placing it in the turned-off oven. Add the loaf to the oven where the steam from the boiling water will create optimal conditions for the loaf to proof.

Preheat the oven to 450°F and place a baking stone in the oven. (If you do not have a baking stone, you can bake directly on the baking sheet.)

Use a sharp knife to score the top of the loaf from left to right with a few straight lines, then slide the loaf onto the baking stone. Use a spray bottle to mist the loaf with water, then bake until golden brown and a thermometer inserted into the center of the loaf registers 195°F, 40 to 45 minutes.

Transfer the loaf to a wire rack to cool for at least 1 hour before slicing.

BAKED

GOODS

Rugelach

MAKES 2 DOZEN RUGELACH

2¾ cups all-purpose flour
½ teaspoon kosher salt
1 (8-ounce) block cream cheese (not whipped), softened
½ cup (1 stick) unsalted butter, softened
¼ cup sour cream
⅓ cup granulated sugar, plus more for topping
Raspberry, Cinnamon, or Chocolate Filling

Each week we make between 9,000 and 12,000 rugelach of assorted flavors. Sold by the pound, these small iconic bites, somewhere between a cookie and a pastry, have developed a loyal and ardent following. And it's easy to see why. The dough is silken and flaky, thanks to the American innovation of using cream cheese and, in our case, a touch of sour cream. (Older versions of rugelach were pareve and relied on yeast.) Spread with fillings—traditionally chocolate, cinnamon, or raspberry—then rolled tightly, sprinkled with sugar, and baked, rugelach is pleasure in nosh form.

In a medium bowl, whisk together the flour and salt.

In the bowl of a stand mixer fitted with a paddle attachment (or using a handheld electric mixer and a large bowl), combine the cream cheese, butter, sour cream, and sugar and beat at medium speed until well combined, about 2 minutes.

Add the flour mixture in two stages, beating on low after each addition and scraping down the sides of the bowl as necessary. Gather the dough and divide it into two equal pieces. Form each piece into a rectangle shape, wrap tightly in plastic, and refrigerate for at least 2 hours, or up to overnight.

Line two large baking sheets with parchment paper and set aside.

Working with one piece of dough at a time, roll out on a lightly floured surface into a 12 by 8-inch rectangle, about ⅛ inch thick. (If the dough is too solid to roll at first, let it sit at room temperature for 5 to 10 minutes before proceeding.) Transfer the dough to one of the baking sheets. Repeat with the remaining dough, then place both baking sheets, uncovered, in the refrigerator to chill for 20 to 30 minutes.

Meanwhile, preheat the oven to 350°F (and make your filling).

Remove the baking sheets from the refrigerator. Follow the instructions in the filling recipe to top the dough pieces. Beginning with a long side of one piece of dough and using the parchment to start the process, roll up the dough around the filling, creating a spiraled log. Repeat with the remaining dough. Lightly dab the top of each log with water and sprinkle generously with more sugar.

Using a sharp knife, cut each log crosswise into 1-inch-thick pieces and arrange on the parchment-lined baking sheets. Bake, rotating the baking sheets back-to-front and top-to-bottom halfway through, until golden brown, 25 to 30 minutes.

The rugelach keeps 7 days at room temperature in an airtight container.

FOR RASPBERRY FILLING

1 cup raspberry jam
½ cup red or dark raisins
½ cup dried currants

FOR CINNAMON FILLING

½ cup (1 stick) unsalted butter, softened
½ cup packed light brown sugar
1½ tablespoons ground cinnamon
½ teaspoon kosher salt
1 cup golden raisins
½ cup cinnamon chips

FOR CHOCOLATE FILLING

½ cup semisweet chocolate chips
2 tablespoons unsalted butter, at room temperature
1 cup chocolate shortbread crumbs
1 tablespoon honey
½ teaspoon coffee extract or instant coffee granules
¼ cup semisweet mini chocolate chips

RASPBERRY FILLING

To top the rugelach dough, divide the jam between the two dough rectangles and spread evenly. Sprinkle half of the raisins and half of the currants over each dough rectangle. Proceed with the recipe.

CINNAMON FILLING

In the bowl of a stand mixer fitted with a paddle attachment (or using a handheld electric mixer and a large bowl), combine the butter and brown sugar and beat at medium speed until fully combined, about 1 minute. Add the cinnamon and salt and beat on low speed to combine.

To top the rugelach dough, divide the cinnamon-butter mixture between the two dough rectangles and spread evenly. Sprinkle half of the golden raisins and half of the cinnamon chips over each dough rectangle. Proceed with the recipe.

CHOCOLATE FILLING

Melt the chocolate chips and butter together in the top of a double boiler over simmering water. Remove from the heat and let cool slightly, then stir in the shortbread crumbs, honey, and coffee extract.

To top the rugelach dough, divide the chocolate-shortbread mixture between the two dough rectangles and spread evenly. Sprinkle 2 tablespoons of the mini chocolate chips over each dough rectangle. Proceed with the recipe.

RUGELACH: HOW TO FILL & ROLL

① ROLL OUT THE DOUGH

Working with one piece of dough at a time, roll out on a lightly floured surface into a 12 by 8-inch rectangle, about ⅛ inch thick. Transfer the dough to one of the baking sheets. Repeat with the remaining dough, then place both baking sheets, uncovered, in the refrigerator to chill for 20 to 30 minutes.

② TOP THE DOUGH

Remove the baking sheets from the refrigerator. Add the filling of your choice on top of the rugelach dough.

③ **ROLL UP THE DOUGH**
Beginning with a long side of one piece of dough and using the parchment to start the process, roll up the dough around the filling, creating a spiraled log. Repeat with the remaining dough. Lightly dab the top of each log with water and sprinkle generously with more sugar.

④ **CUT THE DOUGH**
Using a sharp knife, cut each log crosswise into 1-inch-thick pieces and arrange on the parchment-lined baking sheets.

Black & White Cookies

MAKES ABOUT 18 COOKIES

3 cups cake flour
1 teaspoon baking powder
½ teaspoon kosher salt
½ cup (1 stick) unsalted butter, at room temperature
1½ cups granulated sugar
1 teaspoon grated lemon zest
1 teaspoon vanilla extract
¾ teaspoon almond extract
2 large eggs, at room temperature
½ cup plus 2 tablespoons buttermilk, at room temperature
12 ounces white coating chocolate wafers
12 ounces dark coating chocolate wafers

It's easy to metaphorize the legendary black & white cookie. Among the most iconic New York foods, the black & white cookie has come to symbolize dialectics, racial harmony, finely tuned balance. The cookie was first spotted in New York at Glaser's Bake Shop, a Bavarian bakery in Yorkville founded in 1902. (This is, though, a matter of dispute. Utica's Hemstrought's Bakery also claims the black & white, or *halfmoon*, cookie as their own.) Regardless, today they can be found, often sealed in plastic wrap, in nearly every bodega in the city. But let's not lose sight of what it is. In its ideal form, the black & white cookie is a subtle lemon-scented fine-crumbed drop cake, topped with half-moons of delectable—not cloying—black and white chocolate coatings. Our version of this classic is, well, classic. We use real chocolate, as opposed to the more commonly used icing sugar, and fresh lemon zest and buttermilk, to give the cookies a smooth, moist, and delicate flavor.

Line two large baking sheets with parchment paper and set nearby.

In a large bowl, sift together the cake flour, baking powder, and salt and set aside.

In a stand mixer fitted with the paddle attachment (or using a handheld electric mixer and a large bowl), beat the butter at medium speed for 1 minute. Add the sugar, lemon zest, vanilla extract, and almond extract and beat, scraping down the sides of the bowl as necessary, until light and fluffy, 1 to 2 minutes. Add the eggs, one at a time, beating until incorporated, followed by the buttermilk. It is okay if the mixture looks curdled at this stage.

Add the flour mixture in two stages, beating on low after each, until just incorporated. (Take care not to overmix.)

With a ¼-cup measuring cup, scoop 18 portions of the dough onto the lined baking sheets. Cover the baking sheets with plastic wrap and refrigerate for at least 4 hours, or up to overnight.

Take each portion of chilled cookie dough and, using lightly floured hands, roll into a smooth ball, then return to the baking sheets, leaving 2 inches between each. Using lightly floured hands, gently press each ball into a 3-inch round. Return the baking sheets to the fridge to chill for about 30 minutes.

CONTINUED →

Meanwhile, preheat the oven to 350°F.

Bake the cookies until slightly golden on the bottom but still pale on top, 15 to 18 minutes. Remove from the oven and transfer to wire racks to cool completely.

When ready to decorate: Melt the white chocolate in the top of a double boiler over simmering water, or in the microwave at 20-second intervals, stirring between each, until completely smooth. Use an offset spatula to carefully spread the melted white chocolate on one half of the flat side of each cookie. Repeat the process with the dark chocolate. Place the cookies back on the wire racks, frosted side up, to set, about 10 to 15 minutes.

The cookies can be stored in an airtight container for up to 4 days at room temperature.

Chocolate (or Cinnamon) Babka

MAKES 2 BABKAS

FOR THE DOUGH
1 tablespoon instant dry yeast
2 teaspoons plus ½ cup granulated sugar
2 tablespoons warm water
3½ cups all-purpose flour, plus more as needed
¾ teaspoon kosher salt
½ cup warm whole milk*
1 large egg plus 2 yolks
1 teaspoon vanilla extract
⅓ cup (⅔ stick) unsalted butter, cut into pieces and softened

FOR SHORTBREAD STREUSEL
4 tablespoons (½ stick) unsalted butter, softened
3 tablespoons granulated sugar
½ cup all-purpose flour
⅛ teaspoon kosher salt

FOR ASSEMBLY
Chocolate or Cinnamon Filling (recipes on following page)
1 large egg, for egg wash

*Warm the milk in a small saucepan set over medium heat or in a microwave in 20-second bursts until it reaches 100°F on a digital thermometer.

Like a bagel with lox and the works, chocolate babka is a uniquely American spin on an Old World tradition. The babkas of the Polish shtetlach were essentially a way to use up extra challah dough. They were sweetened, sure, but with fruit jam or cinnamon. Chocolate was, if not unknown, at least prohibitively expensive.

Cut to today, when chocolate babka calls to mind dense bricks of braided yeasty dough deeply marbled with dark chocolate and decadently topped with chocolate streusel. And, of course, the iconic *Seinfeld* episode "The Dinner Party." That's what two generations of affluence and appetite get you.

For years, if you wanted babka on the Lower East Side, you wouldn't need to stop at Russ & Daughters. There were Moishe's and Gertel's and a hundred other bakeries. But as those places gradually shuttered and as we opened up our own bakery in Brooklyn, we decided to step in to fill the babka-shaped void. Our general approach to these matters is not to create some newfangled innovation but to do something much harder: create the Platonic ideal. For babka that means moist, chocolaty, and dense. After a lot of experimentation, we settled on a recipe that avoids palm oil—which all but assures gooey-ness but at what huge human and environmental cost? We focused instead on using the finest ingredients like high-quality chocolate. The result is sweet, of course, but also well-balanced, delicious, and all natural.

In a small bowl, stir together the yeast, the 2 teaspoons sugar, and the warm water and set aside until bubbly, about 3 minutes.

Meanwhile, combine the remaining ½ cup sugar, flour, and salt in the bowl of a stand mixer fitted with the dough hook and briefly mix at low speed.

Add the yeast mixture, warm milk, egg and egg yolks, vanilla, and softened butter and mix at low speed to form a smooth, slightly sticky dough. If the dough looks too wet or sticky, add a little more flour, 1 tablespoon at a time, until the desired texture is reached. Cover the bowl with a damp dish towel and let rise for 30 minutes.

On a lightly floured surface, roll the dough out into a large, ¼-inch-thick rectangle. Cut the rectangle in half, lengthwise, to form two equal pieces. Working with one piece at a time, fold one short end of the dough a third of the way over the dough, then fold the other side on top, like folding a business letter.

CONTINUED →

FOR CHOCOLATE FILLING

- 6 tablespoons unsalted butter, softened
- ⅓ cup granulated sugar
- ⅓ cup packed light brown sugar
- 2 tablespoons cocoa powder
- ½ teaspoon coffee extract or instant coffee granules
- 1 teaspoon vanilla paste

CINNAMON FILLING

- 6 tablespoons unsalted butter, softened
- ⅓ cup granulated sugar
- ⅓ cup packed light brown sugar
- 1 tablespoon light molasses
- 1 teaspoon ground cinnamon

Repeat with the remaining dough. Wrap each folded rectangle of dough in parchment paper, followed by plastic wrap. Refrigerate for at least 2 hours, or up to overnight.

MAKE SHORTBREAD STREUSEL

Combine the butter and sugar in the bowl of a stand mixer fitted with the paddle attachment and beat at medium speed until fluffy, about 2 minutes. Add the flour and salt and beat on low, scraping down the sides of the bowl as necessary, until the mixture is semi-sandy with some larger, soft chunks. (Be careful not to overmix.) Set aside.

TO ASSEMBLE

Line two 9 by 5-inch loaf pans with parchment paper, allowing the paper to hang over on the two opposite long sides.

Working with one piece of dough on a well-floured surface, roll it into a large, ⅛-inch-thick rectangle, about 9 by 12 inches. Scoop half of the filling onto the dough and spread it into a thin, even layer. Starting with one of the short sides of the rectangle, roll up the dough like a jelly roll. Use a sharp knife to cut the roll in half lengthwise, then twist the two halves together and place in one of the loaf pans. Repeat with the second piece of dough and remaining filling. Cover the loaf pans and let rise for 1 hour. The dough will rise a bit, but not double in size.

Preheat the oven to 350°F. Whisk the egg in a small bowl to create an egg wash and brush each loaf evenly with a layer of egg wash. (You will not use all of it.) Sprinkle the top of each loaf with half of the streusel. Bake until golden brown and a digital thermometer inserted into the center of a loaf reaches 195°F, 35 to 40 minutes.

Set the loaf pans on a wire rack to cool completely. Use the overhanging parchment to transfer the babkas to a cutting board for slicing.

Leftover babka can be stored, well wrapped, for up to 1 week at room temperature.

CHOCOLATE FILLING

Combine all the ingredients in the bowl of a stand mixer fitted with a paddle attachment. Beat at low to medium speed until a paste forms. Cover and set aside until needed, up to 48 hours.

CINNAMON FILLING

Combine all the ingredients in the bowl of a stand mixer fitted with a paddle attachment. Beat at low to medium speed until a paste forms. Cover and set aside until needed, up to 48 hours.

BABKA: HOW TO ROLL, FILL & BRAID

① ROLL OUT THE DOUGH

Working with one piece of dough on a well-floured surface, roll it into a large, ⅛-inch-thick rectangle, about 9 by 12 inches.

② ADD FILLING

Scoop half of the filling onto the dough and spread it into a thin, even layer.

3 ROLL UP THE DOUGH
Starting with one of the short sides of the rectangle, roll up the dough like a jelly roll.

4 CUT THE DOUGH
Use a sharp knife to cut the roll in half lengthwise.

5 TWIST THE DOUGH
Twist the two halves together and place in one of the loaf pans.

6 LET RISE
Cover the loaf pans and let rise for 1 hour. The dough will rise a bit, but not double in size.

Challah Bread Pudding

MAKES ONE 9" SQUARE BAKING DISH, 8 TO 10 SERVINGS

Butter, for greasing the baking dish

1 loaf Challah (PAGE 287 or store-bought) or brioche

⅓ cup Grand Marnier

2½ teaspoons water

2⅔ cups heavy cream

4 large eggs

⅓ cup granulated sugar

1½ teaspoons vanilla extract

¼ teaspoon grated nutmeg

⅓ cup dried Turkish apricots, cut into small dice

Challah is one step—or rather, a couple of tablespoons of butter—away from brioche. Both are fluffy eggy enriched breads able, eager in fact, to absorb liquid without disintegrating. That's one reason both brioche and challah make excellent candidates for this decadent bread pudding. What makes this Russ & Daughtersian are the dried apricots, a mainstay of our dried fruit business. In fact, we devote more than one half of our storefront to this picturesque, deeply hued fruit. We carry two kinds, Turkish and Californian. The former are plump and sweet. The latter, of a more reddish orange hue, are flat and tart. Here the sweet Turkish ones complement the rich challah and custard sauce.

Preheat the oven to 350°F. Butter a 9-inch square baking dish.

Remove the crust from the challah, then cut into ½-inch cubes. Spread out evenly on a baking sheet and toast in the oven, stirring halfway, for 5 to 10 minutes, until dry but without developing much color.

Combine the Grand Marnier and water in a small saucepan over medium heat. Bring to a simmer and simmer for 5 minutes, until reduced.

In a large bowl, whisk together the Grand Marnier mixture, cream, eggs, sugar, vanilla, and nutmeg.

Spread the challah evenly in the buttered baking dish, then top with the dried apricots. Carefully pour the custard mix over the challah and apricots, gently pressing down the challah to make sure it is evenly covered. Let soak for 15 minutes.

Cover with aluminum foil and bake for 30 to 40 minutes, or until almost set. Remove the foil and continue baking for about 10 minutes, until the top is lightly browned. Remove the bread pudding from the oven and serve immediately.

Hamantaschen

MAKES ABOUT 3 DOZEN COOKIES

3 cups all-purpose flour, plus more for shaping and rolling
1 teaspoon baking powder
½ teaspoon kosher salt
1 cup (2 sticks) unsalted butter, softened
1 cup granulated sugar
2 large eggs
½ cup sour cream
Poppy Seed Filling (below)

POPPY SEED FILLING
MAKES 2 CUPS

1¼ cups poppy seeds
4 tablespoons (½ stick) unsalted butter, cut into pieces
½ cup granulated sugar
2 teaspoons honey
⅔ cup heavy cream
1 large egg
Grated zest of 1 lemon

The triangular cookie represents the villainous Haman's tricornered hat, or perhaps the pocket in which the king's advisor kept his bribes (*tasche* means pocket), or perhaps the three patriarchs (Abraham, Isaac, and Jacob.) The poppy seed filling tucked safely inside, meanwhile, represents God's hidden presence in the Purim story, or perhaps Queen Esther's vegetarian diet. (Raspberry, apricot, and prune jams are, though delicious, modern variants.) All this might be true. Maybe none of it is. Meaning is, so often, something affixed through the flow of generations in order to further connect traditions to generations past. For those who eat the 4,000 hamantaschen we make each Purim—and those who enjoy Hamantaschen year-round—the pleasure might simply be in the delicate flavors of the flaky dough wrapped around a sweet filling, poppy seed or otherwise.

Whisk together the flour, baking powder, and salt in a medium bowl and set aside.

In the bowl of a stand mixer fitted with the paddle attachment (or using a handheld electric mixer and a large bowl), beat together the butter and sugar at medium speed until light and fluffy, about 2 minutes. Add the eggs, one at a time, beating well after each addition, then beat in the sour cream until combined.

Add the flour mixture to the wet mixture in two additions, beating on low after each and scraping down the sides of the bowl as necessary, until a soft dough forms. Transfer the dough to a lightly floured surface, divide into two equal parts, and form each into a disk. (The dough should be soft and delicate, but if it is too soft to shape, lightly flour your hands.) Wrap each disk in plastic wrap and refrigerate for at least 4 hours or overnight.

Line two large baking sheets with parchment paper and set nearby.

Working with one portion of dough at a time (leaving the other refrigerated), on a floured surface roll out the dough to a ¼-inch thickness. Use a 3-inch round cookie cutter or glass to stamp out as many rounds of dough as possible and transfer them to one of the baking sheets. Gather the dough scraps, reroll the dough, and cut out additional rounds. If the dough gets too warm and soft to work with, place it back in the fridge for 15 minutes to firm up.

CONTINUED →

Spoon a rounded teaspoon of the filling into the center of each dough round. Fold the left side in at an angle, followed by the right side. Fold the bottom flap up, tucking one end under a side flap to make a triangular pocket. (The filling should still be visible in the center.) Pinch the corners to seal. Repeat the rolling and filling process with the remaining dough rounds and filling.

Place the baking sheets in the refrigerator for 15 minutes to allow the cookies to chill. Meanwhile, preheat the oven to 350°F.

Bake the cookies until lightly golden, 17 to 20 minutes. Transfer the cookies to wire racks to cool.

The cookies will keep in an airtight container for up to 5 days.

POPPY SEED FILLING
Working in batches if necessary, pour the poppy seeds into a spice grinder or coffee grinder and pulse until well ground. The poppy seeds should be fluffy and have the texture of slightly damp soil.

Combine the butter, sugar, and honey in a medium saucepan set over medium heat. Cook, stirring occasionally, until the butter is fully melted. Turn the heat to low and, whisking constantly, whisk in the cream, immediately followed by the egg and ground poppy seeds.

Increase the heat to medium and cook, whisking often, until the mixture reaches a simmer and begins to thicken. Remove from the heat and whisk in the lemon zest. Let the mixture cool to room temperature (it will thicken further as it cools), then cover and refrigerate until needed, or up to 2 days.

Sour Cream Coffee Cake

MAKES ONE 9×13" CAKE, 12 SERVINGS

FOR THE CINNAMON FILLING

2 tablespoons unsalted butter, softened
½ cup packed brown sugar
1½ teaspoons ground cinnamon
¼ cup bread flour

FOR THE CRUMB TOPPING

¾ cup (1½ sticks) unsalted butter, room temperature
½ cup granulated sugar
½ cup packed brown sugar
½ teaspoon ground cinnamon
1¼ cups plus 2 tablespoons all-purpose flour
½ teaspoon kosher salt

FOR THE CAKE

2¼ cups plus 2 tablespoons bread flour
¼ teaspoon plus ⅛ teaspoon baking soda
¼ teaspoon baking powder
2 teaspoons kosher salt
1 cup plus 2 tablespoons (2¼ sticks) unsalted butter, softened
2¼ cups plus 3 tablespoons granulated sugar
3 large eggs
2 teaspoons vanilla
1 cup plus 2 tablespoons sour cream

In the days before refrigeration, sour cream (and buttermilk) were the dairy products of choice for baking. Also in the days before refrigeration, as an outgrowth of the Enlightenment, kaffeehaus culture—a fevered caffeine-fueled milieu of ideas—blossomed from Vienna to Prague, Berlin, and Budapest: coffee and the little noshes accompanying them, newspapers, arguments, kibbitzing, revolution. How could a Jew resist? That the confluence of these two trends ensured that a sour cream coffee cake found its way onto the table at your bubbe's house is the fortuitous tale of diasporic taste. In our case, this recipe came from our head baker at the time, Lainie Schleien Rothstein, or more accurately, from her family (and who knows how many generations of Schleiens before her). Dense but not turgid, sweet but not cloying, decadent but not excessive, this classic sour cream coffee cake fortifies you for even the most heated discussions.

CINNAMON FILLING

Cream the butter and brown sugar in the bowl of a stand mixer with a paddle attachment by mixing at a low speed until incorporated. Increase the speed to medium-high and beat for 1 to 2 minutes, until a smooth paste forms. Add the cinnamon and mix to combine. Add the flour and mix until combined. It will be crumbly.

The filling can be made ahead of time and stored in an airtight container in the refrigerator until needed, up to 3 days.

CRUMB TOPPING

Cream the butter, both sugars, and cinnamon in the bowl of a stand mixer fitted with a paddle attachment by mixing at a low speed until just incorporated. Increase the speed to medium-high and beat for 1 to 2 minutes. Scrape down the bowl with a rubber spatula, then add the flour and salt. Mix on medium speed, stopping at 10-second intervals to scrape the bowl to make sure no butter-sugar mixture is stuck to the sides or bottom, until the dough is in small chunks. Be careful not to overmix.

The crumb topping can be made ahead of time and stored in an airtight container in the refrigerator until needed, or up to 3 days.

CONTINUED →

THE CAKE

Preheat the oven to 325°F. Line a 9 by 13-inch baking sheet with parchment paper, then spray with nonstick pan spray.

Sift together the flour, baking soda, baking powder, and salt in a large bowl and set aside.

In the bowl of a stand mixer fitted with a paddle attachment, beat the butter on medium speed for 30 to 60 seconds. Add the sugar and cream the butter at low speed until just incorporated, scraping the bottom and sides of the bowl. Increase the speed to medium-high and beat for 1 to 2 minutes, until light and fluffy. Reduce to low speed and gradually add the eggs and vanilla, occasionally scraping down the sides of the bowl. Once all the eggs have been added, beat on medium until the batter is light and fluffy, 30 to 60 seconds.

Add the sour cream and the flour mixture in small amounts, starting with the dry, alternating between the two, and mixing at low speed, just to incorporate.

In ¼-cup portions, add half of the batter (about 2 cups) to the greased baking sheet, and use a spatula to spread evenly. Carefully distribute the cinnamon filling over the top by crumbling in an even layer and gently pressing down with flat palms. Add the rest of the batter and spread evenly, taking care to not mix in the cinnamon filling. Add the crumb topping and spread evenly.

Bake for about 90 minutes, or until a toothpick inserted in the center of the cake comes out clean. Let cool completely in the pan. Cut into squares and serve.

The coffee cake will keep in an airtight container at room temperature for 2 to 3 days.

Honey Cake

MAKES TWO 9×3" LOAVES

2¼ cups all-purpose flour
1¾ teaspoons baking powder
1¼ teaspoons baking soda
2¼ teaspoons ground cinnamon
¼ teaspoon ground cloves
¼ teaspoon allspice
Scant 1 teaspoon kosher salt
2 large eggs
½ cup granulated sugar
½ cup molasses
¾ cup canola oil
½ cup honey
⅓ cup brewed coffee
1½ teaspoons grated orange zest
⅓ cup orange juice
½ teaspoon vanilla paste

Since the land of, well, milk and honey, honey has been important to the Jews. The introduction of sugar somewhat lessened its primacy; nevertheless when it comes to ceremonial significance, honey still reigns. Usually, anything with honey in it gets yoked to Rosh Hashanah, the Jewish New Year. Honey is sweet; our wish is that the year is sweet. It's why we dip apples in honey and it's why this spiced honey cake, called *lekach* in Yiddish, is so popular during the High Holidays as well. Though the honey is from the Levant, the spiced nature of the lekach has more to do with the Germanic fondness for honey spiced gingerbread (lebkuchen) dating back to the sixteenth century. Often made with brandy, we've added coffee in addition to the warming spices of cinnamon, clove, and allspice, along with orange zest (and juice) for brightness. The result is a treat rich in both symbolism and flavor.

Preheat the oven to 325°F.

Sift together the flour, baking powder, baking soda, cinnamon, cloves, allspice, and salt. Set aside.

Combine the eggs and sugar in the bowl of a stand mixer with a whip attachment. Whip on medium to high speed until ribbons form, about 5 minutes. Add the molasses and continue whipping until incorporated. Then slowly add the canola oil, honey, coffee, orange zest and juice, and vanilla paste.

Add the dry ingredients in two batches, making sure each is incorporated into the batter. Continue whipping until all the ingredients are combined and there are no clumps.

Equally divide the batter between two 9 by 3-inch loaf pans (it should reach about halfway up each). Bake for 45 minutes, until the tops spring back when pressed gently and a thermometer inserted in a cake registers 190°F. The center will be slightly sunken, but this is normal. Let cool. Remove from the loaf pan and enjoy.

The cake, wrapped in plastic, will keep in the refrigerator for 7 days.

Plum (or Apple) Cake

MAKES ONE 9" SQUARE CAKE

2 cups all-purpose flour

2 teaspoons baking powder

1 teaspoon ground cinnamon

1 cup (2 sticks) unsalted butter, softened

1 cup granulated sugar

Grated zest of 3 lemons

4 large eggs

1 tablespoon vanilla extract

⅛ teaspoon kosher salt

2 cups diced pitted fresh plums (about 3 plums), or 2 cups cored Granny Smith apple (about 2 apples)

About 1 tablespoon unsalted butter, melted

1 tablespoon demerara sugar, to finish

Vanilla ice cream, to serve (optional)

* The cake can also be baked in an 8 by 4-inch loaf pan; increase the bake time to 65 to 70 minutes.

In the Old World, since both plums and apples ripen around Rosh Hashanah, they were featured in various cakes and then often associated with the holiday. Both fruits also stand up well to baking, retaining their form and texture. Either adds a lovely flavor—plums being slightly more tart, but both quite sweet. While many traditional Jewish fruit cakes do not use butter—so that they could be eaten after a meal containing meat—as a bakery associated with appetizing, we're free to—and do!—use butter to make a luscious absolutely irresistible fruit cake. Is it fair? Perhaps not. It is delicious? Absolutely.

Preheat the oven to 325°F. Coat a 9-inch square baking pan* with nonstick cooking spray.

Sift together the flour, baking powder, and cinnamon in a large bowl.

In a stand mixer with the paddle attachment, cream the butter, granulated sugar, and lemon zest on medium speed until fluffy. Add the eggs, one at a time, mixing until incorporated. Add the vanilla and salt and beat until the batter is light and uniform.

Add half the dry mixture and beat until mixed. Add the second half and mix until incorporated. Do not overmix.

Gently spread half the batter on the bottom of the prepared pan. Add the plums or apples in a single layer, pressing them down into the batter. Spread the remaining batter over the fruit and gently press down as you smooth the top with a spatula.

Brush with the melted butter and sprinkle with the demerara sugar. Bake for 35 to 40 minutes, until golden brown and set in the middle. Allow to cool to room temperature. Serve on its own or with scoops of vanilla ice cream.

The cake will keep in an airtight container at room temperature for 3 days.

Fruit Strudel

MAKES 1 LOAF, 4 TO 6 SERVINGS

¼ cup raisins
¼ cup chopped dried Turkish apricots
¼ cup chopped dried apple rings
¼ cup chopped dried pear
¼ cup chopped dried peach
1 cup packed brown sugar
1 teaspoon ground cinnamon
¼ to ⅓ cup boiled water
5 sheets frozen phyllo dough (from a 16-ounce package), thawed
5 tablespoons unsalted butter, melted
¼ cup breadcrumbs
½ cup walnuts, chopped
1 large egg yolk, beaten
Powdered sugar, for garnish

The most traditional strudel—a Germanic pastry made by rolling a fruit filling in a laminated dough—is made with fresh apples. But when we decided to make our own we had to look no further than the bins of brightly colored dried fruit that have been an integral part of Russ & Daughters for years, occupying one side of our storefront windows in abundance. Instead of just apples, we use dried apricots, pears, and peaches too. An added benefit from using dried fruit is that—even though it is somewhat rehydrated—the strudel doesn't becomes soggy or loose, a perennial problem when using fresh apples.

In a large bowl, toss all the dried fruits with the brown sugar and cinnamon. Add ¼ to ⅓ cup boiled water, just enough to moisten the fruit. Cover and let sit at room temperature overnight. Remove the frozen phyllo dough and allow it to defrost overnight in the fridge.

Preheat the oven to 350°F. Line a large baking sheet with parchment paper.

Lay one sheet of phyllo dough on the baking sheet. Brush with melted butter and top with a scant tablespoon of breadcrumbs. Add another layer of phyllo dough. Repeat until all layers and all breadcrumbs are used.

Add the chopped walnuts to the fruit filling. Spoon the filling onto the phyllo dough, leaving a few inches bare at each edge. Starting at a long side and keeping the filling in the center, roll up the phyllo dough to enclose the filling, turning it at the end so that the seam is at the bottom. Gently shape the loaf and press down the tail ends of the dough to flatten. Make a crease and neatly fold each end underneath, pressing down gently to seal the strudel.

Brush the strudel with the egg yolk. Bake for 25 to 30 minutes, or until the strudel is golden brown and puffed. Cool for 5 minutes on the sheet. Slice and serve warm, or let cool and serve at room temperature, with a sprinkle of powdered sugar to garnish.

The strudel will keep in an airtight container at room temperature for 2 to 3 days.

ACKNOWLEDGMENTS

THIS BOOK was over one hundred years in the making. If we were to properly acknowledge all of those whom we owe a debt of gratitude, it would be a hundred pages more. So comprehensive this cannot be.

But we must begin with honoring the generations who came before us: Joel Russ, who started what would eventually become Russ & Daughters; his wife, Bella Russ; their daughters, Hattie (Russ) Gold, Ida (Russ) Pulvers, and Anne (Russ) Federman. We also honor their respective husbands, Murray Gold, Max Pulvers, and Herbert (Herbie) Federman, our grandfather.

Which brings us to the third generation, our parents' generation. Nothing we have done so far in our tenure would have been possible without the dedication and hard work of Maria and Mark Russ Federman. Niki's parents (and Josh's aunt and uncle) ran Russ & Daughters and kept it alive for thirty crucial years before we took over. It is thanks to them that the store not only survived but upheld the highest levels of quality. During a trying period, they never wavered or compromised. With Mark and Maria as guardians and champions, the treasure that is our OG shop came to us. They helped instill the core values of our family and our business that guide us today. They continue to be an invaluable resource.

And, as every Russ has known, a family business encompasses the entire family, willing or not, age notwithstanding, paid or unpaid. Our own families deserve all the credit in the world and gratitude we have to give. We know it's not easy. A huge thank-you to Josh's wife, Denise Porcaro Tupper, and their daughters, India and Violet; and Niki's husband, Christopher Meehan, and two children, Maya and Elan. You have all been our biggest supporters, willing taste-testers, toughest critics, and sources of inspiration.

Russ & Daughters would not exist if it weren't for our family of dedicated employees. To them we owe everything. There are too many here to mention but we'd like to start with our "brain trust": Tim von Hollweg, Avi Bromberg, and Emily Cintron have been essential, pouring themselves into the cookbook project in addition to everything else they do on a daily basis. Tim worked diligently on consolidating and refining our recipes and coordinating among everyone who had a hand in bringing this book to fruition. Emily furnished files to our book designer and coordinated marketing efforts as well as making sure the multiday, multilocation, and multifaceted photo shoot unfolded smoothly. Avi has always been our sounding board for tone, context, and accuracy, even running home to pick up Shabbat candlesticks for a photo when we didn't have any on hand.

We'd also like to thank Jamel Harris, the current head chef at Russ & Daughters Cafe; Lainie Schleien-

ACKNOWLEDGMENTS

Rothstein, our head baker during the making of the book; and Johnn Garcia, our production manager. This trio brilliantly helped translate the recipes of the cafe, bakery, and central kitchen for the home chef. Thanks to Alex Linden and Michael Bender, who have been our trusted advisors (not to mention CPAs) through several important moments of transition and change.

And thanks to our heads of state, who so ably and adeptly run each of our locations: Johanna Shipman, Tiffany Rose, Rebecca Zauss, and Justine Shipman gave our team the necessary space to work on this book while also keeping Russ & Daughters running smoothly on a daily basis. Dan Padrick, Julian Bach, Jasmine Anderson, Steven Rodriguez, Michael Nye, and Andy Lantigua, our wonderful team of managers across the company, similarly offered the flexibility and support needed to make this cookbook happen.

To our entire staff, from longtime employees to those who have joined in the last several months, our slicers, our bakers, those on the line, on the floor, and behind the scenes: You have our deepest gratitude. A special thanks to Aliza Gans for sifting through the archives at the American Jewish Historical Society for relevant material and images, and to Betzayda Ponce for contributions to our social media. And a deep thank you to Herman Vargas, our longtime manager, who retired in 2019 but whose soul will forever be part of the store and who graciously shared his story and expertise here.

To our vendors, thank you for supplying us with the ingredients, materials, and services that allow us to do what we do. And our thanks to everyone who shared their stories and quotes with us via interviews, emails, and stopping us to tell us how much we mean to you. You mean as much to us.

This book was also the product of an entire team of folks, each of whom deserves enormous credit. To Jesse Parnell, for his contributions made during his tenure as head chef at R&D Cafe and for returning to help with developing and refining a few of the recipes for the book. To our recipe testers, Lauryn Tyrell and Leah Koenig, who stepped in when needed with their immense expertise, skill, and patience to bring this book to completion. To Andrea Gentl and Marty Hyers of Gentl & Hyers, who, assisted by Coco Hill and Lucy Reback, captured Russ & Daughters' food and spirit so beautifully in images. Thank you to the elegant and talented Mariana Velasquez who, assisted by Brett Statman and Emma Stoloff, ensured our recipes were presented as preciously and styled as timelessly as they deserve.

To Kelli Anderson, for designing the original proposal for this book, and for years of design work together. To King Chong, Deirdre Quinn, and Emily Smith of Lafayette 148, for being great friends and neighbors, always ready to help, including with last-minute alterations for the photo shoot; and a special thank you from Niki for dressing her in beautiful clothes for special occasions when not in a white coat.

To Ruthie Ellenson, a friend and champion, who took it as Code Red when we put out the call for an aesthetically pleasing seder plate for our photo shoot, and to Hannah Ellenson and Becca Israel, who joined Operation Seder Plate and lent us their beautiful plate for the Passover spread.

To Annie Polland, president of the Tenement Museum and esteemed scholar of Jewish American history. Annie is many things to us: friend, neighbor, and historian, not to mention R&D Cafe regular. Annie's work on securing our archives at the American Jewish Historical Society and creating the 2019 exhibition "Russ & Daughters: An Appetizing Story" at the Center for Jewish Studies gave us information and insights into our family and our legacy beyond what we already knew.

To Lauri Freedman and the estate of Jason Polan, for allowing Jason Polan's wonderful illustrations of R&D to be peppered throughout these pages.

To Alex Weiser, Yiddish expert at YIVO, for being inspired years before the cookbook to give us a list of perfect R&D related Yiddish expressions and for being at the ready to answer Yiddish questions.

To Stephanie Hill Wilchfort, president and director of the Museum of the City of New York, for being so responsive and securing from the collection the photo of Joel Russ's apple corer, which is on long-term loan to the museum for its exhibition "New York at Its Core."

Thank you to Melanie Meyers and the American Jewish Historical Society for help in researching stuffed cabbage recipes and being protectors of the

Russ Family Archive; and to cousin Marty Pulvers, for being so generous with his time, memories, and storytelling.

To Naomi Firestone-Teeter of the Jewish Book Council, for her enthusiasm for the book long before it was done and for introducing us to Courtney Gooch.

To Emily Takoudes of Phaidon, for first planting the seed of a potential cookbook in our minds.

To Courtney Gooch, for her expert design work in conceptualizing and bringing this book to life.

To the entire team at Flatiron Books, thank you, especially to Jon Yaged of Macmillan Publishers, whose personal letter to us helped confirm our decision—a correct one—that we picked the right publishing partners. To our editors, Will Schwalbe and Samantha Zukergood, with whom we began this journey, and to Julie Will who brought it home. To Sarah Smith, of the David Black Agency. Sarah was masterful in generating such enthusiasm in our project and for stepping in with grace when needed throughout the process.

And to Joshua David Stein, our coauthor, friend, and honorary Russ. It felt like *bashert* to get to work with Joshua. Before we even knew him as an author, we knew of him and his work. He wrote the very first review of Russ & Daughters Cafe (thanks for the four stars!) when it opened in 2014. Little did we know that we were all secretly hoping that one day we would be lucky enough to work with one another, let alone become friends. Joshua was invaluable in helping us find our voice and structure, and in being a seasoned advisor on how a cookbook comes together.

Finally, we are endlessly indebted to our customers, without whom we simply would not exist. Even the word *customer* doesn't do justice to what you are. Whether R&D has been a part of your life for generations or you've come only once, you are the life and meaning of R&D. Thank you for making R&D part of your life and for sharing stories and feedback about what R&D means to you. May we continue this connection from generation to generation. NIKI RUSS FEDERMAN & JOSH RUSS TUPPER

LIKE EVERYONE READING THIS BOOK and many more who aren't, Russ & Daughters has been an enormously meaningful part of my life for many years. It has connected me to the Lower East Side, to my own roots, to my own shtetl-dwelling ancestors. It has kept me fed and warmed and cared for. In short, it has made me happy. I feel deeply honored to have been able to work on this project and am forever indebted to Niki and Josh for bringing me on board. As Russ & Daughters has modeled a vision of community, Niki and Josh have modeled wisdom, kindness, perspicacity, loyalty, and a certain bravery. They are protectors of their legacy but do not live in its thrall. Thank you both for having faith in me and entrusting me with this project. I thank you and all the ancestors that brought you to this place today.

To the Russ & Daughters family, including but not limited to Jamel, Tim, Johanna, Avi, and Lainie, thank you for being so welcoming and helpful. R&D is a large organization but, thanks to you, I never felt lost navigating it.

To Lauryn Tyrell and Leah Koenig, whose contributions as recipe testers were vast and vital.

To Marty and Andrea, best in the business, this is our second book together and I hope not our last. Working with you two has been, and is always, a pleasure.

To Mariana, an unexpected but most welcome pleasure of this book was getting to work with you on it. I continue to be in awe of your talent.

To David Black, always a relentless advocate, thank you for being both a shepherd and a wolf.

To my own family, my mother, Marcia Lieberman, and my father, Robert Stein; to my sister Rebecca Kunder and nephews Noah and Eli Kunder; to my sons, Augustus and Achilles Heeren Stein; and to my ancestors including my grandparents—may they rest in peace—Frank Stein, Eleanor Bankoff, Morris Lieberman, and Frieda Gollin, who I hope are *shepping naches* over an elaborate spread of appetizing in heaven that their grandson got to work with the illustrious Russes. JOSHUA DAVID STEIN

INDEX

Page numbers in *italics* indicate photographs.

A

alcohol, 250–59
  aperitifs
    Maror Martini, 256
    Smoked Martini, 255
  aquavit
    Schmoozer, 255
  champagne
    caviar and, 100
  chocolate whiskey
    Fershnikit Egg Cream, 241
  Escubac
    Escubac Fizz, 254
    Maror Martini, 256
  gin
    Break Fast Martini, 256
    Lower East Side, 251
    Maror Martini, 256
    Smoked Martini, 255
  Grand Marnier
    Challah Bread Pudding, *310*, 311
  mezcal
    Heads & Tails, 254
  red wine
    Brisket, 215
    Charoset, 209
  slivovitz, 251
  tequila
    Heads & Tails, 254
  triple sec
    Lemon Sorbet with Poppy Seeds, *226*, 227
  vermouth
    Heads & Tails, 254
  vodka
    Bloody Mary, 258, *259*
    caviar and, 100
    Escubac Fizz, 254
    infusions, 258
    Schmaltz & a Shot, 65
    shrubs, 242–43
    Smoked Martini, 255
    sodas, 247–48
  whiskey
    Fershnikit Egg Cream, 241
    Schmoozer, 255
    Smoked Martini, 255
  white wine
    Maror Martini, 256
    Potato Leek Soup, 43
    Roasted Vegetable Stock, 47
    Smoked Whitefish Chowder, 40, *41*
    Vegetarian Stuffed Cabbage, 193–95
almonds
  Everything Spiced Almonds, 161
American *transmontanus* caviar, 97, 98
aperitifs
  Maror Martini, 256
  Smoked Martini, 255
appetizing, definition of, 5
apples
  Apple Cake, 320, *321*
  Apple Compote, 231–32
  applesauce
    Matzo Brei with Applesauce & Sour Cream, 178, *179*
    Potato Latkes, *162*, 163–64, *165*
  Beet, Apple & Herring Salad, 66, 67
  Caramel Apple Ice Cream, 228–29
  Charoset, 209
  Chopped Salad, 168, *169*
  dried apple rings
    Fruit Strudel, *322*, 323
    Tsimmes, 208
  Gravlax, Apples & Honey, *78*, 79
  peeler and corer for, 66, 145
apricots, dried
  Challah Bread Pudding, *310*, 311
  Fruit Strudel, *322*, 323
  Tsimmes, 208
aquavit
  Schmoozer, 255
arugula
  Chopped Salad, 168, *169*
  Shissel Chicken Cutlets with Tartar Sauce, *200*, 201
avocados
  Chopped Salad, 168, *169*
  Sardine Toast with Avocado Mousse & Olive Tapenade, 84, *85*

B

Babka, Chocolate (or Cinnamon), 305–9
  Babka French Toast, 231–32, *233*
bagels, 127–28, 263–81
  Bagel Chips, 280, *281*
  Hot Smoke / Cold Smoke, 80
  Whitefish Croquettes, 88–91
  Cinnamon Raisin Bagels, 274
  Egg Bagels, 275
  Everything Bagels, 271
  on fish platters, 121
  history of, 268
  Plain Bagels, 271
  proofing, 273
  Pumpernickel Bagels, 278
  rolling, 272–73
  sandwiches, 127–37
    A Classic with the Works, 127–29, 131
    Daughters' Delight, *130*, 131
    Fancy Delancey, 136, *137*
    Pastrami Russ, 132, *133*
    Super Heebster, *134*, 135
  Whole Wheat Bagels, 279
barley
  Mushroom Barley Soup, 48, 49
barley malt syrup
  Bagels, 271–79
beef
  Aunt Ida's Stuffed Cabbage, 190–91, *192*
  Brisket, 215
  kashrut and, 5
beets
  Beet, Apple & Herring Salad, 66, *67*
  Chilled Borscht, *50–51*, 52
  Chopped Salad, 168, *169*
  Hot Borscht, 53
  Pickled Beet Juice, 242
    Beet & Lemon Shrub Base, 242
    Escubac Fizz, 254
  Red & Golden Beet Salad, *170*, 171–72
belly lox, 68, 69
beluga caviar, 94, 97, 101
berries
  Babka French Toast, 231–32, *233*
  Blueberry Compote, 223
  Blueberry Kasha Crumble, 230
  Raspberry Rugelach, *296–97*, 298–301
Bialys, 121, *282*, 283–84
bitter orange jam
  Break Fast Martini, 256
bitters
  Schmoozer, 255
Black & White, Caviar Lovers, 104, *105*
Black & White Cookies, 221, *302*, 303–4
  Black & White Cookie Ice Cream, 228–29
Blini, Caviar &, *102*, 103
Blintzes, *222*, 223–24
Bloody Mary, 258, *259*
blueberry
  Blueberry Compote, 223
  Blueberry Kasha Crumble, 230
borowic, 10, 49

INDEX

borscht
    Chilled Borscht, *50–51*, 52
    Hot Borscht, 53
bow tie pasta
    Kasha Varnishkas, *166*, 167
    Kippered Salmon Mac & Cheese, 198, *199*
breads, 285–95
    Challah, 287–89
    Challah Bread Pudding, *310*, 311
    Eggs Benny, *174*, 175–76
    Soft Scrambled Eggs with Caviar, *180*, 181
    on fish platters, 121
    Marble Rye, 294, *295*
    Pumpernickel, *292*, 293
    Red & Golden Beet Salad, *170*, 171–72
    Shissel Rye, 290–91
        Lox, Eggs & Onions (LEO), *182*, 183–84
        Marble Rye Bread, 294, *295*
        Shissel Chicken Cutlets with Tartar Sauce, *200*, 201
    See also bagels
Brisket, 215
brook trout, 83
    roe, 97, 99
    Smoked Trout Mousse, 91
buckwheat
    Blueberry Kasha Crumble, 230
    Caviar & Blini, *102*, 103
    Kasha Varnishkas, *166*, 167
Butter, Clarified, 184
    Gravlax, Apples & Honey, *78*, 79
    Hollandaise Sauce, 175
    Lower Sunny Side, 164
    Lox, Eggs & Onions (LEO), *182*, 183–84
    Nova & Cream Cheese Omelet, 177
    Soft Scrambled Eggs with Caviar, *180*, 181
buttermilk
    Black & White Cookies, *221*, *302*, 303–4

Buttermilk Dressing, 168
Cream Sauce, 61
Buxar Egg Cream, 238

C

cabbage
    Aunt Ida's Stuffed Cabbage, 190–91, *192*
    Cabbage Salad, 115
    Health Salad, 114
    Hot Borscht, 53
    Vegetarian Stuffed Cabbage, 193–95
cake
    Chocolate (or Cinnamon) Babka, 305–9
        Babka French Toast, 231–32, *233*
    Flourless Chocolate Cake, *218*, 219
    Honey Cake, *318*, 319
    Plum (or Apple) Cake, 320, *321*
    Sour Cream Coffee Cake, 315–16, *317*
capers, 128
    A Classic with the Works, 127–29, 131
    Daughters' Delight, *130*, 131
    Fancy Delancey, 136, *137*
    on fish platters, 120
    New Potato Salad, *116*, 117
    Sardine Toast with Avocado Mousse & Olive Tapenade, 84, *85*
    Tartar Sauce, 201
caramel
    Caramel Apple Ice Cream, 228–29
    Chocolate Toffee Matzo, 216, *217*
Caramelized Onions, 183–84
    Chopped Liver, *110*, 111
    Kasha Varnishkas, *166*, 167
    Lox, Eggs & Onions (LEO), *182*, 183–84
caraway
    Pickled Carrots with Cumin & Caraway, 195
    Pumpernickel Bread, *292*, 293
    Schmoozer, 255

Shissel Rye, 290–91
    Lox, Eggs & Onions (LEO), *182*, 183–84
    Marble Rye Bread, 294, *295*
    Shissel Chicken Cutlets with Tartar Sauce, *200*, 201
    Vodka Infusions, 258
carob
    Buxar Egg Cream, 238
carrots
    Brisket, 215
    Fish Stock, 212
    Health Salad, 114
    Hot Borscht, 53
    Matzo Ball Soup, *44*, 45–46
    Mushroom Barley Soup, *48*, 49
    Pickled Carrots with Cumin & Caraway, 195
    Roasted Vegetable Stock, 47
    Smoked Whitefish Chowder, *40*, *41*
    Tsimmes, 208
cauliflower
    Roasted Cauliflower with Garlic Labneh, *202*, 203
caviar, 92–106
    Caviar & Blini, *102*, 103
    Caviar Lovers Black & White, 104, *105*
    on fish platters, 120
    Hasselback Potatoes with Caviar, 106
    history of, 94, 97, *151*
    roe vs., 97, 101
    serving, 100–1
    Soft Scrambled Eggs with Caviar, *180*, 181
    storing, 100, 101
    types of, 97–99, 101
    vodka and, 100
Challah, 287–89
    braiding, 288–89
    Challah Bread Pudding, *310*, 311
    Eggs Benny, *174*, 175–76
    Soft Scrambled Eggs with Caviar, *180*, 181
champagne, 100
Chanukah, 163, 206
    Potato Latkes, *162*, 163–64, *165*

charnushka (nigella seeds)
    Shissel Rye, 290–91
    Marble Rye Bread, 294, *295*
    Shissel Chicken Cutlets with Tartar Sauce, *200*, 201
Charoset, 209
cheese
    cream cheese. *See* cream cheese
    farmer's cheese
        Blintzes, *222*, 223–24
        Noodle Kugel, 225
    goat cheese
        Red & Golden Beet Salad, *170*, 171–72
    kashrut and, 5
    muenster cheese
        Kippered Salmon Mac & Cheese, 198, *199*
        Pastrami Russ, 132, *133*
Cherry Shrub Base, 243
chicken
    Chicken Paprikash, *196*, 197
    Chopped Liver, *110*, 111
    Matzo Ball Soup, *44*, 45–46
    Shissel Chicken Cutlets with Tartar Sauce, *200*, 201
chickpeas
    Vegetarian Chopped Liver, 112
chipotle peppers
    Heads & Tails, 254
    Vodka Infusions, 258
Chips, Bagel, 280, *281*
    Hot Smoke / Cold Smoke, 80
    Whitefish Croquettes, 88–91
chives
    with caviar, 101
    on fish platters, 120
    Hasselback Potatoes with Caviar, 106
    Hot Smoke / Cold Smoke, 80
    Potato Leek Soup, 43
chocolate
    Black & White Cookies, *221*, *302*, 303–4
    Chocolate Babka, 305–9
        Babka French Toast, 231–32, *233*

chocolate (cont.)
Chocolate-Covered Macaroons, 220
Chocolate Egg Cream, 237
Fershnikit Egg Cream, 241
Chocolate Rugelach, *296–97*, 298–301
Chocolate Toffee Matzo, 216, *217*
Flourless Chocolate Cake, *218*, 219
Ganache, 219
Chopped Liver, *110*, 111
Vegetarian Chopped Liver, 112
Chopped Salad, 168, *169*
Chowder, Smoked Whitefish, 40, *41*
chub, 82
cinnamon
Cinnamon Babka, 305–9
Babka French Toast, 231–32, *233*
Cinnamon Raisin Bagels, 274
Cinnamon Rugelach, *296–97*, 298–301
Honey Cake, *318*, 319
Sour Cream Coffee Cake, 315–16, *317*
Clarified Butter, 184
Gravlax, Apples & Honey, *78*, 79
Hollandaise Sauce, 175
Lower Sunny Side, 164
Lox, Eggs & Onions (LEO), *182*, 183–84
Nova & Cream Cheese Omelet, 177
Soft Scrambled Eggs with Caviar, *180*, 181
cocktails, 250–59
Bloody Mary, 258, *259*
Break Fast Martini, 256
Escubac Fizz, 254
Heads & Tails, 254
Lower East Side, 251
Maror Martini, 256
Schmoozer, 255
Smoked Martini, 255
Coconut Macaroons, 220
coffee
Chocolate Babka, 305–9

Chocolate Rugelach, *296–97*, 298–301
Coffee Soda, 247
Honey Cake, *318*, 319
coffee cake. *See* cake
coleslaw
Cabbage Salad, 115
condensed milk
Coconut Macaroons, 220
cookies
Black & White Cookies, *221*, *302*, 303–4
Hamantaschen, 312–14
Rugelach, *296–97*, 298–301
cornichons
Classic New Catch Holland Herring Sandwich, *64*, 65
Tartar Sauce, 201
cream, heavy
Challah Bread Pudding, *310*, 311
Flourless Chocolate Cake, *218*, 219
Hamantaschen, 312–14
Ice Creams, *226*, 228–29
Kippered Salmon Mac & Cheese, 198, *199*
Potato Leek Soup, 43
Smoked Whitefish Chowder, 40, *41*
cream cheese, 127, 128
bagel sandwiches
A Classic with the Works, 127–29, 131
Daughters' Delight, *130*, 131
Fancy Delancey, 136, *137*
Super Heebster, *134*, 135
belly lox and, 69
on fish platters, 121
Kippered Salmon Mac & Cheese, 198, *199*
Noodle Kugel, 225
Nova & Cream Cheese Omelet, 177
Rugelach, *296–97*, 298–301
Sardine Toast with Avocado Mousse & Olive Tapenade, 84, *85*
Cream Sauce, 61, 71
Curry Sauce, 62

crème fraîche
Babka French Toast, 231–32, *233*
Caviar & Blini, *102*, 103
Caviar Lover's Black & White, 104, *105*
Croquettes, Whitefish, 88–91
Croutons, Pumpernickel, 171
Red & Golden Beet Salad, *170*, 171–72
cucumbers
in drinks
Jasmine Cucumber Soda, 248
Lower East Side, 251
Gazpacho, 42
Sour (& Half-Sour) Pickles, 109
cumin
Brisket, 215
Chicken Paprikash, *196*, 197
Gazpacho, 42
Pickled Carrots with Cumin & Caraway, 195
currants
Raspberry Rugelach, *296–97*, 298–301
Curry Sauce, 62

D
dairy products, kashrut and, 5
Daughters' Delight, *130*, 131
delicatessens, appetizing vs., 5
Demerara Syrup, 255
desserts. *See* sweets
dill
A Classic with the Works, 127–29, 131
in drinks
Bloody Mary, 258, *259*
Jasmine Cucumber Soda, 248
Lemon-Lime Soda, 247
Lower East Side, 251
Mango Shrub Base, 243
Vodka Infusions, 258
on fish platters, 120, 121
Health Salad, 114
Matzo Ball Soup, *44*, 45–46
Mustard Dill Sauce, 62
Beet, Apple & Herring Salad, 66, *67*

New Potato Salad, *116*, 117
Red & Golden Beet Salad, *170*, 171–72
Salmon & Whitefish Gefilte Fish, *210*, 211–12
Sour (& Half-Sour) Pickles, 109
Tartar Sauce, 201
dinners, 188–203
Aunt Ida's Stuffed Cabbage, 190–91, *192*
Brisket, 215
Chicken Paprikash, *196*, 197
Kippered Salmon Mac & Cheese, 198, *199*
Potato Kugel, 213
Roasted Cauliflower with Garlic Labneh, *202*, 203
Shissel Chicken Cutlets with Tartar Sauce, *200*, 201
Vegetarian Stuffed Cabbage, 193–95
See also soups
dressings
Buttermilk Dressing, 168
Sherry Vinaigrette, 171
Yogurt Goat Cheese Dressing, 171
See also sauces
dried fruit, 13
Challah Bread Pudding, *310*, 311
Fruit Strudel, *322*, 323
Mango Shrub Base, 243
Tsimmes, 208
drinks, 235–59
cocktails, 250–59
Bloody Mary, 258, *259*
Break Fast Martini, 256
Escubac Fizz, 254
Heads & Tails, 254
Lower East Side, 251
Maror Martini, 256
Schmoozer, 255
Smoked Martini, 255
egg creams, *236*, 237–41
Buxar Egg Cream, 238
Chocolate Egg Cream, 237, *240*
Fershnikit Egg Cream, 241
Malt Egg Cream, 238
Vanilla Egg Cream, 241

INDEX

shrubs, 242–43, *244–45*
   Beet & Lemon Shrub Base, 242
   Cherry Shrub Base, 243
   Mango Shrub Base, 243
   Pineapple Shrub Base, 243
sodas, *246*, 247–48
   Coffee Syrup, 247
   Ginger Lavender Syrup, 248
   Grape Syrup, 248
   Jasmine Syrup, 248
   Lemon-Lime Syrup, 247
dumplings
   Potato Knishes, *158*, 159–60

E
egg creams, *236*, 237–41
   Buxar Egg Cream, 238
   Chocolate Egg Cream, 237, *240*
   Fershnikit Egg Cream, 241
   Malt Egg Cream, 238
   Vanilla Egg Cream, 241
eggplant
   Romanian Eggplant Salad, 113
eggs, 173–84
   in cocktails
      Break Fast Martini, 256
      Escubac Fizz, 254
   Egg Bagels, 275
   Eggs Benny/Florentine, *174*, 175–76
   of fish. *See* caviar; roe
   hardboiled, 118
      with caviar, 101
      Chopped Liver, *110*, 111
      Chopped Salad, *168*, 169
      Egg Salad, 118
   Lower Sunny Side, 164
   Lox, Eggs & Onions (LEO), *182*, 183–84
   Matzo Brei with Applesauce & Sour Cream, 178, *179*
   Nova & Cream Cheese Omelet, 177
   Soft Scrambled Eggs with Caviar, *180*, 181
Escubac
   Escubac Fizz, 254
   Maror Martini, 256
Everything Spice Mix, 271
   Bagel Chips, 280, *281*
   Everything Bagels, 271
   Everything Spiced Almonds, 161

F
Fancy Delancey, 136, *137*
farfalle
   Kasha Varnishkas, *166*, 167
   Kippered Salmon Mac & Cheese, 198, *199*
fennel
   Jasmine Syrup, 248
   Mango Shrub Base, 243
   Roasted Vegetable Stock, 47
   Vegetarian Stuffed Cabbage, 193–95
fenugreek
   Vodka Infusions, 258
fermentation, 109
Fershnikit Egg Cream, 241
fish, 5, 54–91
   brook trout, 83
      Smoked Trout Mousse, 91
   chub, 82
   eggs (roe), 92–106
   herring, 56–67
      Beet, Apple & Herring Salad, 66, *67*
      Classic New Catch Holland Sandwich, 58, *64*, 65
      Health Salad, 114
      on platters, 120–21
      sauces for, 60, 61–62, *63*
         Cream Sauce, 61
         Curry Sauce, 62
         Mustard Dill Sauce, 62
         Plain Sauce, 61
         Schmaltz & a Shot, 65
      types of, 58–59
   mackerel, 83
   plattering of, 120–21
   sable, 83
   salmon, 68–81
      bagel sandwiches, 127–33
      A Classic with the Works, 127–29, 131
      Daughters' Delight, *130*, 131
      Pastrami Russ, 132, *133*
      Eggs Benny, *174*, 175–76
      Gravlax, Apples & Honey, *78*, 79
      Hot Smoke / Cold Smoke, 80
      Kippered Salmon Mac & Cheese, 198, *199*
      Lox, Eggs & Onions (LEO), *182*, 183–84
      Nova & Cream Cheese Omelet, 177
      Salmon & Whitefish Gefilte Fish, *210*, 211–12
      slicing, 72–75
      types of, 69–71
      Whitefish & Baked Salmon Salad, *86*, 87
      Super Heebster, *134*, 135
   sardines
      Sardine Toast with Avocado Mousse & Olive Tapenade, 84, *85*
   stock, 212
   sturgeon, 82
   eggs. *See* caviar
   whitefish, 82
      Chopped Salad, *168*, 169
      Salmon & Whitefish Gefilte Fish, *210*, 211–12
      Smoked Whitefish Chowder, 40, *41*
      Whitefish & Baked Salmon Salad, *86*, 87
      Super Heebster, *134*, 135
      Whitefish Croquettes, 88–91
   yellowfin tuna, 83
      Fancy Delancey, 136, *137*
fizz drinks
   Escubac Fizz, 254
Flourless Chocolate Cake, *218*, 219
flying fish roe, wasabi-infused, 97, 99
   Fancy Delancey, 136, *137*
   Super Heebster, *134*, 135
Fox's U-Bet chocolate syrup
   Chocolate Egg Cream, 237
   Fershnikit Egg Cream, 241
French smoked herring, 59
French Toast, Babka, 231–32, *233*
Fruit Strudel, *322*, 323

G
Ganache, 219

garlic
   Brisket, 215
   Roasted Cauliflower with Garlic Labneh, *202*, 203
   Romanian Eggplant Salad, 113
   Sour (& Half-Sour) Pickles, 109
   See also Everything Spice Mix
Gaspe Nova, 70
   A Classic with the Works, 129, 131
   Daughters' Delight, *130*, 131
   Eggs Benny, *174*, 175–76
   Lower Sunny Side, 164
   Lox, Eggs & Onions (LEO), *182*, 183–84
   Nova & Cream Cheese Omelet, 177
Gazpacho, 42
Gefilte Fish, Salmon & Whitefish, *210*, 211–12
gin
   Break Fast Martini, 256
   Lower East Side, 251
   Maror Martini, 256
   Smoked Martini, 255
ginger
   Brisket, 215
   Charoset, 209
   Ginger Lavender Soda, 248
   Escubac Fizz, 254
goat cheese
   Red & Golden Beet Salad, *170*, 171–72
Grand Marnier
   Challah Bread Pudding, *310*, 311
Grape Soda, 248
gravlax, 69
   Gravlax, Apples & Honey, *78*, 79
Greek yogurt
   Gravlax, Apples & Honey, *78*, 79
   Red & Golden Beet Salad, *170*, 171–72
green beans
   Vegetarian Chopped Liver, 112

INDEX

greens
    Chopped Salad, 168, *169*
    on fish platters, 120

H

hackleback caviar, 97, 98
Halvah Ice Cream, 228–29
Hamantaschen, 312–14
Heads & Tails, 254
Health Salad, 114
heavy cream
    Challah Bread Pudding, *310*, 311
    Flourless Chocolate Cake, *218*, 219
    Hamantaschen, 312–14
    Ice Creams, *226*, 228–29
    Kippered Salmon Mac & Cheese, 198, *199*
    Potato Leek Soup, 43
    Smoked Whitefish Chowder, 40, *41*
herring, 56–67
    Beet, Apple & Herring Salad, 66, *67*
    Classic New Catch Holland Sandwich, 58, *64*, 65
    Health Salad, 114
    Herring Pairing events, 62
    history of, 9–10, 56
    plattering of, 120–21
    sauces for, *60*, 61–62, *63*
        Cream Sauce, 61
        Curry Sauce, 62
        Mustard Dill Sauce, 62
        Plain Sauce, 61
    Schmaltz & a Shot, 65
    types of, 58–59
Hollandaise Sauce, 175
    Eggs Benny, *174*, 175–76
honey
    Gravlax, Apples & Honey, *78*, 79
    Honey Cake, *318*, 319
horseradish
    Bloody Mary, 258, *259*
    horseradish cream cheese
        Fancy Delancey, 136, *137*
        Super Heebster, *134*, 135
    Salmon & Whitefish Gefilte Fish, *210*, 211–12

I

Ice Creams, *226*, 228–29
    Black & White Cookie Ice Cream, 228
    Caramel Apple Ice Cream, 228–29
    Halvah Ice Cream, 228
Irish smoked salmon, 70

J

Jasmine Syrup, 248

K

Kaluga caviar, 101
kasha
    Blueberry Kasha Crumble, 230
    Kasha Varnishkas, *166*, 167
kashrut, 5, 59, 112, 211
kippered hot-smoked salmon, 71
    Hot Smoke / Cold Smoke, 80
    Kippered Salmon Mac & Cheese, 198, *199*
    Whitefish & Baked Salmon Salad, *86*, 87
Knishes, Potato, *158*, 159–60
kosher laws, appetizing and, 5, 59, 112, 211
kugel
    Noodle Kugel, 225
    Potato Kugel, 213

L

Labneh, Garlic, 203
lactose intolerance, 228
Latkes, Potato, *162*, 163–64, *165*
    Caviar Lovers Black & White, 104, *105*
    Lower Sunny Side, 164
lavender
    Escubac Fizz, 254
    Ginger Lavender Soda, 248
leeks
    Potato Leek Soup, 43
    Roasted Vegetable Stock, 47
Lekach (Honey Cake), *318*, 319
lemon
    in drinks
        Beet & Lemon Shrub Base, 242
        Break Fast Martini, 256
        Escubac Fizz, 254
        Lemon-Lime Soda, 247
        Heads & Tails, 254
    Lemon Sorbet with Poppy Seeds, *226*, 227
    with fish, 120
lettuce
    Chopped Salad, 168, *169*
    on fish platters, 120
limes
    Lemon-Lime Soda, 247
    Heads & Tails, 254
    Lower East Side, 251
liver
    Chopped Liver, *110*, 111
    Vegetarian Chopped Liver, 112
Lokshen Kugel, 225
Lower East Side (cocktail), 251
lox, 68
    belly lox, 68, 69
    Gaspe Nova, 70
    A Classic with the Works, 129, 131
    Daughters' Delight, *130*, 131
    Eggs Benny, *174*, 175–76
    Lower Sunny Side, 164
    Lox, Eggs & Onions (LEO), *182*, 183–84
    Nova & Cream Cheese Omelet, 177
    gravlax, 69
    Gravlax, Apples & Honey, *78*, 79
    Pickled lox, 71
    slicing, 72–75
    Western Nova, 68, 71

M

Mac & Cheese, Kippered Salmon, 198, *199*
Macaroons, Coconut, 220
mackerel, 83
malted milk
    Malt Egg Cream, 238
mangoes, dried
    Mango Shrub Base, 243
Manischewitz
    Charoset, 209
martinis
    Maror Martini, 256
    Smoked Martini, 255
matjes herring, 59
matzo
    Chocolate Toffee Matzo, 216, *217*
    Chopped Salad, 168, *169*
    Matzo Brei with Applesauce & Sour Cream, 178, *179*
    on fish platters, 121
    toppings for
        Charoset, 209
        Chopped Liver, *110*, 111
        Gravlax, Apples & Honey, *78*, 79
matzo meal
    Matzo Ball Soup, *44*, 45–46
    Potato Kugel, 213
    Potato Latkes, *162*, 163–64, *165*
    Salmon & Whitefish Gefilte Fish, *210*, 211–12
mayonnaise
    Chopped Salad, 168, *169*
    Curry Sauce, 62
    Egg Salad, 118
    Hot Smoke / Cold Smoke, 80
    Smoked Trout Mousse, 91
    Tartar Sauce, 201
    Whitefish & Baked Salmon Salad, *86*, 87
meat, kashrut and, 5
See also beef; chicken; fish
mezcal
    Heads & Tails, 254
milk
    Egg Creams, *236*, 237–41
    sweetened condensed milk
        Coconut Macaroons, 220
    See also buttermilk; heavy cream
Mock Chopped Liver, 112
mohn, 227
    Hamantaschen, 312–14
mousse
    Sardine Toast with Avocado Mousse & Olive Tapenade, *84*, 85
    Smoked Trout Mousse, 91
mushrooms
    Brisket, 215
    Mushroom Barley Soup, *48*, 49
    Mushroom Sauce, 194
    Vegetarian Chopped Liver, 112

Vegetarian Stuffed Cabbage, 193–95
mustard
  Curry Sauce, 62
  Mustard Dill Sauce, 62
    Beet, Apple & Herring Salad, 66, *67*
    New Potato Salad, *116*, 117
    Pastrami Russ, 132, *133*
    Red & Golden Beet Salad, *170*, 171–72

N
New Catch Holland herring, 58
  Classic New Catch Holland Herring Sandwich, *64*, 65
New Potato Salad, *116*, 117
nigella seeds
  Shissel Rye, 290–91
    Marble Rye Bread, 294, *295*
    Shissel Chicken Cutlets with Tartar Sauce, *200*, 201
noodles
  Kasha Varnishkas, *166*, 167
  Kippered Salmon Mac & Cheese, 198, *199*
  Noodle Kugel, 225
Norwegian smoked salmon, 71
nova lox
  A Classic Bagel with the Works, 129, 131
  Daughters' Delight, *130*, 131
  Eggs Benny, *174*, 175–76
  Lower Sunny Side, 164
  Lox, Eggs & Onions (LEO), *182*, 183–84
  Nova & Cream Cheese Omelet, 177

O
oats
  Blueberry Kasha Crumble, 230
olives
  on fish platters, 120
  Sardine Toast with Avocado Mousse & Olive Tapenade, 84, *85*
onions, 127, 129
  Bialys, 121, *282*, 283–84
  Caramelized Onions, 183–84
    Chopped Liver, *110*, 111
    Kasha Varnishkas, *166*, 167
    Lox, Eggs & Onions (LEO), *182*, 183–84
  on fish platters, 121
  Marble Rye Bread, 294, *295*
  Pumpernickel Bread, *292*, 293
  red onions
    caviar and, 101
    A Classic with the Works, 127–29, 131
    Fancy Delancey, 136, *137*
    pickled red onion, 59, 79
    Schmaltz & a Shot, 65
  Shissel Rye Bread, 290–91
  See also Everything Spice Mix
orange jam
  Break Fast Martini, 256
osetra caviar, 94, 98

P
pancakes
  Blintzes, *222*, 223–24
  Caviar & Blini, *102*, 103
  Potato Latkes, *162*, 163–64, *165*
  Caviar Lovers Black & White, 104, *105*
  Lower Sunny Side, 164
paddlefish caviar, 99
paprika
  Chicken Paprikash, *196*, 197
parsley
  Chilled Borscht, *50–51*, 52
  Maror Martini, 256
  New Potato Salad, *116*, 117
  Sardine Toast with Avocado Mousse & Olive Tapenade, 84, *85*
Passover, 2, 195, 204–20
  Brisket, 215
  Charoset, 209
  Chocolate Toffee Matzo, 216, *217*
  Chopped Liver, *110*, 111
  Coconut Macaroons, 220
  Flourless Chocolate Cake, *218*, 219
  Gravlax, Apples & Honey, *78*, 79
  Maror Martini, 256
  Matzo Ball Soup, *44*, 45–46
  Matzo Brei with Applesauce & Sour Cream, 178, *179*
  Potato Kugel, 213
  Salmon & Whitefish Gefilte Fish, *210*, 211, 212
  Tsimmes, 208
pasta
  Kasha Varnishkas, *166*, 167
  Kippered Salmon Mac & Cheese, 198, *199*
  Noodle Kugel, 225
pastrami-cured salmon, 70
  Pastrami Russ, 132, *133*
peaches, dried
  Fruit Strudel, *322*, 323
pears, dried
  Fruit Strudel, *322*, 323
peppers, bell
  Gazpacho, 42
  Romanian Eggplant Salad, 113
phyllo dough
  Fruit Strudel, *322*, 323
pickles
  cabbage
    Cabbage Salad, 115
  cornichons
    Classic New Catch Holland Herring Sandwich, *64*, 65
    Tartar Sauce, 201
  Pickled Beet Juice, 66
    Beet & Lemon Shrub Base, 242
    Escubac Fizz, 254
  Pickled Carrots with Cumin & Caraway, 195
  Pickled Herring, 59, 61–62, 66
    Beet, Apple & Herring Salad, 66, *67*
    Health Salad, 114
  pickled lox, 71
  pickled red onion, 79
    Gravlax, Apples & Honey, *78*, 79
  on fish platters, 120–21
  Sour (& Half-Sour) Pickles, 109
    Beet, Apple & Herring Salad, 66, *67*
    Pastrami Russ, 132, *133*
  See also capers; shrubs
Pineapple Shrub Base, 243
Plain Sauce, 61, 71
platters, assembling, 120–21
Plum (or Apple) Cake, 320, *321*
poppy seeds
  on bagels, 268
    Egg Bagels, 275
    Plain Bagels, 271
    Whole Wheat Bagels, 279
  Bialys, 121, *282*, 283–84
  Hamantaschen, 312–14
  Lemon Sorbet with Poppy Seeds, *226*, 227
  See also Everything Spice Mix
potatoes
  Beet, Apple & Herring Salad, 66, *67*
  Hasselback Potatoes with Caviar, 106
  New Potato Salad, *116*, 117
  Potato Knishes, *158*, 159–60
  Potato Kugel, 213
  Potato Latkes, *162*, 163–64, *165*
    Caviar Lovers Black & White, 104, *105*
    Lower Sunny Side, 164
  Potato Leek Soup, 43
  Schmaltz & a Shot, 65
  Smoked Whitefish Chowder, 40, *41*
  Whitefish Croquettes, 88–91
prunes
  Tsimmes, 208
pumpernickel
  Pumpernickel Bagels, 278
  Pumpernickel Bread, *292*, 293
    Sardine Toast with Avocado Mousse & Olive Tapenade, 84, *85*
  Pumpernickel Croutons, 171
    Red & Golden Beet Salad, *170*, 171–72
Purim
  Hamantaschen, 312–14

INDEX

R
raisins
  Aunt Ida's Stuffed Cabbage, 190–91, *192*
  Charoset, 209
  Cinnamon Raisin Bagels, 274
  Fruit Strudel, *322*, 323
  Noodle Kugel, 225
  Rugelach, *296–97*, 298–301
  Tsimmes, 208
Raspberry Rugelach, *296–97*, 298–301
Reuben sandwich
  Pastrami Russ, 132, *133*
rice
  Aunt Ida's Stuffed Cabbage, 190–91, *192*
  Vegetarian Stuffed Cabbage, 193–95
Roasted Cauliflower with Garlic Labneh, *202*, 203
Roasted Vegetable Stock, 47
  Chilled Borscht, *50–51*, 52
  Hot Borscht, 53
  Mushroom Barley Soup, *48*, 49
  Potato Leek Soup, 43
roe, 97, 99
  on bagel sandwiches
    Daughters' Delight, *130*, 131
    Fancy Delancey, 136, *137*
    Super Heebster, *134*, 135
  sturgeon. *See* caviar
roll mops (herring), 59
Romanian Eggplant Salad, 113
Rosh Hashanah, 206
  Gravlax, Apples & Honey, *78*, 79
  Heads & Tails, 254
  Honey Cake, *318*, 319
  Tsimmes, 208
  whitefish, 120
Rugelach, *296–97*, 298–301
  Cinnamon Filling, 299
  Chocolate Filling, 299
  Raspberry Filling, 299
  rolling, 300–1
Russ & Daughters
  Bakery, 5, 28, 38, 263–64
    recipes from, 260–323
  Cafe, 2, 28, 149–53, 206, 215, 242, 247, 251
    recipes from, 146–259
  collaborators with, 62, 68
    Anderson, Laurie, 206–7
    Arze, Nico, 152
    Bachman, Andy, 206
    Baynon, Jeff, 263
    Bengtsson, Ulrika, 62
    Biezunski, Eléanor, 206
    Bloomfield, April, 62
    Brooklyn Grange, 42
    Costello, Elvis, 206
    Dufresne, Wylie, 62
    Freestyle Love Supreme, 206
    Gutman, Hank, 263
    Kings County Distillery, 241
    Kohn, Daniel, 206
    Let There Be Neon, 264
    Maddy, Matthew, 152
    Sklamberg, Lorin, 206
    Sono, Chikara, 206
    Stone, Jeremiah, 62
    Streit's, 216
    Vega, Suzanne, 206
    Volfson, Yana, 153
    von Hauske, Fabian, 62
    Walter the Seltzer Guy, 142
  events hosted by, 2, 62, 206–7
  family
    Federman, Anne Russ, *6*, *7*, 11–15, *18*, 24–25, 227
    Federman, Herbie, *x*, 13–15, *18*, 65, 94, 97, 150
    Federman, Maria Carvajal, 6, *7*, 15, 17, *18*, 23, 26–27, 42
    Federman, Mark Russ, 9, 14–17, *19*, 23, 25, 26–28, 68, 97, 141
      changes under, 61, 62, 66, 127, 145
      food preferences of, 150, 197
      press coverage of, 6, 7
    Federman, Niki, 15, 17, *19*, 22–23, 26–28
      food preferences of, 61, 100, 104
    Federman, Noah, *15*, 15
    Federman, Tara, 14, *15*, 24–25
    Gold, Hattie Russ, 6, 10, *11*, 12–13, 15
    Gold, Murray, *x*, *3*, 13, 15
    Gold, Nina, *18*
    Pulvers, Ida Russ, 6, 10, *11*, 12–13, 190
    Pulvers, Marty, 190
    Russ, Bella Spier, 10, 12, 13
    Russ, Joel (founder), *x*, 1, *3*, 5–14, 65, 66, 82, 150
      foods sold by, 49, 56, 58, 84
    Tupper, Josh Russ, *15*, 17, *19*, 23, 24–28, 72
      food preferences of, 61, 88, 100, 135, 255
  fans of
    Anderson, Laurie, 40, 206–7
    Bachman, Andy, 206
    Cohen, Paula, 211
    Ginsburg, Ruth Bader, 12
    Glaser, Milton, *4*, 17, *141*, 150
    Hall, Marcellus, 150
    Kalman, Maira, 38
    Newhouse, Alana, 59
    Peskowtiz, Josh, 83
    Polan, Jason, 150
    Sacks, Oliver, 62
    Shallwani, Pervaiz, 58
    Shefi, Naama, 58
    Squadron, Daniel, 80
    Stewart, Martha, 17
    Trillin, Calvin, 17, 142, 150
    Waxman, Ben, 175
  history of, 1–29
    documentary about, 12
    first generation of, 9–13, 49, 56, 66, 68, 127, 150
    locations of, 2, 5, 10, 11, 13, 28, 149–50, 263–64
    memorabilia from, *139–45*
    previous names of, 10
    second generation of, *6*, 12–15, 68, 82, 94
    third generation of, *7*, 15–17, 23, 27–28, 62, 68, 97, 127, 141
    fourth generation of, 2, 5, 17, 22–28, 68, 149–53, 206–7, 263–64
  kashrut and, 5, 59, 112, 211
  non-family staff of, 14, *18–19*, 153, 326–27, *329–31*
    Jacques, David, 128
    Reyes, Jose, 14, *18*, 25
    Reynosa, Walter, *19*
    Riccio, Ron, *19*
    Sheffi, Alina, 113
    Starr, Autumn, *19*
    Vargas, Herman, 14, *19*, 23, 25, 121, 136
  press coverage of, 6–7, 17
  New Yorker, The, 17, 62
  New York magazine, *4*, 17, *141*
  New York Times, The, 22, 104
  Store, 1, 37–38, *139–45*
    recipes from, 39–137
rye bread
  Marble Rye, 294, *295*
  Shissel Rye, 290–91
  Lox, Eggs & Onions (LEO), *182*, 183–84
  Shissel Chicken Cutlets with Tartar Sauce, *200*, 201
  See also pumpernickel

S
Sabbath
  Challah, 287–89
sable, 83
salads
  Cabbage Salad, 115
  Chopped Salad, 168, *169*
  Egg Salad, 118
  Health Salad, 114
  New Potato Salad, *116*, 117

INDEX

Red & Golden Beet Salad, *170*, 171–72
Romanian Eggplant Salad, 113
salmon, 68–81
    bagel sandwiches
        A Classic with the Works, 127–29, 131
        Daughters' Delight, *130*, 131
        Pastrami Russ, 132, *133*
        Super Heebster, 134, *135*
    Eggs Benny, *174*, 175–76
    Gravlax, Apples & Honey, *78*, 79
    Hot Smoke / Cold Smoke, 80
    Kippered Salmon Mac & Cheese, 198, *199*
    Lower Sunny Side, 164
    lox, as term, 68
    Lox, Eggs & Onions (LEO), *182*, 183–84
    Nova & Cream Cheese Omelet, 177
    plattering, 120
    roe, 97, 99
        Daughters' Delight, *130*, 131
    Salmon & Whitefish Gefilte Fish, *210*, 211–12
    slicing, 72–75
    types of, 69–71
    Whitefish & Baked Salmon Salad, *86*, 87
        Super Heebster, 134, *135*
Salt, Spiced, 254
sandwiches
    on babka, 288
    on bagels, 127–37
        A Classic with the Works, 127–29, 131
        Daughters' Delight, *130*, 131
        Fancy Delancey, 136, *137*
        Pastrami Russ, 132, *133*
        Super Heebster, *134*, 135
    on bread
        Sardine Toast with Avocado Mousse & Olive Tapenade, 84, *85*

on buns
    Classic New Catch Holland Herring Sandwich, *64*, 65
on latkes, 163
    Lower Sunny Side, 164
on matzo
    Charoset, 209
    Gravlax, Apples & Honey, *78*, 79
sardines
    Sardine Toast with Avocado Mousse & Olive Tapenade, 84, *85*
sauces
    Blueberry Compote, 223
    Caramel Sauce, 229
    Cream Sauce, 61
    Curry Sauce, 62
    Garlic Labneh, 203
    Hollandaise Sauce, 175
    Mushroom Sauce, 194
    Mustard Dill Sauce, 62
    Plain Sauce, 61
    Stuffed Cabbage Sauce, 190–91
    Tartar Sauce, 201
    Vinegar Sauce, 115
    See also dressings
sauerkraut
    Hot Borscht, 53
schmaltz herring, 1, 56, 58
    Schmaltz & a Shot, 65
Schmoozer, 255
Scottish smoked salmon, 70
    Hot Smoke / Cold Smoke, 80
seltzer, 142
    Egg Creams, *236*, 237–41
    Matzo Ball Soup, *44*, 45–46
    shrubs, 242–43
    sodas, 247–48
sesame seeds
    on bagels, 268
        Egg Bagels, 275
        Plain Bagels, 271
        Whole Wheat Bagels, 279
    See also Everything Spice Mix
sevruga caviar, 94, 101
Shabbat
    Challah, 287–89

Shavuot
    Blintzes, *222*, 223–24
Sherry Vinaigrette, 171
ship caviar, 94
Shissel Rye, 290–91
    Lox, Eggs & Onions (LEO), *182*, 183–84
    Shissel Chicken Cutlets with Tartar Sauce, *200*, 201
shrubs, 242–43, *244–45*
    Beet & Lemon Shrub Base, 242
    Cherry Shrub Base, 243
    Mango Shrub Base, 243
    Pineapple Shrub Base, 243
Siberian caviar, 98
sides, 107–21
    Everything Spiced Almonds, 161
    on fish platters, 120–21
    Kasha Varnishkas, *166*, 167
    Pickled Carrots with Cumin & Caraway, 195
    Potato Knishes, *158*, 159–60
    Potato Kugel, 213
    Sour (& Half-Sour) Pickles, 109
    Tsimmes, 208
    See also salads; soups; spreads
Simple Syrup, 251
    Break Fast Martini, 256
    Buxar Egg Cream, 238
    Lower East Side, 251
slicing fish, 72–75, 142
slivovitz, 150, 251
smoked and cured fish. *See* fish; *specific fish*
Smoked Martini, 255
smoked pepper
    Vodka Infusions, 258
Smoked Trout Mousse, 91
sodas, *246*, 247–48
    Coffee Syrup, 247
    Ginger Lavender Syrup, 248
    Escubac Fizz, 254
    Grape Syrup, 248
    Jasmine Syrup, 248
    Lemon-Lime Syrup, 247
    Heads & Tails, 254
Sorbet, Lemon with Poppy Seeds, *226*, 227

soups, 39–53
    Chilled Borscht, *50–51*, 52
    Gazpacho, 42
    Hot Borscht, 53
    Matzo Ball Soup, *44*, 45–46
    Mushroom Barley Soup, *48*, 49
    Potato Leek Soup, 43
    Roasted Vegetable Stock, 47
    Smoked Whitefish Chowder, 40, *41*
sour cream
    Chopped Salad, 168, *169*
    Cream Sauce, 61
    Hamantaschen, 312–14
    Hot Smoke / Cold Smoke, 80
    Matzo Brei with Applesauce & Sour Cream, 178, *179*
    Noodle Kugel, 225
    Rugelach, 296–97, 298–301
    Sour Cream Coffee Cake, 315–16, *317*
Spiced Salt, 254
spinach
    Chopped Salad, 168, *169*
    Eggs Benny, *174*, 175–76
spreads
    Avocado Mousse, 84, *85*
    Charoset, 209
    Chopped Liver, *110*, 111
    Egg Salad, 118
    Hot Smoke / Cold Smoke, 80
    Olive Tapenade, 84, *85*
    Smoked Trout Mousse, 91
    Vegetarian Chopped Liver, 112
    Whitefish & Baked Salmon Salad, *86*, 87
    See also cream cheese
stock
    Fish Stock, 212
    Roasted Vegetable Stock, 47
        Chilled Borscht, *50–51*, 52
        Hot Borscht, 53
        Mushroom Barley Soup, *48*, 49
        Potato Leek Soup, 43
Strudel, Fruit, *322*, 323
Stuffed Cabbage, *322*, 323
    Aunt Ida's Stuffed Cabbage, 190–91, *192*
    Vegetarian Stuffed Cabbage, 193–95

sturgeon, 82, 94
  eggs. *See* caviar
Super Heebster, *134*, 135
Svekolnik (Chilled Borscht), *50–51*, 52
sweetened condensed milk
  Coconut Macaroons, 220
sweet potatoes
  Tsimmes, 208
sweets, 221–33, 296–323
  Apple Compote, 231–32
  Black & White Cookies, *221*, *302*, 303–4
  Blueberry Kasha Crumble, 230
  Blintzes, *222*, 223–24
  Candied Walnuts, 231–32
  Challah Bread Pudding, *310*, 311
  Chocolate (or Cinnamon) Babka, 305–9
    Babka French Toast, 231–32, *233*
  Chocolate Toffee Matzo, 216, *217*
  Coconut Macaroons, 220
  Egg Creams, *236*, 237–41
    Buxar Egg Cream, 238
    Chocolate Egg Cream, 237, *240*
    Fershnikit Egg Cream, 241
    Malt Egg Cream, 238
    Vanilla Egg Cream, 241
  Flourless Chocolate Cake, *218*, 219
  Fruit Strudel, *322*, 323
  Hamantaschen, 312–14
  Honey Cake, *318*, 319
  Ice Creams, *226*, 228–29
    Black & White Cookie Ice Cream, 228
    Caramel Apple Ice Cream, 228–29
    Halvah Ice Cream, 228
    Lemon Sorbet with Poppy Seeds, *226*, 227
  Noodle Kugel, 225
  Plum (or Apple) Cake, 320, *321*
  Rugelach, *296–97*, 298–301
  Sour Cream Coffee Cake, 315–16, *317*

syrups
  Coffee Syrup, 247
  Demerara Syrup, 255
  Ginger Lavender Syrup, 248
    Escubac Fizz, 254
  Grape Syrup, 248
  Jasmine Syrup, 248
  Lemon-Lime Syrup, 247
    Heads & Tails, 254
  Malt Syrup, 238
  Simple Syrup, 251
  Vanilla Syrup, 241

T
Tapenade, Sardine Toast with Avocado Mousse &, 84, 85
Tartar Sauce, 201
  Shissel Chicken Cutlets with Tartar Sauce, *200*, 201
  Whitefish Croquettes, 88–91
tequila
  Heads & Tails, 254
Toffee, Chocolate Matzo, 216, *217*
tomatoes
  Brisket, 215
  Chicken Paprikash, *196*, 197
  A Classic Bagel with the Works, 127–29, 131
  Aunt Ida's Stuffed Cabbage, 190–91, *192*
  Fancy Delancey, 136, *137*
  on fish platters, 121
  Gazpacho, 42
  Roasted Vegetable Stock, 47
tomato juice
  Bloody Mary, 258, *259*
triple sec
  Lemon Sorbet with Poppy Seeds, *226*, 227
Tsimmes, 208
trout, 83
  roe, 97, 99
  Smoked Trout Mousse, 91
Tu B'Shevat
  Buxar Egg Cream, 238
tuna, yellowfin, 83
  Fancy Delancey, 136, *137*

V
Vanilla Egg Cream, 241
Vegetable Stock, Roasted, 47
  Chilled Borscht, *50–51*, 52
  Hot Borscht, 53
  Mushroom Barley Soup, *48*, 49
  Potato Leek Soup, 43
vermouth
  Heads & Tails, 254
vinegar
  Chilled Borscht, *50–51*, 52
  Hot Borscht, 53
  Sherry Vinaigrette, 171
  Vinegar Sauce, 115
  See also pickles; shrubs
vodka
  Bloody Mary, 258, *259*
  caviar and, 100
  Escubac Fizz, 254
  infusions, 258
  Schmaltz & a Shot, 65
  shrubs, 242
  Smoked Martini, 255
  sodas, 247

W
walnuts
  Candied Walnuts, 231–32
  Charoset, 209
  Fruit Strudel, *322*, 323
  Red & Golden Beet Salad, *170*, 171–72
  Vegetarian Chopped Liver, 112
wasabi-infused flying fish roe, 99
  Fancy Delancey, 136, *137*
  Super Heebster, *134*, 135
watercress
  Red & Golden Beet Salad, *170*, 171–72
Western Nova, 68, 71
whiskey
  chocolate
    Fershnikit Egg Cream, 241
  rye
    Schmoozer, 255
  Scottish
    Smoked Martini, 255

whitefish, 82, 120
  Chopped Salad, 168, *169*
  roe, 97
  Salmon & Whitefish Gefilte Fish, *210*, 211–12
  Smoked Whitefish Chowder, 40, *41*
  Whitefish & Baked Salmon Salad, *86*, 87
  Super Heebster, *134*, 135
  Whitefish Croquettes, 88–91
Whole Wheat Bagels, 279
wine
  red wine
    Brisket, 215
    Charoset, 209
  white wine
    Maror Martini, 256
    Potato Leek Soup, 43
    Roasted Vegetable Stock, 47
    Smoked Whitefish Chowder, 40, *41*
    Vegetarian Stuffed Cabbage, 193–95

Y
yellowfin tuna, 83
  Fancy Delancey, 136, *137*
Yiddish proverbs, 327
  on appetite, 120
  on borscht, 52
  on chicken, 197
  on herring, 56
  on kugel, 213
  on matzo balls, 46
  on meat and fish, 68
  on work, 11
  on worries, 47
yogurt
  Gravlax, Apples & Honey, *78*, 79
  Red & Golden Beet Salad, *170*, 171–72
  Roasted Cauliflower with Garlic Labneh, *202*, 203
  Yogurt Goat Cheese Dressing, 171
Yom Kippur, 206
  Break Fast Martini, 256

NIKI RUSS FEDERMAN is the fourth-generation co-owner of Russ & Daughters. At the age of twenty-seven, Russ Federman chose to return to the shop in which she grew up. Together with her cousin Josh, she has grown Russ & Daughters into what it is today while preserving its cultural and culinary legacy. Russ Federman has been featured in *The Sturgeon Queens*, the award-winning documentary about Russ & Daughters; television shows such as *Taste the Nation with Padma Lakshmi* and *Anthony Bourdain: No Reservations*; and publications including *The New York Times*, *The New Yorker*, *Food & Wine*, *Zagat*, *Vogue*, and *W*. She was inducted into the Manhattan Jewish Hall of Fame and has an encyclopedic entry in the Jewish Women's Archive. She is a member of the Independent Restaurant Coalition and Les Dames d'Escoffier. She lives in Brooklyn with her husband, Christopher, and two children.

JOSH RUSS TUPPER is the fourth-generation co-owner of Russ & Daughters. Raised in an ashram in upstate New York, Russ Tupper was working as an engineer in Portland, Oregon, when the opportunity arose to join his family business. Since 2009, he has been leading Russ & Daughters with his cousin Niki. He has been featured in media outlets such as NPR, Food Network, Travel Channel, *Forbes*, *The Cut*, *Kinfolk*, *Lucky Peach*, *The New Yorker*, and *Vogue*. He is also one of the subjects of the documentary *The Sturgeon Queens*. Called the "Babka Baron" by *The New York Times*, Russ Tupper has been honored by the Museum of Food and Drink for his contributions to NYC food culture. He has taught at the YIVO Institute for Jewish Research and Astor Center. Russ Tupper lives with his wife, Denise, and two daughters.

JOSHUA DAVID STEIN is a cookbook and children's book author, journalist, and restaurant critic. His work includes *Notes from a Young Black Chef* and *My America*, with Kwame Onwuachi; *Il Buco: Stories & Recipes*, with Donna Lennard; *The Nom Wah Cookbook*, with Wilson Tang; *Vino: The Essential Guide to Real Italian Wine*, with Joe Campanale; *Jang: The Soul of Korean Cooking*, with Mingoo Kang and Nadia Cho; *Why I Cook* with Tom Colicchio; and many more. Among his children's books are *What's Cooking?*, *Can I Eat That?*, *Brick: Who Found Herself in Architecture*, *Solitary Animals: Introverts of the Wild*, and *The Catalogue of Hugs*. He lives in Brooklyn with his sons, Augustus and Achilles.